Criminal Justice
Recent Scholarship

Edited by
Nicholas P. Lovrich

A Series from LFB Scholarly

Domestic Violence and Mandatory Arrest

Influences on Police Officer Actions

John F. Waldron

LFB Scholarly Publishing LLC
El Paso 2012

HUMBER LIBRARIES LAKESHORE CAMPUS
3199 Lakeshore Blvd West
TORONTO, ON. M8V 1K8

Library of Congress Cataloging-in-Publication Data

Waldron, John F. (John Francis), 1954-
  Domestic violence and mandatory arrest : influences on police officer
actions / John F. Waldron.
      p. cm.
  Includes bibliographical references and index.
  ISBN 978-1-59332-581-7 (hardcover : alk. paper)
  1. Family violence--New Jersey. 2. Family violence--Law and
legislation--New Jersey. 3. Police--New Jersey. 4. Arrest--New
Jersey. I. Title.
  HV6626.22.N5W35 2012
  364.15'5509749--dc23

                                    20120322515

ISBN 978-1-59332-581-7

Printed on acid-free 250-year-life paper.

Manufactured in the United States of America.

Dedication

To my father John M. Waldron, a police officer for 36 years, who taught me much of what there was to know about law enforcement. He was my mentor, guide, and advisor about almost everything and anything in life. He often unselfishly went without, to give to his family. He encouraged my love of reading, something that has served me well in my later academic pursuits. As an early product of the LEEP program, he was a shining example and a role model for me of the educated practitioner for both law enforcement and criminal justice. I truly miss our lively discussion, debates, and even the occasional disagreements. What I have achieved, is but a reflection of his wisdom, patience, and leadership by example.

Table of Contents

Acknowledgements

First and foremost, to my wife, Barbara Ann Waldron, she has endured countless hours of inconvenience, separation, and rereads of my papers in the course of my academic pursuits. Barbara has served as the primary editor throughout my academic career, and for this book specifically. Edward Barth, a former police partner and a fellow academic/practitioner with whom I earned both my undergraduate and Master's degrees. Simply put, he was the best cop I ever worked with. He also served as a sounding board and editor for this book and I am eternally in his debt.

To my sons John Joseph and Kevin Patrick who have basically never known their father not to be attending school in one form or another for their entire lives. For using their considerable powers of persuasion to open door and gain access to those who could make this research possible, Michael Waldron, and Joseph DeBaise.

To Dr. Maki Haberfeld, whose guidance and wisdom were and are still instrumental in my life and to my achievements. The tenacity in every project she undertakes and accomplishes is but a reflection of her steely inner strength of character and highest personal integrity. Thanks also to Dr. Barry Spunt and Dr. Larry Sullivan whose insightful suggestions and recommendations have helped produce this finished product. Thanks to all of you for your time and efforts on my behalf.

To the many police officers, past and present members of the Union County, New Jersey Police Department and the Sayreville, New Jersey Police Department with whom I had the honor and pleasure to serve with and work beside, during my 26 years in law enforcement.

To Dr. Nicholas P. Lovrich, who is an exceptional editor, and showed great patience in revising the original draft of this book. Mr.

Leo Balk of LFB Publishing must also be recognized for suggesting, encouraging, and promoting this undertaking.

To the many educators who have inspired, challenged, promoted, and honed my critical and analytical thinking over the years. Of particular note are: William Calathes from Jersey City State College; Janet Fishman, William Heffernan, Richard Lovely, Dorothy Moses Schulz, Bernard Cohen, James J. Fyfe, Candice McCoy, and Robert Louden from John Jay College of Criminal Justice; Steven Brier and Joan Greenbaum from the Graduate Center of CUNY. Thank you all for forever being a part of my education and making me a better student through your teachings.

Finally, to the police departments, police chiefs, public safety directors, and the 425 study participants, all of whom shall remain anonymous, who allowed me to conduct this important research without reservations or preconditions. You are a credit to the law enforcement profession and I am eternally in your debt.

CHAPTER 1
Introduction to the Mandatory Arrest for the Crime of Domestic Violence

IMPLICATIONS OF DECISIONS IN DOMESTIC VIOLENCE

Domestic violence enforcement poses numerous far reaching and potentially life or death consequences and implications for all parties involved. For the police who are called upon to intervene, most often at the residence of the victim and/or the attacker, the situation is fraught with a multitude of unknown factors that are most often potentially dangerous, and on occasion life-threatening. The actions taken and decisions a police officer makes at these volatile encounters can have a lasting impact on his/her agency's reputation as well as their own professional image. They can have criminal and civil implications for the officer, and beside the obvious effects on both the victim and the offender the potential impact on the children of the involved parties can be profound. They are too often the unintended victims of domestic violence incidents as they witness the abuse and subsequent police actions taking place in their homes.

For the victims, the direct result of a police intervention is the immediate end to the abuse taking place at the time. Additional benefits can include the education of the victim as to their legal rights under the domestic violence laws in their particular state, and their options for relief, temporary and/or permanent, to prevent the commission of further acts of domestic violence against them. It is also a goal that of police intervention that the attacker desists from the commission of further acts of domestic violence. For the attacker, the effective enforcement of domestic violence laws by the police can lead to the imposition of legal sanctions from arrest, to conviction, and to the imposition of criminal sanctions. The hoped for goal of the nation's domestic violence laws is to change the behavior of offenders, preferably through education and rehabilitation, but by the imposition of sanctions (monetary fines and incarceration) if necessary.

Unfortunately, the record of domestic violence enforcement by law enforcement has been mixed at best. Not all the blame for the suboptimal outcomes can be laid on the lower levels of police agencies entrusted with enforcement; past-established public policy broadly encouraged the view that incidents of domestic violence were primarily private matters best resolved between spouses. A good deal of research (Bard, 1970) also contributed to this policy of non-intervention that encouraged mediation and resolution rather than the imposition of criminal sanctions. These attitudes and researcher recommendations influenced police practices and policies for decades. In addition, the perception that handling domestic disputes was not "real police work" and not part of the crime fighting model of police work made popular during the 1930's and 40's added to the inclination to minimize attention to domestic violence. This tendency persisted well into the 60' & 70's and is even evident in some police agencies to this day.

However, over the last quarter century domestic violence laws have been enacted and policies have been developed to treat domestic violence as a serious crime necessitating an appropriate criminal justice response. Court decisions have also had an influential impact on policy and practices, often serving as a catalyst for change in the direction of strengthening the protection of the rights of victims of domestic violence. These changes have included everything from mandatory arrest laws for domestic violence offenses, the compilation of extensive report filing systems to track domestic violence, the requirement of mandatory in-service training on an annual basis for police officers, the establishment of specific domestic violence units in many prosecutorial offices, and the provision of specific training for judges on the intricacies of domestic violence laws. There has been an unprecedented mobilization of the criminal justice system in the area of domestic violence, from the 911 operators who receive the initial call for help to the judges who sit in preside over the outcome. Nowhere has this change in priorities and concern been more pronounced than on the law enforcement officers working on the front lines of this struggle to protect the victims who are all too often the least capable of fighting back and defending themselves.

It is against this background that this research examines some of the social and legal influences that affect the decision making process of police officers in domestic violence incidents. New Jersey was chosen as the site for this research due to a number of considerations. First, there is a specific enumeration of the mandatory arrest criteria in the state laws pertaining to domestic violence. Second, the heavy influence of the State of New Jersey Attorney General's Office in the establishment of policies and procedures that all police officers are directly responsible for knowing and following and that all law enforcement agencies are encouraged to make part of their standard operation procedures. Third, the diversity of population and housing in the state allows for comparisons between police agencies by urban, urban-suburb, large suburban, and small suburban settings. Finally, the long-established concept of home rule and the fact that each municipality has its own individual police department, allows for variations not characteristic of large monolithic agencies most often studied in police research. The vast majority of officers spend their entire careers or a good portion of them in a single organizational setting. While this is the case, only limited research has been done to determine the context to which organizational norms and practices influence police officer behavior in highly discretionary areas of policing such as domestic violence.

LEGISLATIVE INTENT OF NEW JERSEY DOMESTIC VIOLENCE LAWS

The New Jersey State Legislature, in the enactment of The Prevention of Domestic Violence Act included a statement of legislative intent which reads in part at *N.J.S.* 2C:25-18 that:

> domestic violence is a serious crime against society; that there are thousands of persons in this State who are regularly beaten, tortured and in some cases even killed by their spouses or coinhabitants; that a significant number of women who are assaulted re pregnant; that the victims come from all social

and economic backgrounds and ethnic groups; that there is a positive correlation between spousal abuse and child abuse; and that children, even when they are not themselves physically assaulted, suffer deep and lasting effects from exposure to domestic violence. It is, therefore, the intent of the Legislature to assure the victim of domestic violence the maximum protection from abuse the law can provide....

It is the intent of the Legislature to stress that the primary duty of a law enforcement officer when responding to a domestic violence call is to enforce the laws allegedly violated and to protect the victim....

It is further the intent that the official response to domestic violence shall communicate the attitude that violent behavior will not be excused or tolerated, and shall make clear the fact that the existing criminal laws and civil remedies created under this act will be enforced without regard to the fact that the violence grows out of a domestic situation.

NEW JERSEY'S DOMESTIC VIOLENCE LAWS

The New Jersey Criminal Justice Code Title, 2C, establishes the general purpose and defines the specific criminal offenses that comprise the State's criminal code. Chapter 25 of the Code is known as The Prevention of Domestic Violence Act. This Act establishes and identifies the three primary elements of domestic violence acts, relationships that activate domestic violence procedures, and specific offenses that activate mandatory arrest procedures by law enforcement. As this research takes place in New Jersey and the participants are full-time sworn police officers serving in various jurisdictions over a two-county area of the State, the legal definitions of domestic violence as defined by the Criminal Code are the only ones applicable to this research. Federal statutes directly applicable to law enforcement officers nationwide in the enforcement of domestic violence specifically the Full Faith and Credit provisions of the Violence Against Women Act (VAWA), 18 *U.S.C.A.* 2265, are also used in this research.

For the purposes of this research, the working operational definitions of domestic violence will be the statutory definitions as explained in the State of New Jersey Code of Criminal Justice under

N.J.S. 2C 25-19. This section recognizes 14 crimes as offenses under the domestic violence laws, the crimes are:

Homicide	2C: 11-1
Assault	2C: 12-1
Terroristic threats	2C: 12-3
Stalking	2C: 12-10
Kidnapping	2C: 13-1
Criminal restraint	2C: 13-2
False imprisonment	2C: 13-3
Sexual Assault	2C: 14-2
Criminal sexual contact	2C: 14-3
Lewdness	2C: 14-4
Criminal mischief	2C: 17-3
Burglary	2C: 18-2
Trespass	2C: 18-3
Harassment	2C: 33-4

For the purposes of this research, the working operational definition of victims of domestic violence will be defined by the New Jersey Criminal Code 2C: 29, which specifies any person:

who is 18 years of age or older, or
who is an emancipated minor,

a minor is considered emancipated from his or her parents when the minor;
has been married;
has entered military service;
has a child or is pregnant;
has been previously declared by the court or an administrative agency to be emancipated.
and who has been subjected to an act of domestic violence by:

spouse
former spouse
any other person who is a present or former household member, or

who, regardless of age has been subjected to domestic violence by a person:

with whom the victim has a child in common, or
with whom the victim anticipates having a child in common, if one of the parties is pregnant, or
who, regardless of age, has been subjected to domestic violence by a person with whom the victim has had a dating relationship.

A victim of domestic violence may be below the age of 18.

The domestic violence assailant must be over the age of 18, or emancipated at the time of the offense.

For the purposes of this research, the definition of a mandatory arrest under the domestic violence statutes will be defined in the Guidelines on *Police Response Procedures in Domestic Violence Cases* Issued October 1991 and revised November 1994. It states that a police officer must arrest and take into custody a domestic violence suspect and must sign the criminal complaint against that person if:

A. The victim exhibits signs of injury caused by an act of domestic violence.
1. The word "exhibits" is to be liberally construed to mean any indication that a victim has suffered bodily injury, which shall include physical pain or any impairment of physical condition. Probable cause to arrest also may be established when the police officer observes manifestations of an internal injury suffered by the victim.
2. Where the victim exhibits no visible sign of injury, but states that an injury has occurred, the officer should consider other relevant factors in determining whether there is probable cause to make an arrest.
3. In determining which party in a domestic violence incident is the victim where both parties' exhibit signs of injury, the officer should consider:
a. the comparative extent of injuries suffered;

        b.   the history of domestic violence between the parties, if any, or

        c.   other relevant factors.

    4.   Police shall follow standard procedures in rendering or summoning emergency treatment of the victim, if required.

   B.   There is probable cause to believe that the terms of a "no contact" court order have been violated. If the victim does not have a copy of the court order, the officer may verify the existence of an order with the appropriate law enforcement agency.

   C.   A warrant is in effect.

   D.   There is probable cause to believe that a weapon as defined in N.J.S. 2C:39-1r. has been involved in the commission of an act of domestic violence.

For the purposes of this research, the definition of a discretionary arrest in a domestic violence situation is defined by the New Jersey Criminal Code in 2C:25 as a situation where a police officer may arrest a person or may sign a criminal complaint against that person, or may do both, where there is probable cause to believe that an act of domestic violence has been committed but none of the conditions for a mandatory arrest exist.

While the law is relatively long and extensive in scope, the above description is the basis for the current research, intended to explore the legal and social justifications for actions police officers take in domestic violence situations. The mandatory arrest provisions of the Domestic Violence Act are the legislature's means of attempting to deter future acts of domestic violence, to hold abusers accountable, and to afford the maximum protection legally allowed to the victims of domestic violence.

ROLE OF ATTORNEY GENERAL IN DOMESTIC VIOLENCE ENFORCEMENT

The New Jersey State Attorney General plays a pivotal law enforcement role within the criminal justice system in the promulgation, dissemination, and provision of training regarding domestic violence enforcement. *N.J.S.* 52:17B-97 the "Criminal Justice Act of 1970" establishes as public policy the intent "to provide for the general supervision of the criminal justice system by the Attorney General as the chief law enforcement officer in the State, in order to secure the benefits of a uniform and efficient enforcement of the criminal law and the administration of criminal justice throughout the State." *N.J.S.* 17B-112b further holds that "It shall be the duty of the police officers of the several counties and municipalities of this State and all other law enforcement officers to cooperate with and aid the Attorney General and the several county prosecutors in the performance of their respective duties."

The result of the enactment of this statute has been the development of a series of guidelines formulated by the office of the Attorney General covering a wide variety of law enforcement related issues. Some of the subjects covered by these guidelines are Bias Incident Investigation Standards, Standards to Ensure the Rights of Crime Victims, the Statewide Narcotics Action Plan, the Semi-Annual Firearms Qualification and Requalification Standards for New Jersey Law Enforcement, Internal Affairs Policy and Procedures, Missing and Unidentified Persons Investigations, Use of Force including Deadly Force by Law Enforcement Officers, Vehicular Pursuit Policy, and the Guidelines on Police Response Procedures in Domestic Violence Cases. The Guidelines on Police Response Procedures in Domestic Violence Cases were originally issued in 1991, and then revised in 1994. In addition, the State of New Jersey Domestic Violence Procedures Manual issued under the authority of the Supreme Court of New Jersey and the Attorney General of the State of New Jersey was published to provide procedural guidance to law enforcement, government officials, judges, and judiciary staff on the implementation of the Prevention of Domestic Violence Act. Originally issued in 1991 it was first revised in 1998 and most recently in 2004 to reflect changes in the law and to incorporate relevant judicial decisions.

N.J.S.A. 2C:25-20 requires annual in-service training of at least four hours on domestic violence. Initial training now occurs as part of the Basic Course for Police Officers. The Attorney General's office provides training materials to police agencies to fulfill this requirement. It also conducts training sessions for officers to become certified instructors in domestic violence for their agencies and police training academies.

PROFILE OF THE STATE OF NEW JERSEY AND STUDY SITES

New Jersey is situated on the east coast of the United States and is located between the major markets of New York and Philadelphia. New Jersey is considered a corridor state in that major highways cross the state both North to South along the Atlantic Seaboard and East to West cross country to and from her ports and New York City through the Mid-west, and even to the West Coast. The state is comprised of 21 counties and it contains 566 incorporated municipalities. While New Jersey ranks 46th in geographic land size with 7,495 square miles, it had a 2010 population of 8,791,894 ranking it 11th, and a density of 1195.5 individuals per square mile, making it the most densely populated state in the nation.

The Department of Community Affairs, Division of State and Regional Planning for the New Jersey Bureau of Statewide Planning have compiled a list of municipal characteristics and descriptions for each geographic category. The State Police use this classification in their reporting of crime statistics, and this system will be used by this research as well. The categories are listed below with their accompanying descriptions.

Urban Center	Densely populated with extensive development.
Urban Suburban	Near an urban center but not as extremely developed and more residential areas.
Suburban	Predominantly single family residential, within a short distance of an urban area.
Rural	Scattered small communities and isolated single family dwellings.
Rural Center	High density core area with surrounding rural municipalities.

For the purposes of this research, the category of suburban has been further broken down into large and small suburban agencies inasmuch as there is a wide variation within this specific classification as to the number of officers employed in municipal police departments. The cutoff point for inclusion in the small suburban designation was 50 officers. There are no Rural, or Rural Centers, that chose to participate in this study. Participation by specific police agencies and individual police officers was strictly voluntary. This research was conducted over a two-county area of New Jersey. The names of the counties and the names of individual municipalities, as well as individual subjects that participated in the study, are being kept confidential due to the sensitive nature of the study. However, some general statistics of the participating sites can be provided.

Fourteen out of potential forty-seven police agencies from a two-county area of New Jersey participated in the study. This represents a response rate of 30 percent of the possible departments. Combined, these agencies have 1,042 sworn officers of which 425 participated in the study producing a response rate of 41 percent. There are clear differences between settings in almost every category of Table 1. The two urban settings, while geographically small in size and with smaller population totals, are several times more densely populated than the two suburban settings. The total crime rates per 1,000 residents exhibit a stark contrast across the four settings. The urban police departments report a violent crime rate almost 12 times higher and a non-violent crime rate almost 3 times higher than the small suburban agencies.

When the number of domestic violence incidents reported are examined as a function of population, it was found that these crimes in the urban settings were almost three times higher than in large suburban settings and six times more likely than in small suburban settings. Surprisingly, the urban suburb communities in the study had a slightly higher reported domestic violence crime rate than even the urban settings.

The number of sworn officers per square mile is another indication of the concentration of police personnel in urban settings. Urban participating study sites had police concentrations almost five times as high as large suburban study sites and over seven times that of small suburban sites. Urban suburb study sites had police officer concentrations over three times greater than large suburban, and almost five times that of the small suburban study sites.

The overall findings of Table 1 indicate an expected high concentration of population, sworn police personnel and crime, as well as domestic violence crimes in the Urban and Urban Suburb study sites. The large suburban study sites were considerably larger geographically and in total population. The small suburban study sites were the most sparsely populated of all the settings and reflected substantially lower crime rates per 1,000 population in all categories. They also had the lowest concentrations of sworn officers and reported domestic violence incidents.

Table 1: Demographics of Participating Police Agencies by Setting*

2008	Urban	Urban Suburb	Large Suburban	Small Suburban
Geographic size square miles	10.55	8.2	100.2	57.1
Population	95,350	50,202	222,666	73,528
Population per square mile	9,037	6,099	2,528	2,198
Crime Index Total offenses	3,353	1,315	4,703	779
Crime rate per 1,000	35.17	26.2	21.1	10.6
Violent crimes	667	164	433	41
Violent crime rate per 1,000	7.1	3.3	1.9	.6
Nonviolent crimes	2,676	1,151	4,270	738
Nonviolent crime rate per 1,000	28.07	22.9	19.2	10.0
Domestic violence crimes	920	528	745	109
Number of sworn officers	268	134	446	194
Number of sworn officers per sq mi	25.4	16.3	5.3	3.4

* Sources 2008 US Census Bureau and N.J. State Police Uniform Crime Reporting Unit.

SURVEY METHODOLOGY

This research was conducted by self-report surveys of individual police officers. It is understood that this is a non-probability sample, and as such, safeguards must be taken concerning sampling error. During 2008, there were 21,715 municipal police officers employed in the state of New Jersey. Over 3,000 of these were eligible for inclusion in this study, on the condition the chief law enforcement officer of their agency approved and the individual officers agreed to participate. The reason for this universe is multi-faceted. First, with over 3,000 police officers employed within these two selected counties working different shifts and various schedules a random sample would suffer from either an inability to contact selected subjects, an inability to coordinate an effective administration of questionnaire, and/or overcoming a poor response rate. By working with the various police agencies and bringing the study questionnaires to the police officers primarily responsible for the enforcement of domestic violence offenses, this procedure allowed for a more secure collection of data on the variables measured with a wide pool of potential study participants.

Self-administered questionnaires have been found to have higher rates of return when a researcher delivers and picks up the completed questionnaires. The principal investigator was present at all sessions at which the questionnaires were distributed; he remained on-site during the completion of the survey, and he personally collected and secured all completed surveys. No individuals from the participating police agencies were given access to completed surveys. This process enhanced the security and confidentiality as only the principal investigator alone had access to the raw data and was able to monitor all the security protocols of this research.

Since the survey instrument has the potential to document findings in responses that could represent actual violations of state laws and departmental regulations, the survey was completed anonymously. In order to obtain accurate data, the survey only collected basic and limited information concerning an officer's background. To avoid identification, especially for officers working in smaller agencies, years of service of participating police officers were grouped by three-year increments. Nowhere on the questionnaire was the officer's individual department identified to ensure anonymity. All responses for agency were categorized by the New Jersey State Police designation for the type of police agency, of which there will be several in each category. Participation in the survey was strictly voluntary by individual officers after the approval of their Police Chief. This fact was stressed both by the principal investigator in person prior to the distribution of the survey and in the informed consent letter that accompanied the questionnaire which every research subject was required to read and sign prior to participation in the research.

All New Jersey police officers operate under the same laws and Attorney General Guidelines for the handling of domestic violence laws. New Jersey police officers are mandated to make an arrest in many situations similar to those posed in the hypothetical situations found in the questionnaire. If and why they decide to deviate from this standard of conduct is at the crux of this study.

The survey instrument consists of two parts. The first phase of the survey entails a series of 30 multiple choice questions, including several qualifying and sorting questions pertaining to officer and department demographics, a series of questions concerning the officers opinion concerning current domestic violence laws, department philosophy, and general departmental training and domestic violence training specifically received. The second phase of the survey process involves a series of six hypothetical domestic violence incidents which require the officer to determine how he or she would handle the scenarios on their next tour of duty. Each scenario represents complications that are commonly encountered in domestic violence situations, uncooperative victims, obvious physical injuries, suspects that have left the scene prior to police arrival, responding to the scene of repeat domestic offenses, the use of weapons in escalating domestic situations, the presence of potentially dangerous weapons, and injuries to both parties. The respondents were then asked to sort through 25 potential courses of action, some of which are mandated by the Attorney General Guidelines and New Jersey State Law and others that are optional, and some that are legally incorrect under the circumstance. The respondents are asked to explain the reasoning underlying their decisions on each scenario.

Participants were advised that there were no right or wrong answers, and the researcher is only interested in how they think, feel, and would likely react to the scenarios. They were asked to give honest reactions to the questions posed. In evaluating the responses, the benchmark employed will be the letter of the law in the State of New Jersey according to the 2C:25-17, The Prevention of Domestic Violence Act of 1991 and the Attorney General Guidelines on *Police Response Procedures in Domestic Violence Cases* revised November 1994. While there is somewhat of a contradiction inherent in asking anyone-especially police officers-about the potentially hypothetical non-compliance with the criminal laws, there was no easy way to resolve this inherent conflict within this research.

As the scenarios are all hypothetical situations and officers are not being asked to reveal any actual acts of malfeasance, misfeasance, or nonfeasance; no real harm is either measured or recorded. It would serve no legitimate purpose to ask officers to recite the letter of the law on the questionnaire and then attempt to investigate deviation from those standards. Only by attempting to learn how officers actually handle hypothetical incidents of domestic violence, and then measuring their decisions against an established benchmark that all officers are required to know, are trained in, and be in compliance with, can the deviation from the established standards be measured. To simply test the officer's level of knowledge of the law, rather than his or her application to the law would be of little utility. Instead asking about dynamic situations and about the justification they offer for these actions provides clear insight into the realities of domestic violence enforcement.

CHAPTER 2

The History of Domestic Violence

DOMESTIC VIOLENCE: THE MIDDLE AGES TO THE 1970'S

Domestic violence is not a recent phenomenon that was only addressed in the late Twentieth Century. The basis for the patriarchal, male dominated society extends back to Biblical times and can be seen in The Bible itself (Genesis 3:16, Ephesians 5:22-23, Num. 5:29-30). Blackstone's codification of the common law in 1768 asserted that a husband had the right to "physically chastise" an errant wife, provided the stick was no bigger than his thumb (Straus & Gelles, 1986). This patriarchal concept of the right for a husband to chastise his wife with a whip or rattan no bigger than his thumb around was upheld in a Mississippi court in *Bradley v. State* (1824). However, this was one of only three nineteenth century American appellate court rulings that held that a husband had a right to beat a wife in "moderation" (Sherman, 1992). The structural element of patriarchy can be seen in the low status that women generally held relative to men in the family, and in the economic, educational, political, and legal institutions of the times. The legitimacy of male dominance in the patriarchal society is clearly reflected in the values, beliefs, and norms of the times and American society (Yllo and Straus, 1984).

Balancing these facts is evidence that there are three distinct eras when attempts to outlaw spousal abuse by men have occurred in North America over the past three centuries. In 1642, American Puritans in the Massachusetts Bay Colony drew up their own criminal code, which provided:

"Everie marryed woman shall be free from bodilie correction or stripes by her husbund, unless it be in his own defence upon her assault" (Pleck, 1989, p. 22).

Several years later, an amendment to this element of the criminal code prohibited husband beating was also enacted into law. The laws provided for penalties of fines, whipping, or both. Magistrates relied heavily on "holy watching" by neighbors as a deterrent to further violence. Church courts also "shamed offenders and decided whether to expel them from the congregation" (Sherman, 1992, p. 46). This public focus on family violence diminished in the eighteenth century as the distinction between public and private conduct widened. Cultural values increasingly treated the family as a private institution and as a result, spousal abuse as a private matter not subject to public or legal scrutiny.

In the late nineteenth century, with the rising concerns over immigration, crime and general social disorder again brought the issue of family violence to prominence. By the 1870's, many of the larger cities in the United States had created police departments. A broad reform movement began to hold the police responsible for enforcing public laws and reinforcing private morality. A number of innovative policies were developed for the control of domestic disputes and for the maintenance of public order. Two of these programs included: Tort liability laws for saloonkeepers were enacted within the United States by 20 states, between 1873 and 1891. The laws permitted injured victims to sue saloonkeepers or owners for damages inflicted by people who became intoxicated in their establishments. In some states, only battered wives could sue. (Pleck, 1989, p. 42). Another effort to reduce incidents of spousal abuse included the extreme measure of implementing the use of whipping posts for wife-beaters. This measure was legislatively enacted in Maryland during 1882, Delaware in 1901, and in Oregon as late as 1906 (Caldwell, 1947, p. 131)

By World War I, however, the concern over family violence had again faded, although the problem remained. While it is difficult to obtain reliable estimates of how much change there was in the volume or rates of domestic violence, there is no reason to believe that it had substantially abated (Zimring, Makherjee, & Van Winkle, 1983).

DOMESTIC VIOLENCE: EARLY CRIMINAL JUSTICE RESEARCH AND VICTIMS RIGHTS:

Wolfgang found (1958) in an investigation of homicides occurring between 1948 and 1952 that spouses accounted for 18 percent of the crimes. He concluded there was virtually no difference between the percent of husbands and wives who were the offending party. According to FBI statistics, 15 percent of the homicides in 1975 were between husband and wife. In 7.8 percent of the cases, the husbands were the victims and 8 percent of the victims were wives (Steinmetz, 1978).

In 1967, in one of the first U.S. Department of Justice grants for law enforcement assistance, CUNY psychology professor Morton Bard designed a new method of police response to domestic disturbances. The Bard Method required that all domestic calls be directed to officers specially trained in conflict management skills. The unit was named the Family Crisis Intervention Unit, or FCIU. The techniques used by officers stressed mediation of conflict, much like a marriage counselor on the spot, rather than the assessment of possible law-breaking taking place. Arrest was reserved for cases of serious injury or assaults on police, consistent with past practices (Sherman, 1992). The consequence of this program in some cities was that fewer arrests were made than before the mediation-focused training (Wylie, Basinger, Heinecke, & Reuckert, 1976). Many of the early claims of success for the method were unsubstantiated according to later day scholars (Liebman & Schwartz, 1973).

A national survey of large police agencies (with over 100 employees) conducted in 1977 found that 71% of them reported a family crisis intervention program in operation (Bard & Connolly, 1978). This widespread adoption of mediation helped establish a bias in favor of mediation and against arrest (Sherman, 1992). Crisis intervention programs assumed that violence within the family was an interpersonal matter, not a criminal matter. Consequently, even when criminal sanctions were clearly warranted the police seldom invoked them (Wermuth, 1983). The response of law enforcement throughout the 1970's and early 1980's reflected the views of American society, the laws of the time, and their professional training. Domestic violence was seen as a private matter, ill-suited to public intervention (Burzawa & Burzawa, 2003). Domestic violence calls were considered unglamorous, unrewarding, and not real police work in the eyes of many in law enforcement.

Police agencies that did have written policies on domestic violence in the 1970's, promoted a clear non-arrest policy. An example of such a policy is the Oakland Police Department's 1975 *Training Bulletin on Techniques of Dispute Resolution,* which read:

The police role in a dispute situation is more often that of a mediator and peacekeeper than enforcer of the law....The possibility that... arrest will only aggravate the dispute or create a serious danger for the arresting officers due to possible efforts to resist arrest...is most likely when a husband or father is arrested in his home....Normally officers should adhere to the policy that arrests are to be avoided...but when one of the parties demands arrest, you should attempt to explain the ramifications of such action (e.g., loss of wages, bail procedures, court appearances) and encourage the parties to reason with each other (Martin, 1981).

In the 1970's, the third era of resurgence for domestic violence as a problem that needed to be addressed by society again brought the issue to the attention of the public. The feminist movement of this period addressed spouse assault as a major woman's issue. Frustrated by a failure of police to arrest even those husbands who committed felony assaults, domestic violence rights activists recognized the need to concentrate their efforts in two areas. First, they focused on forcing the police to enforce the few laws that did exist to help battered woman (Schechter, 1982). Secondly, activists and advocates for women's rights began lobbying state legislatures to turn police policy away from mediation and towards arrest (Sherman, 1992).

In 1976, the New York Legal Aid organization and the Center for Constitutional Rights filed a class action lawsuit on behalf of battered woman against the New York City Police Department. In a suit captioned *Bruno v. Codd* (1977), the plaintiffs alleged that the actions of the NYPD with respect to their failure to arrest husbands who had battered their wives were improper. The suit claimed the wives had been denied police protection to which they were entitled to under the law. Although the Court of Appeals dismissed several counts of the suit, the police department entered into a consent judgment. The judgment provided that the police would accept a duty to respond, and henceforth would respond to every woman's request for protection against acts of domestic violence (Zorra, 1992). In 1979, more than 3 years after the filing of a class action lawsuit by the Legal Aid Society of Alameda County in Oakland, a suit captioned *Scott v. Hart*, (filed October, 1976), led to the parties agreeing to a settlement. Under the terms of the settlement, the police agreed to institute new policies, which required:

1. The police to make an arrest whenever there was probable cause to believe a felonious assault had occurred or that a misdemeanor had been committed in the presence of a police officer
2. The decision to make an arrest would not consider factors traditionally used to justify inaction.
3. The police would not use the threat of adverse financial consequences for the couple to justify inaction or to urge the victim not to pursue the case.
4. The police would inform victims that she had the right to make a citizen's arrest and to assist the victim if she chose to do so.
5. The police to acknowledge its affirmative duty to enforce civil restraining orders.

DOMESTIC VIOLENCE: MANDATORY ARREST

By the early 1980s, three competing perspectives on the best way to handle and reduce domestic violence came into prominence. The traditional law enforcement view was to take as little formal action as possible to prevent escalation of the violence and to allow the parties to cool off. The clinical psychological approach was to stress mediation and to arbitrate the disputes (Sherman, 1992). Meanwhile, advocates for woman and victim's rights began to instigate policy changes that would characterize domestic violence as a crime rather than a family crisis, and as such, would lead to the development of mandatory arrest policies (Ellis, 1987).

In response to the controversy over how to best deal with domestic violence incidents, the first controlled experiment involving the arrest of suspects of misdemeanor assaults was conducted in Minneapolis. Perhaps the most influential and misunderstood research conducted concerning domestic violence was the Minneapolis Domestic Violence Experiment (Sherman & Berk, 1984). This scientifically controlled test attempted to determine if arrest, mediation, or temporarily separating assailants and victims was the most effective at reduced recidivism in misdemeanor domestic violence assaults. The random assignment of the three treatment responses were termed arrest, advise, or send. The victims were then followed up on a bi-weekly basis for a period of 24 weeks by telephone and in-person interviews to determine the effectiveness of the intervention employed. Of the three police responses tested, arrest was found to be the most effective of the three methods with respect to reduced future incidents of domestic violence. Data from 314 cases were collected, over an 18-month period.

This finding was seized on by a wide variety of political and social organizations from both ends of the political spectrum as positive proof that mandatory arrest policies for misdemeanor domestic violence offenses was the mean of reducing domestic violence. While conservatives saw mandatory arrest as part of a program to get tough on crime, liberals and women rights activists promoted the same policies as empowering and protecting women's rights. What almost all readers failed to heed was the author's major caveat to their own research findings:

> "It may be premature to conclude that arrest is always the best way for police to handle domestic violence, or that all suspects in such situations should be arrested. A number of factors suggest a cautious interpretation of the findings" (Sherman & Berk, 1984.)

The same can be said for the three major recommendations made by the authors the first two of which were warmly embraced while the third was ignored. They were:

1. Police officers should probably employ arrest in most cases of minor domestic violence.
2. That the Minneapolis Domestic Violence experiment should be replicated to see if it would hold up in other cities with many different kinds of people.
3. An explicit recommendation against the adoption of mandatory arrest laws.

There were many methodological issues, which also arose during and after the completion of the experiment that gave concern about the published results and the supposed conclusions of this study. First, while the designed treatment "arrest" was delivered 98.9% of the time, the designed treatment "advise" was only delivered 77.8% of the time with "arrest" being the preferred alternative in 17.6% of the cases. Similarly, the designed treatment "separate" was only delivered 72.8% percent of the time, with again "arrest" being the alternative employed in 22.8% of these cases. There was also considerable attrition among the police officers involved requiring the training of eighteen additional police officers to supplement the original 33 involved in the study. In fact, three officers accounted for 28% of all the cases included the study. Even more disturbing was the low initial follow-up interview completion rate of 62%. This dropped to only 161 victims who completed all twelve follow-up interviews or a 49% response rate (Sherman & Berk 1984.)

Perhaps the greatest criticism of the methodology of the Minneapolis Domestic Violence Experiment was the experiments lack of generalizability due to a single city with the many unique limitations of that specific community (Lempert, 1984.) Yet, the results and findings were to have an immediate and long reaching impact on domestic violence policy nationwide.

In part due to the surprising and somewhat controversial conclusions found by Sherman and Berk in the Minneapolis Domestic Violence Experiment, five follow-up studies were funded and conducted. In the five subsequent follow-up studies, the original conclusions were severely called into question. They were: Omaha, Milwaukee, Miami-Dade, Colorado Springs, and Charlotte. The original conclusions of Minneapolis could only be replicated in two of the five follow-up studies as measured by victim interviews. In only one of the five follow-up studies was deterrence, as measured by official measures, effective at the six-month period. The most startling finding was an escalation effect in domestic violence for arrested unemployed offenders and a deterrence effect for employed offenders in three of the follow-up studies (Sherman, 1992.)

Researchers Meeker and Binder (1990) suggested that the experiment had "indirect effects in modifying police policy by its effects on legislators, lobbyist, and general advocates of feminist positions." Researchers also called for an increased involvement of the criminal justice system as the appropriate response to domestic violence (Sherman & Berk, 1984; Dutton & McGreggor, 1991; Jolin, 1983). Primarily, because of Sherman and Berk (1984) Minneapolis Domestic Violence Experiment, a wave of pro-arrest policies swept the nation and with them programs established to assist the victims. By 1988, 90% of police agencies either "encouraged" or "required" arrests for misdemeanor domestic violence (Sherman, 1992).

DOMESTIC VIOLENCE: THE FEDERAL RESPONSE

The United States Attorney General's Task Force on Family Violence Final Report (1984) is often cited as one of the primary reasons for changes in arrest policies in law enforcement agencies across the nation. The goal of the task force was to help determine what role the government should be in combating the domestic violence problem. The report made specific recommendations to law enforcement agencies that included:

1. Written policies be instituted.
2. Arrest be considered the preferred response to domestic violence incidents.
3. A system be devised to track orders of protection.
4. That there be no delay in the response of law enforcement to incidents of domestic violence.
5. That orders of protection be made available by the access of forms at all police and sheriff offices.
6. That all violations of pretrial release conditions are documented.

During this time another avenue which was taken to protect victims of domestic violence were the attempts by advocates of woman's rights to use the courts to provide greater protection under the law. Since 1978, an increasing number of plaintiffs have sought to use 42 U.S.C. § 1983 as a means to redress wrong and injuries inflicted by municipal officials including the police. 42 U.S.C. § 1983 (1882) states:

> Every person who, under color of any statute, ordinance, regulation, custom, or usage, of any State or Territory or the

District of Columbia, subjects, or causes to be subjected, any citizen of the United States or other person within the jurisdiction thereof to the deprivation of any rights, privileges, or immunities secured by the Constitution and laws, shall be liable to the party injured in an action at law, suit in equity, or other proper proceeding for redress.

Suits charging that police department policies have deprived female victims of domestic violence equal protection of the law have been the most consistently successful type of failure to protect claims. In failure-to-protect cases, the policy or custom can either be a formal police department policy, or an informal "pattern or practice" implicitly condoned by the city through its failure to halt it. These equal protection suits rely on the principal that although a municipality has no obligation to provide police protection to its citizens, once it undertakes to provide these services it may not do so in a discriminatory fashion.

Thurman v. City of Torrington 595 F. Supp. 1521 (Dist. Conn. 1984) was the first case that sought to extend section 1983 protection to redress discriminatory treatment of domestic violence victims. In this case, the police refused to accept a complaint from a woman whose ex-husband repeatedly threatened her with violence (Thurman at 1530). A few days later, the police stood by while the ex-husband screamed threats at the plaintiff in her car; they refused to intervene until he broke her windshield. When the plaintiff later attempted to have her ex-husband arrested for threatening to shoot her and violating a parole condition that he refrain from future threats against the plaintiff, the police told her to return in three weeks. Three weeks later, she was told to come back after the holiday weekend; and when she returned at that time, she was informed that the only police officer who could help her was on vacation (Thurman at 1524-25).

The court held that the consistent failure of the police to respond to plaintiff's complaints, repeated over a lengthy period, demonstrated an ongoing "pattern of deliberate indifference" to persons in the plaintiff's position. It also raised an inference that there was a municipal custom or policy of extending lesser protection to women victims of domestic violence. The court had no difficulty finding that these events constituted an informal policy of denying police services to abused women (Thurman at 1527). The court found that Torrington's policy of indifference amounted to sex discrimination. By refusing to afford plaintiff protection over an eight-month period, the police were in effect operating in a discriminatory fashion. A federal jury awarded Tracey Thurman and her son $2.3 million because the police were negligent in failing to protect her from her abusive husband (Buzawa & Buzawa, 1990). *Thurman* was a landmark case, establishing the requirements for a domestic violence equal protection claim under section 1983.

Two years later, *Watson v. City of Kansas City* (1988) clarified the two types of discrimination claims that may be made in the domestic violence failure-to-protect context and the level of evidentiary proof needed to withstand summary judgment on each. The two types of claims are discrimination against the class of victims of domestic violence, and sex discrimination. In *Watson* (1988), attempts were made to apply the Fourteenth Amendment and the equal protection provisions to female victims of domestic violence. The basis for these lawsuits was the assertion that woman in domestic violence assaults were not being treated fairly and that the custom and practices of the police agencies failed to provide the victims to constitutional guaranteed protections. This case has provided the clearest statement of the requirements for equal protection claims to date.

In this case, the plaintiff, who prevailed on her equal protection claim, produced statistics showing that the arrest rate in domestic assault cases in Kansas City was half that for non-domestic assaults (Watson, 695). The statistical evidence in *Watson* was effective because it was local and it analyzed police response based on the same classification that the plaintiff claimed existed (domestic compared with non-domestic assault victims) so that disparities could easily be seen. The plaintiff in *Watson* also offered evidence that police training for domestic violence situations was oriented toward mediation, with arrest as a last resort (Watson, 696). The court held that the statistical evidence, coupled with the training curriculum, constituted sufficient evidence of a municipal policy to withstand a motion for summary judgment and to render the municipality a proper party to the suit.

The police defendants originally maintained that the statistics showing different arrest rates were not applicable to the case because the statistics did not take into account the determination of probable cause. The *Watson* court rejected this argument, however, stating that the determination of probable cause could also be influenced by the same discriminatory motives that the plaintiff alleged; and thus probable cause was not an objective standard. In other words, "the failure to account for probable cause does not necessarily undermine the probative value of the statistics (Watson, at 695).

Although equal protection claims continue to be asserted in section 1983 failure-to-protect cases, due process claims have provided an additional theory of recovery. Due process claims allow an avenue of recovery for the plaintiff who can show that she was injured by action taken pursuant to a municipal policy or custom, but who may not be able to prove the discriminatory effect or intent needed for an equal protection claim.

Due process failure-to-protect cases concern the issue of whether a state can be liable under the fourteenth amendment for failing to act. Traditionally, the state must take some affirmative action that deprives an individual of life, liberty, or property in order to trigger the protection of the due process clause. In failure-to-protect cases however, the deprivation is caused by state inaction. The challenge for plaintiffs seeking to bring due process claims lies in showing that the state's failure to act violated the fourteenth amendment. Two approaches have been developed to resolve this action/inaction dilemma.

The first approach is the special relationship theory. This theory postulate that in certain circumstances the state has an obligation to act, and by failing to act, the state violates the constitutional rights of the person toward whom it owes the obligation. However, this approach was rejected by the Supreme Court in *DeShaney v. Winnebago County Department of Social Services* (1989). The second approach holds that the creation of an arbitrary governmental policy of inaction toward certain citizens itself constitutes state action. Domestic violence failure-to-protect cases may be construed as involving affirmative state action in one of two ways. One form of state action is the creation of a municipal policy, such as a policy of nonintervention in domestic violence cases. When a city creates a policy that results in an individual being deprived of a fundamental right, it affirmatively acts in a way that may give rise to a valid substantive due process claim. A second form of state action exists when a state law grants citizens a right to expect a particular level of police protection. If the police summarily refuse to render that level of protection to an individual, the deprivation of protection is state action that violates procedural due process. The two types of claims are distinguished here primarily based on the kind of right invaded. Substantive due process claims are based on the deprivation of fundamental constitutional rights, while procedural due process claims focus on the deprivation of rights created by state law without due process.

Thus far, the section 1983 failure-to-protect cases that have been brought are based upon equal protection and the due process special relationship theory. The equal protection theory remains strong, having been reaffirmed in *DeShaney v. Winnebago County Department of Social Services,* (1989). However, the two types of equal protection claims must be distinguished and each has their separate requirements, using the Watson (1988) two-track analysis. As for due process theories, while *DeShaney* (1989) struck down the due process special relationship claims outside of the custodial context. However, claims based on affirmative state action offer a valid alternative. A strong substantive due process argument can be made that municipal policy making itself constitutes state action. Procedural due process theory offers another potential cause of action, but only in those states with statutes granting an identifiable level of protection to domestic violence victims (McFarlane, 1991).

The *DeShaney* Court addressed the question of whether a state, through its officials and governmental entities, has an affirmative constitutional duty under the due process clause to protect a citizen from private violence. If so, a state's failure to protect would render it liable under section 1983. The Court held that "a State's failure to protect an individual against private violence simply does not constitute a violation of the Due Process Clause" (*DeShaney,* at 1004.) Further, the Court denied the existence of a special relationship triggering the state's affirmative duty to protect because the child victim was not in the state's custody when his father abused him *(DeShaney,* at 1004).

Battered women plaintiffs have relied upon Section 1983 to seek federal redress for their constitutional deprivations resulting from the state's failure to intervene in domestic abuse situations. Because of this close analogy, battered women plaintiffs have felt the impact from *DeShaney's,* particularly those asserting substantive due process claims. The Court's significant narrowing of the special relationship doctrine to state custodial relationships effectively forecloses this due process avenue for battered women. In *DeShaney,* however, the Court kept the equal protection avenue open, thus signaling its continued availability as a legal avenue to recovery for battered women

In a post-*DeShaney* domestic violence case, *McKee v. City of Rockwall*, Texas, (1989), the Fifth Circuit provided the first indication of *DeShaney's* impact by confirming the apparent foreclosure of substantive due process claims (*McKee v. City of Rockwall,.* at 413). The court suggesting that if McKee had claimed a due process violation, her section 1983 suit would have been "directly barred by the holding in *DeShaney.*" The plaintiff, a domestic assault victim, sued responding police officers and the city under section 1983 for injuries resulting from the police officers' refusal to arrest her boyfriend-assaulter. *McKee* asserted an equal protection violation, alleging that this "non-arrest was the result of a [city] policy that discriminated on the basis of gender" because it discouraged officers from making arrests in domestic violence situations (*McKee v. City of Rockwall* at 401).

DOMESTIC VIOLENCE: THE VICTIMS AND BATTERERS

Family violence, family abuse, or battering are the most encompassing and inclusive of the many terms occasionally used surrounding the issue of domestic violence (Straus and Lincoln, 1985). Battering has be defined by researchers Healey, Smith and O'Sullivan (1998) as a constellation of physical violence, sexual, and psychological abuses that may include physical violence, intimidation, threats, emotional abuse, isolation, sexual abuse, manipulation, the using of children, economic coercion, and the assertion of male privilege. Victims of family violence can either share kin, intimate, or domestic relationships with their offenders. This all-encompassing term can include such varied offenses as child and elderly abuse or sibling, dating relationship and roommate violence (Weis, 1989). Definitions can be based on the form or pattern of coercive control action used or threatened to be used and forced upon the victim, these actions can include any combination of the following: physical violence, sexual violence, emotional/ psychological violence, psychological battering, destruction of property and pets, and economic control.

Gelles (1974) asked the question, "Why would a woman who has been abused by her husband remain with him?" His analysis suggests that there are three major factors influencing wife's decision to leave her abusing husbands:

1. The less the severity and the frequency of the violence.

2. The more the wife experienced violence as a child.
3. The fewer the resources and power the wife has, the more likely she is to stay with her husband.

The definition of the term violence or abuse also stirs debate as to the appropriate context of each of the terms. Spousal abuse has been expanded from its earlier definition of acts of physical violence directed toward woman by their spouses or partners (Martin, 1981) to one including sexual abuse, marital rape, and pornography (London, 1978). Researchers Gelles and Strauss (1978) defined violence as "an act carried out with the intention or perceived intention of physically pain or injury to another person."

Victims of domestic violence also face multiple situational obstacles to leaving the batterer. Because of the isolation imposed by the abusive partner, abused woman often have no friends to turn to for assistance. Their families will often offer little support and may even encourage the victim to return to their abusive partners. Some religious beliefs do not favor separation or divorce. Among the many difficult choices they may face some can include; living in poverty, going on public assistance, living in a neighborhood that is less safe for the victim's children, and/ or living out on the streets

The bonding that takes place between the batterer and the victim as a survival mechanism for the victim is similar to the dynamics that occur between hostages and captors. Applying the Stockholm Syndrome to domestic violence would mean that the victim tolerates the psychological abuse from the batterer because she sees herself through her abuser. The victims of domestic violence often have no incentive to leave because she defines herself through him. The domestic violence victim is afraid to show disloyalty to her abuser because he threatens her survival. Even when let free, the victim fears her abuser will get her again.

The repeated experience of violence may produce specific characteristics in women who are victims of domestic violence. This condition has been termed "The Battered Woman Syndrome." Women suffering battered women's syndrome have low self-esteem, strong feelings of personal guilt over their failing marriages, and self blame for the violence that their mates inflict upon them (Walker, 1979). The battered woman syndrome can be divided into two categories: First, there are those victims suffering from Learned Helplessness. Repeated battering, in addition to the victim's failed attempts at leaving the relationship reduce her/his self-esteem to a point where the victim becomes powerless. The victim accepts the inevitable that she is helpless to stop the violence against her (Walker, 1979). In the second categories are the victims of Post-Traumatic Stress Disorder. In this situation the continued abuse a victim is subjected to may lead to post-traumatic stress symptoms, such as nightmares, flashbacks, numbness, memory impairment, hyper-vigilance, and exaggerated startle response. The victim may deny and minimize the extent of the violence. This denial is necessary as a defense against anxiety and as a method of daily survival (Walker, 1991).

DOMESTIC VIOLENCE: MANDATORY ARREST AND THE POLICE

Descriptive research studies suggest that there are multiple profiles of batterers, and therefore one generic approach is not appropriate for all offenders (Chalk & King, 1998). Mandatory arrests increase domestic violence among the unemployed, but no arrests increases domestic violence among the employed (Sherman, 1992). Studies of batterers in treatment suggest conditions of impaired cognition or mental disorder (Dutton, 1995). The logic of deterrence is compromised among batterers whose behavior is patterned over time, and for whom rational calculations are not possible during the arousal associated with violent assault (Fagan, 1996).

A retrospective research study was conducted by Bourg and Stock (1994) of 1,870 domestic violence reports from a Florida county sheriff's department. In this jurisdiction, the police agency was determined to have a pro-arrest policy, limited training, and no organized community approach. The researchers found only 28.8% of cases ending in arrests. The authors concluded that future research needed to consider the adverse impact of some pro-arrest policies in addition to the effectiveness of these programs.

Past research has measured the impact of mandatory arrest policies on police through surveys (Walker, 1981; Breci, 1989; and Bellknap & McCall, 1994). Feder (1997) conducted a study of a larger southern Florida police department with a pro-arrest policy. The author found those individual police officers possessing positive attitudes toward intervention and women were positively associated with the likelihood of arrest. In addition, correct knowledge of the pro-arrest policy was found significant in accounting for the variation in the probability of police to arrest.

Researchers have examined the reluctance of police officers to enforce domestic violence legislation in detail and have noted a series of influences that have affected police agencies' response (Wallace, 1996). Some researchers have looked to feminist theories of criminal justice for an explanation of domestic violence and deviance from the law. They have looked at the male dominated law enforcement structure and declared that domestic violence is yet another example of the male dominated patriarchal society. Researchers have also looked at behavioral differences among officers within the same department and investigated education and training effects (Buzawa & Buzawa, 1990). Past research has theorized that police behavior is primarily a result of socialization within the police sub-culture, producing a similarity of values and expectations and behavioral norms (Gross, 1984).

Recently, developments include the expansion of domestic violence laws to protect victims in dating relationships and to punish those who would use stalking as a weapon in domestic settings. Another development has been the recognition and greater emphasis placed on expanded victim services. Yet, despite the increased and intensified response, there continues to be considerable criticism to the response of law enforcement and their failure to act with respect to domestic violence.

On one side of the equation, there are victims' advocacy groups and legislative mandates eliminating police discretion in acts of domestic violence. Diametrically opposed to this concept is the theory of community policing and the need for the police to empower residents to make their own decisions regarding the criminal justice process. The community-policing model, which allows for a greater emphasis on a wider range of discretion, places law enforcement in a clear dilemma in the domestic violence area. The dynamics of domestic violence include the interpersonal relationship between the victim and the offender and the reluctance of victims to pursue legal recourse of their own accord. Caught in the middle are the police, often faced with uncooperative victims and called on to enforce the letter of the law despite the potential of greater harm to the victim (Sherman, 1992).

Several studies (Dunford et el. 1990, Hirschel & Hutchinson, 1991) within the field have come to identify new factors that may actually place victims at increased risk in incidents involving misdemeanor assaults and mandatory arrests. These findings call into question the entire concept of mandatory arrests within situations of domestic violence. Yet, the vast body of current research supports the mandatory arrest provisions of domestic violence laws. Prior to any wholesale changes in the mandatory arrest laws of domestic violence, research should be conducted that will establish the answers to a number of questions surrounding domestic violence.

We can see in the feminist movement and the application of the criminal law to the problem of domestic violence and the deconstructing of the traditional values of the patriarchal male-dominated society that existed in Western Culture from the Middle Ages until the 1970's virtually unabated. By rejecting the mediation approach of Bard (1970) and promoting a change in the attitude of the society toward domestic violence, the feminist movement brought out into the open that which had remained hidden and literally behind closed doors and brought to the forefront an issue of importance and concern for millions of women and their families.

In the late 1970's, state laws expanded protection of domestic violence victims, shelters and other services for domestic violence victims (Buzawa & Buzawa, 1990). Throughout the 1970's and early 1980's police officers were taught and believed that domestic violence was a private matter, ill-suited to public intervention (Gillespie, 1989). Prior to the early 1980s, most police agencies discouraged their officers from arresting perpetrators of domestic violence (Goolkasian, 1986). Many officers would make an arrest only if in their estimation the injury to the victim was severe. It illustrates the thinking and reluctance of the police to intervene in a "family argument" (Buzawa and Buzawa, 1990).

In the early 1980s, advocates for women's and victim's rights began to instigate policy changes that would establish domestic violence as a crime rather than viewing it as a family crisis (Ellis, 1987). The Supreme Court of New Jersey, in *State v. Smith* (1981) declared that a husband could be criminally liable for the rape of his wife. The reaction to the 1984 Minneapolis Experiment was the rapid enactment in a number of states, including New Jersey, embracing mandatory arrest in domestic violence offences. It was hypothesized that arresting the batterer would have the effect of exposing the offender to negative sanctions which would counteract any rewards associated with the battering (Jolin & Moose, 1997). The United States Attorney General's Task Force on Family Violence endorsed the Minneapolis Domestic Violence Experiment findings and recommended that state and local agencies adopt a pro-arrest policy towards domestic violence. By 1988, 90% of police agencies either "encouraged" or "required" arrests for misdemeanor domestic violence (Sherman, 1992).

Since that time, multiple studies have decried the ineffectiveness or the lack of a concerted effort by police to resolve the problem of domestic violence. Past research has found that only 10% of domestic violence criminal incidents led to arrests (McLeod, 1984; Roy, 1977). In jurisdictions that mandated arrest it has been found that arrests statistics are as low as 18% (Ferraro, 1989). Even where there is extensive injury to the victim, studies have indicated a rate of arrest rarely falls outside of the 11% to 23% range (Bowker, 1982; Balos & Trotzky, 1988). In a study of homicide and domestic violence, Friedman and Shulman (1991) found 3,000 women are murdered yearly by their boyfriends or husbands notwithstanding the heightened attention to violence against women.

In the past, limited research measured the impact of mandatory arrest policies on police through surveys (Walker, 1981; Breci, 1989; and Belknap & McCall, 1994; Logan, Shannon & Walker, 2006) which have focused on various aspects of problem. Walker (1981) conducted interviews with 30 police officers in a small northeastern city and explored both their perceptions and approaches to handling domestic violence disturbances. She found that many of the police officers interviewed were frustrated and believed that little in the way of positive accomplishments could be achieved through their intervention in domestic disputes.

Another researcher (Breci, 1989) conducted studies in four police agencies, two in the southeast, and two in the Midwest. A total of 242 respondents completed survey questionnaires that sought to measure police training and assess attitudes regarding domestic disturbances. The findings of this research concluded that in comparison to untrained officers that trained officers were more likely to have a service-oriented perspective on their role in handling domestic disputes. Officers with little training on the other hand were more likely to view their role in terms of dispassionately enforcing the law. This research concluded that the more training the officers received, the more likely they were to resent guidelines and policies that limit their ability to use alternative interventions to resolve domestic disputes.

Belknap and McCall (1994) surveyed 324 police officers in a large mid-western metropolis to determine the number and types of police referrals in incidents of domestic violence. It also surveyed the officer's personal characteristics and attitudes toward domestic violence to determine if these factors influenced the type of referrals they made.

Feder (1997) conducted a study of a larger southern Florida police department with a pro-arrest policy. The author found those individual male police officers possessing positive attitudes toward intervention and the female gender were positively associated with the likelihood of arrest. In addition, correct knowledge of the pro-arrest policy was found to be a significant factor in accounting for the variation in the probability of police to arrest.

DOMESTIC VIOLENCE: RECENT RESEARCH AND DEVELOPMENTS

Logan et al. (2006) surveyed a municipal police agency and collected data from over 300 respondents to examine the police officers' attitudes toward sanctions, including fines, hard labor, or incarceration, and toward the use of treatment for domestic violence offenders. This study also examined police officers attitudes for domestic violence offenders, their substance abuse, and the imposition of sanctions. The results of this study was that officers preferred to handle domestic violence cases with treatment rather than arrest. This study also found that sanctions were favored by officers when confronted by domestic violence offenders with drug or alcohol involvement, while treatment was the favored option for offenders who were not substance abusers.

Over the last ten years researchers have begun to explore the decision making process of law enforcement in the handling of domestic violence laws, and in particular organizational characteristics than influence officers decision-making process. Researchers Buzawa & Buzawa (2003) examined the response of the criminal justice system to domestic violence laws and in particular, the evolving police response and the role of prosecutors and the courts. Among the situational and incident characteristics involved, the researchers identified the following major influence:

- The absence of the offender upon police arrival
- Who initiated the call to the police
- The presence of weapons
- The potential threat to victim's or present children's safety
- Degree of injury
- The victim-offender relationship
- Victims preference for arrest

Dugan (2003) uses data collected from the National Crime Victimization Survey to examine how legislation influences police involvement and arrest when compared to cases not reported to the police. The research found that all the legislative initiatives had at least some marginal significance with one or more forms of domestic violence. There was only one contradictory finding in that violent males are more likely to retaliate if they lose custody of their children. Another surprising finding of this research was that in states with a mandatory arrest policy the police were less likely to be called to the scene of domestic violence incidents. Hall (2005) examined the role of suspect availability in the domestic violence arrest decision-making process. This research was conducted in three upstate jurisdictions within New York and found on-scene arrests in one location at over 90%. However, in all three sites the absence of a suspect at the scene diminished the likelihood of arrest.

The use of dual arrest in domestic violence incidents is another area of research that has concentrated on the decision making process of police officers. This situation has been identified as very problematic, as it often results in true victims who, on a particular occasion, retaliate or who are perceived by the police as the aggressor in a domestic violence situation even when in fact they are not. An unintended consequence of the nationwide enforcement efforts of mandatory arrest policies in domestic violence has been the marked rise in the number of women being arrested. This is often as the result of dual arrest of both the victim and the offender after the implementation of a preferred or mandatory arrest law (Buzawa & Burzawa, 2003.) Martin (1997b) found that some prosecutors encouraged the use of dual arrest in domestic disputes to allow the courts to make the factual determination of guilt or self-defense in such cases. In Delaware, researcher Miller (2001) found the police employed dual arrest to leave the decision making process of whom to charge in the hands of the prosecutor.

Research conducted by Connolly, Huzurbazar, & Routh-McGee (2000) found that the impact of extralegal factors is significantly different for multiple party domestic violence incidents as compared to single offender incidents, and that these factors such as marital status impact arrest differently. Finn, Blackwell, Stalans, Studdard, and Dugan (2004) examined the influence of departmental policies on the dual arrests decision-making process. The researchers found that the perception by officers of official support by their superiors for dual arrest increased the likelihood of this option to resolve domestic violence disputes, especially among older officers. In addition, the presence of injuries to both parties in a dispute was a factor that tended to lead to dual arrest. Finn & Bettis (2006) examined dual arrest in a preferred arrest jurisdiction in Georgia. The researchers concluded that there were to two primary justifications for the use of dual arrests. First, officers cited as justification for dual arrest the admissions of both parties to fighting, claims of injuries and the provisions under state law. Second, this research found that by invoking dual arrest the criminal justice process would help the couple obtain the necessary services and access to resources to resolve their problem.

Researchers Frye, Haviland, & Rajah (2007) examined dual arrest and three other unintended consequences of mandatory arrest by examining data collected from a random sample of callers to a domestic violence victims call line in 1997. The findings of this study included that dual arrests were over three times as likely to be making more than $30,000 per year. In addition, the callers were found to have more likely to have been involved in previous documented domestic violence situations. According to O'Dell (2007) informal observations at the San Diego Police Department suggest that an acceptable rate of mutual combat arrests is a maximum of about 3% of all DV-related arrests.

New Jersey strongly discourages the use of dual arrest in domestic violence situations as can be seen by the directives in the Attorney General's Guidelines for Domestic Violence Cases, which states:

"In determining which party in a domestic violence incident is the victim where both parties exhibit signs of injury, the officer should consider:

    a. the comparative extent on injuries suffered
    b. the history of domestic violence between the parties, if any, or
    c. other relevant factors." (Sect II A, sub sec. 3)

The New Jersey Division of Criminal Justice Domestic Violence Instructors Manual (Module 2, 1/95) reinforces this concept in noting that "the officers should not automatically arrest both parties in a domestic violence incident (where both parties are injured). An officer should attempt to determine who was the victim and who was the assailant." (p.11)

Recent research by Finn et al. (2004) found that departmental policies that appeared to support dual arrest resulted in a greater willingness by police officers to use this option in mutual injury domestic violence incidents. This research also found that experienced officers were more likely to utilize the dual arrest option than novice officers. Finn, & Bettis (2006) explored police officers' justifications for using dual arrest, finding that officers often cited requirements under the laws and the desire to implement counseling for both parties as justification for their dual arrest actions.

Another area of research that is receiving considerable attention explores the perceptions of the victims of domestic violence in evaluating police performance, this is known as the victim-centered approach to domestic violence. Davis and Taylor (1997) conducted research of the New York City Police Department and a coordinated police and social services response to domestic violence. Their findings were that victims were more likely to report future acts of violence; as a consequence ,there was no reduction in recidivism associated with the program. The researchers concluded that increased victim confidence in reporting subsequent incidents was due to the positive impression of the police response. Research by Barnett, Miller-Perrin, & Perrin, (1997) focused on the reluctance by victims of domestic violence to evoke criminal justice sanctions against their attackers. The commonly cited justifications by female victims include economic dependency, relationship issues, lack of social support, and the concept of learned helplessness. Other research Stephens & Sinden (2000) found that victims want the police to show empathy for them and their situation. The researchers also found that victims of domestic violence wanted the police to treat them as worthy of police concern and intervention.

A third area of recent study that is closely associated to this study involves the development of systematic and encompassing domestic violence programs that go beyond the simple mandatory arrest policies currently in place in many states including New Jersey. White, Goldcamp, & Campbell (2005) examined a California Police Department that designed and implemented a program that sought to increase successful prosecutions and reduce recidivism in domestic violence offenses. This was accomplished by integration of victim support services working with the investigating police to provide enhanced response to victims' needs and an increased emphasis on victimless prosecutions. Enhanced prosecutorial involvement and communication also sought to improve the quality of case preparation and courtroom presentation.

Another researcher (Humphries, 2002) has called for an integrated criminal justice response with greater emphasis on victim preference and a broader range of punitive and treatment options. She proposes to monitor closely, but keep the offender out of jail and in intensive supervision probation or halfway houses to remain a viable taxpaying member of society. The researcher also proposes greater dedication of resources to support the victims of domestic violence through a wide array of enhanced social and legal services.

This research builds upon many earlier empirical studies that have examined a wide variety of the various aspects of theoretical perspectives of police work, including domestic violence, criminal law, police discretion, police training, and police services administration. While informed by various theoretical approaches and perspectives, much of what is examined in this study is not widely known outside of the closely guarded circle of practitioners within the law enforcement community. This research attempts to merge these two divergent and sometimes conflicting perspectives of criminology theory and the criminal justice apparatus at work in its practical application into a cohesive framework on domestic violence enforcement by the police in a mandatory arrest environment.

Zora (2011) maintains that Restorative Justice, as currently practiced in the United States, is not beneficial to victims of domestic violence. The author maintains that the tenants of Restorative Justice are incompatible with patterns of repetitive abuse and the insincerity of a willingness to change behavior exhibited by many domestic violence abusers.

CHAPTER 3
Research Design

The purpose of this research is to examine the social and legal determinants that affect a police officer's decisions and actions in domestic violence incidents in both mandatory and discretionary arrest situations within the state of New Jersey. This study investigates the effect of variation based on years of police service, education, departmental size, working environment (urban or suburban), training, police experience, departmental policy, supervisory preferences, discipline employed by individual departments, managerial style of individual departments, and requirements under the law.

It is important to clarify the terminology used by this researcher, in particular to operationalize the concept of "determinants" as referred to in this study. Determinants of domestic violence enforcement by police officers in this research pertains to a wide variety of factors that are at work both on the surface and behind the scenes to produce both expected and unanticipated outcomes in these situations. The traditional discretion common for much of police work is limited, sometimes severely, by the mandatory arrest provisions that exist in current domestic violence legislation.

Some of these determinants are orientations or personal attitudes of the individual officer being studied. Others factors investigated include those associated with the formal nature and structure of police organizations and their policies and procedures that are the result of a combination of the enacted laws and administrative directives. Still another determinant examined in this research is the geographical setting in which a police officer operates. There are four major hypotheses set forth here, each with several research questions that explore this phenomenon.

RESEARCH QUESTIONS AND HYPOTHESES

H 1 There are geographic determinants which influence and affect the enforcement of domestic violence laws by police officers.

Crank & Wells (1991) and Weiseheit, Wells & Falcone (1999) found that officers from larger, more urban police departments spend more time on crime control than officers in smaller agencies. Conversely, it was found that officers in smaller police agencies expended significantly more resources providing services than did larger agencies. Meager (1985) found significant variation in police activities by city size in a national study of 249 municipal agencies. How does this translate into the actions of the police in domestic violence situation? This research hypothesizes that police officers working in urban settings will display less strict adherence to the legal requirements of domestic violence situations and will justify their actions on personal justifications. Urban officers will differ significantly from how officers in other geographic working environments perform their duties and differ in their justifications for their actions.

Research Question 1. Does the size and type of municipality where a police officer is employed affect his/her enforcement of domestic violence laws? Are police agencies in urban settings more focused on violent felony crimes than on misdemeanor domestic violence crimes?

Research Question 2. Does the working environment of the individual police officer have a direct effect on the enforcement of mandatory arrest domestic violence situations? Do police officers in urban settings focus more on violent felony domestic violence offenses than on misdemeanor domestic violence crimes?

Research Question 3. Does the larger number of officers assigned to a shift or squad have a positive effect on a police officer's enforcement of domestic violence laws within a specific geographical setting?

Research Question 4. Do police officers working in urban areas display an adverse reaction to the strict enforcement of misdemeanor domestic violence crimes compared to officers in either urban suburb or suburban municipalities?

H 2 There are variances in the enforcement of domestic violence laws by police officers based on level of in-service training and self-motivated learning that officers pursue and are exposed to.

Studies were conducted of four police agencies (Breci, 1989), two in the Southeast and two in the Midwest, featuring a total of 242 respondents in which questionnaires measured police training and attitudes regarding domestic disturbances. The findings of this research indicated that trained officers were more likely to have a service-oriented perspective on their role in handling domestic disputes. Officers with little training, on the other hand, were more likely to view their role in terms of enforcing the law. This research concluded that the more training the officers received, the more likely they were to resent guidelines and policies that limit their ability to use alternative interventions to resolve domestic disputes. This research runs counter to the express intent of the State of New Jersey mandating four hours of annual training in domestic violence. The current research study hypothesizes that training will have a positive effect on an officer's attitudes and actions toward adherence to and enforcement of domestic violence laws.

Research Question 5. Does the frequency and amount of time an officer receives in-service training positively affect an officer's attitude toward the enforcement of domestic violence laws?

Research Question 6. Do police officers who has studied for a promotional exam with a formal study group show a more positive attitude in his/her enforcement of domestic violence laws?

Research Question 7. Does an increased level of formal education that a police officer possesses correlate to his/her enforcement of domestic violence laws?

H 3 There are social determinants, which will influence the enforcement of domestic violence laws by police officers.

Department leadership, attitudes of direct supervisors, and the work environment of the various police agencies will each affect how police officers perform their duties in domestic violence situations. Herbert (1998) found that formal and informal regulations commingle in ways that merit close investigation. Legal and bureaucratic rules partially determine police activity; however, officers have the ability to interpret these rules in different ways. There is a need to examine how formal rules become real in daily practice. This question is tested in several of the scenarios as conflicting demands for police services complicate the officer's response in domestic violence situations.

Research Question 8. Does the impression given by a police agency on strict adherence to the letter of the law correlate with a positive effect an officer's attitude toward the enforcement of domestic violence laws?

Research Question 9. Does a police officer's years of service have a negative effect his/hers attitudes toward the enforcement of domestic violence laws?

H 4 There are variances in the enforcement of domestic violence laws based primarily on a police officer's justification for initiating and sustaining a specific course of action.

The subculture of normative orders, as described by Herbert ((1998) based on the works of Parsons (1951), which attempt to capture the importance of internalized values for structuring individual behavior will be examined for police officers participating in this study. This hypothesis will be tested by an officer's actual actions in a given scenario and his/her rationalization as allowed in the second question for each scenario where the officer must justify and give some insight as to his/her reasoning for their chosen course of action. It is one thing for an officer to say that he abides by the law and another to do so in practice- and be able to justify and articulate one's reasons. This process of choice and rational provision will allow the principal investigator to test leadership, training, and the police officer's attitudes against his/her actions and justifications.

The patrol officer has been long recognized as having a great deal of discretion in carrying out his/her law enforcement duties. Yet, when it comes to domestic violence, particularly in New Jersey with extensive and specific mandatory arrest laws and guidelines, that discretion would seem to be rather limited. However, there are circumstances both within and beyond the control of the police officer on patrol which can confound and conspire against even the best of intentions. Uncooperative victims, defendants that know how to manipulate the system, the need to prioritize responses and handle other pressing requests for police services, and reluctance by prosecutors and courts to enforce sanctions all conspire to have police officers seek and sometimes utilize alternative solutions to that of arresting offenders.

Research Question 10. Do the justifications given by a police officer for the actions he/she initiates explain their actions taken in the enforcement of domestic violence laws under State and Federal law?

SURVEY RESEARCH

Survey research is one of the best and preferred vehicles by which to collect original data from a population too large to observe directly. It also eliminates the Hawthorne effect, where participant's actions are effected by and respond to the attention given them by the direct observation of researchers. The use of a standardized questionnaire in the scenario part of the survey allows for meaningful comparisons between respondents. Self-administered questionnaires are also appropriate in a group format to respondents gathered at a central location simultaneously. This research was required to adapt to the limitations and restrictions of 15 different police agencies in the location and times when the survey could be distributed, it would have been almost impossible to complete this research if not for the ability to do so in-group settings.

Four primary methods were used to collect the data for this research. Many agencies permitted this researcher to address their police officers at roll call either prior to or directly after their tour of duty. This option was available primarily due to overlapping shifts that maintained police coverage, while still allowing adequate time for officers to complete the questionnaire. Second, several agencies had scheduled in-service training days during the course of the data collection phase of this research and allowed this officer to address officers in this format. Third, some agencies allowed officers to return to headquarters and complete the survey in small groups as workload and work force allowed. Finally, this researcher was given access to a room at several agencies primarily used for conferences or roll call and permitted to use the office for walk-in participants and solicit departmental members assigned to specialized units to participate in this research.

ETHICAL CONSIDERATIONS

The potential harm to subjects in this research project is minimal. It is a routine activity for police officers to respond to domestic disputes and violations of the domestic violence laws of the State of New Jersey. The questions focus on hypothetical situations, questions about the officers' opinions toward domestic violence, or general questions regarding the police agency by which the officer is employed.

The demographic information collected was specifically designed so that no individual police officer could ever be identified from his or her answers to the survey questionnaire. Special considerations include the fact that no identifying information such as name, age, badge number, or even gender were asked on the questionnaire. Departments that participated in the study are not individually identified and are known only to the principal investigator.

The principal investigator of this research was present at all sessions where the questionnaire were distributed, read the informed consent to all potential participants, answered any and all concerns prior to the participants signing the informed consent forms. All potential participants were advised as to the strictly voluntary nature of their participation and that no repercussions would result from their refusal to participate in this study prior to the distribution of the surveys. The principal investigator remained present while the surveys were completed and collected.

As all responses are strictly confidential and the survey is anonymous, there is minimal risk of discomfort, embarrassment, or anxiety from a subject's participation in this project. The benefits of a subject's participation are that, in the future, there may be more information available on how and why police officers undertake the actions they do in domestic violence situations.

DATA COLLECTION PROCEDURES

This study was conducted by the completion of an anonymous survey questionnaire by full-time police officers employed within a two county area of New Jersey. All municipalities within this area were available for inclusion in this research. There are 21 counties in New Jersey, and the two counties that agreed to participate in this study have a population of 1.3 million of the 8.7 million of the New Jersey population (or 15% of the state population). It must be stressed that this is a convenience sampling of available police agencies and voluntary participation of individual police officers.

Preliminary contact was made through the Police Chief's Associations for each of the selected counties. A brief 15-minute presentation was conducted at a monthly meeting and a package of information concerning the research was distributed to all Police Chief's, Deputy Chief's and/or Pubic Safety Directors. The executives of the police agencies were next given the option of completing a form to agree or decline to participate in the study. If a police chief agreed to participate in the study, they were asked to designate a contact person for the principal investigator to contact and arrange the best method for the distribution of the questionnaires for that particular department. All jurisdictions within these counties were contacted either at these Police Chief meeting or by follow-up letter and offered the opportunity to participate in this research. It was entirely up to the individual police chiefs or chief executive to grant permission for the officers under his command to participate in the study. Fourteen of forty-six possible police agencies participated in this study.

At each session where potential subjects were asked to participate in the study, the principal investigator would follow the same procedure of introducing himself, distributing the approved informed consent forms for the police officers to read, and then explained the informed consent form to those present. The anonymous and strictly voluntary nature of each officer's participation in this research was stressed in every session. The principal investigator then asked for questions and answered them as needed. Officers who agreed to participate in the study signed the informed consent forms and only then given a questionnaire. Officers who declined to participate were released and allowed to resume their normal duties.

All questionnaires were personally administered by the principal investigator to assure anonymity to participants and eliminate any uncertainty and inconsistency that might affect the results of the questionnaire. This precaution helped assure consistent extraneous and environmental conditions were controlled for and that sufficient time is allotted to complete the questionnaire. At the completion each officer's participation study subjects were given a copy of the IRB consent form to keep. They were also given the opportunity to sign a separate mailing list to receive the results of the research when it became available.

DATA COLLECTION INSTRUMENT

The data collection instrument was a 10-page questionnaire. It consists of 2 distinct sections, the first with 30 questions and the second with twelve questions. Section 1 was comprised of one sorting question regarding the officer's status as a full time police officer and 14 demographic questions concerning the officer and his agency. There are 7 questions on the respondent officer's attitude towards current domestic violence laws. Six of these questions were rated on a four-point, Likert-type scale. One question had a numerical value for the frequency of dual arrest in domestic violence situations.

There were a series of 5 questions concerning the police officer's support for the replacement of mandatory arrest by the process used for dealing with disorderly person's offenses of simple assaults in incidents of domestic violence. There were 5 questions on the officer's opinion of the general and specific training that he/she received from the police department, attitude toward the department, and the enforcement of domestic violence by his or her agency. Three of these questions used a four-point, Likert-type scale; the other two questions employed numerical values determining the quantitative number of days training provided by the officer's department. There were two questions on the officer's opinion on support provided by both the administration and his immediate supervisor for the strict enforcement of domestic violence laws. These questions used a four-point, Likert-type scale. There was 1 question on the severity of his agencies departmental discipline using a four-point, Likert-type scale format for response. There was a series of 3 questions on the respondent's attitude towards his municipal court system's handling of domestic violence incidents. Here, each response was rated on a four-point, Likert-type scale.

The second part of the questionnaire featured a series of six scenario questions. First, the respondents were asked to identify who they felt was the offender in each situation. The second segment of the scenario-based questions examined the dependent variable "Action taken by police officer in domestic disputes." Twenty-five possible courses of action are made available to the officer. The legally correct answers were as follows: In five of the scenarios, the answer "arrest the suspect" was the correct course of action with respect to New Jersey Law. In one of the scenarios, "Take no action, not a crime of domestic violence" was the correct course of action.

There was a second question after each scenario asking the respondent to list those factors they felt were most important to take into consideration in making his/her decision.

This question was used to determine the officer's justification and assess the degree of compliance between his/her chosen course of action and the requirements under the Domestic Violence laws of New Jersey. There are seven possible justifications, and survey respondents were requested to rank at least two but not more than five in order of importance from 1 to 5, with 1 being the most important and five the least.

CHAPTER 4

Research Findings

For the sake of clarity, the findings are discussed in the following order: First, the demographic data for the participants is examined, followed by the officers' opinions of their personal policing style and their departmental policies and practices. Next, the subjects' overall training and departmental and judicial support for domestic violence enforcement are examined. Finally, the officers' philosophies concerning domestic violence enforcement are explored. This completes the examination of the self-report first phase of the questionnaire.

The second part of the questionnaire consists of six potential hypothetical domestic violence scenarios in which the officers were asked to handle as if they occurred on their next tour of duty. In each scenario officers were asked to identify the offender, and then, they were asked how often they would take one of the 25 potential actions listed in the circumstances portrayed in the six scenarios. Some of these 25 actions are mandatory under the current New Jersey Criminal Code and the Attorney General Guidelines, while other actions are discretionary; finally some actions would be violations of state law. There is a follow-up question to each scenario solicits the motivation for each officer's actions in each given situation.

PART I: DEMOGRAPHIC SURVEY RESPONSES

Appendix Table 4.1 identifies the rank of the participating police officers (N=425) by the setting in which the officer works. The setting is broken down into four categories: **Urban, Urban Suburb, Large Suburban, and Small Suburban.** The first three of these settings are designations used by the New Jersey State Police in their annual Uniform Crime Reports to distinguish among types of municipalities. The **Suburban** category was broken up due to the wide variety in the size of police agencies participating in the study. An arbitrary division at 50 police officers was made by the principal investigator for the purposes of this research. Two police departments are represented in the **Urban** setting, three police departments in the **Urban Suburb,** four departments in the **Large Suburban,** and five departments in the **Small Suburban.**

As depicted in Appendix Table 4.1, within the **Urban** setting of the 98 respondents 57 (or 58.2%) of the participants held the rank of police officer, 11 (or 11.2%) were detectives, 20 (or 20.4%) were sergeants, six (or 6.1%) were lieutenants, and four (or 4.1%) held the rank of captain or police chief. In the **Urban Suburb,** the smallest of the four settings, there were fifty-eight respondents, of which 42 (or 72.4%) identified themselves as police officers, one (or 1.7%) as corporals, 12 (or 20.7%) were sergeants, and three (or 5.2%) were lieutenants. The **Large Suburban** setting was the largest setting of respondents with 192 participants. The breakdown by rank for this setting was 142 (or 74%) police officers, 30 (or 15.6%) as sergeant, 15 (or 7.8%) as lieutenant, and two (or 1%) were either a captain or chiefs of police. The **Small Suburban** setting was comprised of 77 respondents, of which 50 (or 64.9%) were police officers, one (or 1.3%) was a detective, three (or 3.9%) were corporals, 11 (or 14.3%) sergeants, nine (or 11.7%) lieutenants, and three (or 3.9%) as captains or chief of police. It must be noted that the ranks of corporal and detective are titles not recognized by the New Jersey Department of Personnel (Civil Service), as an official rank and is one reason for the low number of officers identifying themselves as such by rank. This is different from Appendix Table 4.2, which identifies an officer's current assignment and may explain the disparity between the fifteen participants of the study who identified themselves by rank as detectives and the fort-eight participants who identified their assignment as detective.

The assignment of a police officer to a particular unit within the agency is, as just explained, an entirely different designation than that of an officer's rank. There are many different organizational designs for police agencies that can affect the designation of a particular officer's assignment. Some of the more frequently identified structural types include line, line and staff, functional and matrix and combinations or hybrids of these designations (Swanson, Territo, & Taylor, 2005). To accommodate variances between agencies, participants were given five general primary choices for assignments and the option for specifying another designation if they so desired. Nine particular assignment designations were reported by 425 participants as found in Appendix Table 4.2.

Across all four settings 325 (or 76.5%) of respondents reported their assignment as patrol, 48 (or 11.3%) as detective, 27 (or 6.4%) as administration, ten officers (or 2.4%) as traffic, six (or 1.4%) as narcotics officers, four (or .9%) as juvenile officers, two (or .5%) as both community policing and internal affairs, and one (or .2%) as a domestic violence officer.

As shown in Appendix Table 4.2 there was considerable variance between settings as to the assignment of officers participating in this research. The **Urban** setting exhibited the greatest variance in the range of assignments for their officers, most likely a direct result of the degree of specialization and the size of the agencies compared to the other three settings. Fifty-nine (or 60.2%) of respondents in the **Urban** setting were assigned to patrol, the lowest percentage of the four settings, while 20 (or 20.4%) of participants were detectives. Seven officers(or 7.1%) were assigned to administration, and six (or 6.1%) of officers in this setting were assigned to narcotics, two officers (or 2%) self-reported as either juvenile or internal affairs officers and one (or 1.0%) as domestic violence or traffic.

The **Urban Suburb** setting with 49 (or 84.5%) of participants reported their assignment as patrol; this was the highest percentage among the settings in this research. Of the remaining nine officers in this setting designation, four (or 6.9%) were detectives, three (or 5.2%) were assigned to traffic and two (or 3.4%) officers were classified as administration. Within the 192 **Large Suburban** research subjects in this study, 153 (or 79.7%) were assigned to patrol, 20 (or 10.4%) of the officers reported their assignment as detective and ten (or 5.2%) were assigned to administration, while five (or 2.6%) were designated as traffic, and two officers (or 1%) reported being assigned to either juvenile or community policing. Within the **Small Suburban** setting, 77 respondents were broken down by assignment as 64 (or 83.1%) in patrol, eight (or 10.4%) as administration, four (or 5.2%) as detective, and one officer reporting as assigned to traffic.

Appendix Table 4.3 examines the number of officers assigned to participant's shift. For the officers from the **Urban Suburb** and **Small Suburban** police agencies who participated in the study the most frequent response was four officers per shift. The **Urban** setting's most frequent response was seven officers per shift, with 66.2% of all responses found between six and ten officers per shift. The **Large Suburban** setting the most frequent response was six officers per shift, with 64.1% of all respondents within this setting reporting that there were between five and eight officers assigned to their shift.

All police officers, regardless of their current assignment, should be aware of the requirements of the Domestic Violence laws as part of their basic police knowledge. However, as the handling of domestic disturbances calls is primarily a function of the patrol division, this difference due to specialization is of particular interest in examining the responses to the hypothetical situations found in Part Two the of this research. In Appendix Table 4.4, 101 (or 32%) of officers who regularly respond to domestic disturbance calls report that over the past 6 months they answered "less than 10" such calls for service. This was the largest response within this grouping. Just over one-fourth of officers (or 83 respondents) answered they had answered between "ten and 19 domestic calls" in the past six months. The category of "20 to 29 domestic calls" had 61 respondents (or just fewer than 20%) of all study participants, the smallest response grouping for this question. The final response of "30 or more domestic calls" in the past six months elicited 71 responses (or just over 20%). In total, the count of 316 of officers who report they regularly respond to domestic disturbances represented 74% of all study participants. For the remaining 26% of the study participants, the overwhelming majority of 106 of 109 (or better than 97%) of officers, who in the course of their regular duties do not respond to domestic calls reported answering "less than 10" domestic calls in the past 6 months.

Urban police officers who regularly respond to domestic calls were evenly distributed at around 25% for each of the four responses, with "less than 10" having the lowest response rate at 22.7% and "30 or more" having the highest at 27%. **Urban Suburb** officers reported regularly responding to domestic calls ranged from a low of 20.8% in the "less than 10" category. This group recorded the largest responses at 28.3% for both the "10 to 19" and "30 or more" categories. **Large Suburban** police officers reported the least responses in the "20 to 29" category at 20.7% and the most in the "10 to 19" grouping at 29.3%. **Small Suburban** participants were highly concentrated in the "less than 10" category, with an over 75% response rate. The setting respondents in this category fell off sharply with only two participants (or 4%) in each of the categories "20 to 29" and "30 or more."

Appendix Table 4.4 examines the issue of officers who regularly respond to domestic disturbances in the course of their normal police duties, and the frequency with which they do so. The numbers are quite similar to those for Table 4.2, and with good reason. In most police agencies the primary responsibility for responding to calls for service falls upon the patrol division. The only officers assigned to the patrol division, who might consider they do not regularly respond to domestic calls, would be supervisors whose primary responsibilities are to be in charge of police headquarters during their tour of duty.

Appendix Table 4.5 displays the years of service for the police officers participating in this research. There are 11 categories; the first 10 are equally divided into 3 years of service intervals, while the last category collects all officers with more than 30 years of service. Police officers in New Jersey can retire with benefits after 25 years of service, at the time of this study and after 30 years of service a police officer cannot improve the percentage of his base salary on which his pension is based. This in part explains why there is such a precipitous drop in the last three categories of the chart. The reason why the years of service were broken down into categories rather than record the years of service of a participant was to give greater anonymity to participants, especially those from smaller police departments who often only hire a few officers in any given year and who, as a result, could be more readily identified by their responses.

The hiring of new police officers is contingent upon a number of factors, including the number of positions open due to retirements, resignations, and terminations, economic factors of the community, available federal funding, and grant approvals, as well as other external factors. Civil Service police agencies must give their entrance exams on the cycle determined by the Department of Personnel, which may not be on an annual basis, while non-Civil Service police agencies can administer a test whenever they desire.

Years of police service was used as a measure rather than age. Age as a measure could be used to identify an individual officer, especially in a smaller police agency. The confidential nature of this research was needed to safeguard and to protect study participant identities. The additional safeguard was taken to group years of service by three-year increments, further guarding against the possibility of attributing any survey responses to a particular study subject.

The screening and selection process for new police officers is both expensive and time- consuming. After passing the written exam portion of the selection process, police candidates undergo a battery of additional tests and examinations. These may include character and background examinations, physical agility tests, medical examinations, psychological testing, and personal interviews (Fyfe, Klinger, & Flavin 1997, Swanson, Territo, & Taylor 2005, Bennett & Hess, 2007).

There has been and there continues to be an ongoing debate within academic and law enforcement circles on the value of formal education for police officers. Researchers and commissions have decried the lack of higher standards for many of the ills within policing in the past (Fosdick, 1920; Presidents Commission, 1968; Vollmer, 1972; National Advisory Commission, 1973; Sherman et al., 1978*)* and as an impediment to future advances such as community policing (Shernock, 1992; Smith & Flanagan, 2000). Some researchers have concluded that college-educated police officers are a valuable asset that needs to be encouraged and promoted (Carter, Sapp & Stephens (1989), Cohen & Chaiken (1973), and Kappeler, Sapp & Carter (1993). Researchers Carter, Sapp, & Stephens (1986*)* cited several hypothetical advantages for police officers obtaining college educations, including:

1. The development of a broader base of information for decision making by college educated officers.
2. College education engenders the officer with the ability to flexibly handle difficult or ambiguous situation with greater creativity.
3. Higher education develops greater empathy for diverse populations.
4. An officer with a less rigid decision making process and one that more readily accepts and adapts to organizational change.
5. Police officers with a college education exhibit more "professional" demeanor and performance.

6. College educated police officers would tend to be less authoritarian and less cynical within the milieu of law enforcement.

There are important differences between education and training, both of which are examined as possible factors in determining police actions within the scope of this research. Haberfeld (2002) differentiates between education and training within the police environment by the following criteria:

Training:

- Training prepares a person with a ready response in case of an emergency.
- Programmed responses can be attained through intensive training.
- Research is used to determine the best responses.
- Training makes people feel more confident.
- Training leads to quicker and more efficient responses.
- Training leads to more consistent responses that are in accordance with the authority.
- The training process is concentrated and inexpensive.
- Skills that require hands-on training are acquired efficiently.
- Training provides an alternative solution to people who do not have the interest or ability to find their own solutions.
- Training decreases the likelihood of being sued because of the appropriate training to specific situations.

Education:

- Skills can be applied to various situations.
- Education results in a wider range of knowledge, and more intelligent communication skills.

- Education provides knowledge of how to create good training programs.
- Education may result in more worldly knowledge and thereby more tolerance of differences.
- Education takes the student through an extensive program that prepares him for a wide range of occupations.
- Education provides greater awareness of contemporary and historical events.
- Education provides people with better logical solutions.
- Education provides problem-solving skills, critical thinking, and communication skill

Appendix Table 4.6 displays the level of education for the police officers participating in the study. It should be noted that at most police academies in New Jersey some college academic credit is available as an optional part of the curriculum. New Jersey municipalities, covered by Civil Service, have as a minimum basic requirement a high school diploma in order to take the entrance exam for police officer. Non-civil service departments are free to have their own educational requirements. Often, even if there is no formal advanced academic requirement, advanced academic standing can be one of many factors used in determining an applicant's success in non-civil service police agencies.

The status of whether or not a police agency is covered by Civil Service regulations extends far beyond entrance requirements. The New Jersey Department of Personnel also administers promotional exams to Civil Service police departments. Police departments not covered by Civil Service do not participate in Department of Personnel promotional exams, but they are free to set their own criteria and develop their own testing procedures. Table 4.7 shows the study's participants covered by Civil Service Regulation.

A substantial number of officers who study for promotional exams in the State of New Jersey do so with the assistance of formal study groups. Study groups are available for both Civil Service and non-civil service police agencies. Some study groups are open to any officer wishing to participate; others are limited by recommendation or other means of selection. These study groups have been around for at least fifty years in one form or another and are a subject of considerable controversy and debate.

There is a constant chess game going on between the New Jersey Department of Personnel and the study groups as each side attempts to counter the efforts of the other regarding issues of test integrity and the security of test questions used in the testing procedure. Test subjects and study group organizers, on the other hand, claim of a lack of due process and the frequent use of unfair, and blatantly improper test questions. Study groups can be extremely intensive and expensive investments in both an officer's time and money, and they are no guarantee of success or promotion. What they do accomplish is to make the study group participant, who seriously undertakes his or her involvement, keenly aware of a wide scope of police administration theories and practices, relevant New Jersey and U. S. case law and statutes, and the New Jersey Attorney General Guidelines-including those on domestic violence. The study groups in New Jersey also have a very good record of accomplishment of placing participants at or near the top of many departmental promotional lists on a regular basis. Still, many officers decide to forego the formalized instruction of organized study groups and prepare for promotional exams on their own. Some officers choose to walk in with little or no preparation and multiple guess their way through the testing process.

With respect to Civil Service departments, the normal testing cycle for promotional exams is three years; this is why this period was used to ask study participants about their involvement with study groups. Appendix Table 4.8 illustrates the considerable role study groups play in preparing officers in this study for promotional exams. For Civil Service police agencies, there were 266 officers in this study, of which 36.8% (or 98) chose to participate in study groups. Officers choosing not to participate in study groups within Civil Service departments represented 63.2% (or 168) of study participants. For participants found in this cohort 63 (or 37.5%) studied on their own for their last promotional exam, while 105 or (62.5%) did not study or participate in a study group.

Study participants in non-Civil Service police agencies comprised 159 (or 37%) of all police officers taking part in this research. Only 31 or (19.5%) of this cohort participated in study groups. This is about half the rate of participation as found in Civil Service departments. Part of this difference might be explained by the diversity of exams given by the non-Civil Service police departments and the difficulty in preparing a study program to meet the needs of such a small number of potential promotional candidates. Civil Service promotional exams are given on a yearly cycle, and as such are predictable and test roughly one-third of all promotional candidates. Several of the large promotional study groups hold multiple sessions weekly for up to 3 months and can prepare 1,000 officers or more in a given testing cycle.

Another issue of interest in this research is a police officer's perception of the departmental philosophy. Participants were asked what their perception was of the philosophy of the police department as shown in Appendix Table 4.9. This information is sometimes found in the mission statement for the agency or is the result of a concerted and ongoing effort by a particular department to foster a specific work environment.

Traditional policing is perhaps best described as a model comprised of crime control and criminal apprehension (Kelling & Moore, 1988). First conceived by August Vollmer in the beginning of the twentieth century, this model came to prominence under O.W. Wilson and William H. Parker and became refined into the concept of crime control through motorized preventive patrol and radio-dispatched responses to reported crime (Fyfe, Greene, Walsh, Wilson, McLaren, 1995).

Conversely, community policing consistently involves some measure of community participation and involvement, particularly in the identification and prioritizing of problems as well as being an involved partner in public safety solutions (National Research Council, 2004). Community policing is an organization-wide philosophy and management approach that promotes: community, government, and police partnerships; proactive problem solving to prevent crime; and community engagement to address the causes of crime, fear of crime, and other community issues (Bennett & Hess, 2007). Community policing seeks to have the police become proactive so that they can anticipate and prevent crime rather than reacting after the fact as in traditional policing. Haberfeld (2002) noted "there are as many versions of community-oriented policing as there are police chiefs."

Discipline within a law enforcement agency can have many meanings, among the definitions authors (Fyfe et al. 1995) found that discipline is a state in which an organization's members behave in ways that best serve its goals and purposes. Other authors, (Schroeder,

Lombardo, & Strollo, 1995) differentiate between various forms of discipline. Overall, discipline is defined as the combined results of the administration of positive and negative discipline. Negative discipline refers to the meting out of forms of punishment for wrong or inappropriate job-related conduct. Positive discipline refers to the training and counseling of subordinates that result in willing commitment and voluntary compliance with the rules and regulations of an organization.

Appendix Table 4.10 displays the study participant's opinions on the types of discipline prevailing in the officer's department. This question evoked an obvious and often verbal reaction in almost every session where the questionnaire was distributed. Most officers just chuckled or made short declaratory statements, while others voiced their consternations. One primary concern was that the administration or police chief would not learn of the officer's answer to this question. Secondly, officers asked if I really wanted their honest answer to this question. Thirdly, officers asked for reassurance that the survey was anonymous and that they could not be identified. Finally, there were concerns by participants if their department's administration had seen this question and or knew of its inclusion. Officers were reassured that all answers were strictly confidential and completely anonymous. To the final question of the department's preview of the questionnaire the officers were informed that all officers were given the opportunity to participate in the study and that no police chief or administration official had asked for or been given a preview or advance copy of the survey in order to maintain the integrity of the process. The officers' concern was not without good reason. Several of the senior administrative police officers who participated in the study commented afterwards that they would love to have their department's answer to this particular question. Their requests were, of course, denied by the researcher in accord with a deep commitment to the provision of survey respondents' anonymity.

In Appendix Table 4.10 it is documented across all four settings that the category of "somewhat strict" had the largest percentages of responses ranging from a high of 62.1% for **Urban Suburb** to a low of 42.7% for **Large Suburban**. The lowest category was "very loose" across all four settings, which scored highest in the **Urban** at only 12.2% and the lowest in **Urban Suburb** with no responses. The results of this table need to be taken into consideration with other survey items that address particular components of discipline, including overall training, domestic violence training and policing style, for a more complete picture of the environment in which police officers operate within a given setting.

One component of training for New Jersey police officers is the need for police departments to keep their officers current with changes to criminal statutes, Attorney General Guidelines, and both New Jersey case law and new Federal rulings. Each of these can affect the officer's performance of their duties in critical ways. Some of the better managed police departments accomplish this by distributing periodic newsletters published through the County Prosecutor's Offices to each officer, undated departmental policies and procedures to reflect changes in the law, and ongoing and comprehensive in-service training programs.

Unfortunately, as can be seen in Appendix Table 4.11, 140 (or almost one-third) of the police officers who participated in this study responded "never" or "sometimes" to the question "I am regularly kept abreast of changes in the law by my department." It is perhaps encouraging that two-thirds of the respondents felt that their police agencies often or always kept them abreast of changes in the law. It is interesting to note that the smaller police agencies **Urban Suburb** at 53.4% and **Small Suburban** at 35.1% displayed considerably higher percentages that the **Urban** at 23.5% or **Large Suburban** at 25% of officers by setting for the response "always".

In New Jersey there are several key components to ongoing training. For 2008, when this research was conducted, the list of mandatory training topics for New Jersey police officers included the following subjects. First, there is firearms requalification, next the use of deadly force, and motor vehicle pursuit policies which, according to the Attorney General Guidelines (Division of Criminal Justice, rev. 2000), occur on a mandatory, semi-annual basis and should be given in the same 8-hour block of instruction. Secondly, there is domestic violence training which is required on an annual basis for at least four hours. Thirdly, there are a series of mandatory training sessions that must occur on an annual basis due to a particular assignment or duty. These training subjects include blood borne pathogens, hazardous materials, right-to-know (hazardous substances), breathalyzer recertification, 911 dispatcher or call taker update training, K-9 in-service training, Emergency Medical Technician recertification, confined space training, self-contained breathing apparatus training, and even fire extinguisher training. For Terminal Agency Coordinators (TAC) who monitor their department's participation in the National Crime Information System there is also (N.C.I.C/S.C.I.C recertification). Participants in this research were asked "How many days a year do you have programs of in-service training excluding firearms" to examine this essential and required component of police training. Appendix Table 4-12 displays the results of this survey question. Between all settings 55.5% of respondents received 3 days or less of in-service training. The median number of days of training, by setting, showed considerable difference across settings. The median number of days of training reported for the **Urban** setting was 3.0, for the **Small Suburban** 4.0, for the **Large Suburban** 6.0 and for the **Urban Suburb** 6.5. Perhaps more surprising was the variance in the means between the settings. Police officers in the **Urban** setting had a mean of 3.28 days of training compared to 4.65 for **Small Suburban**, 5.61 for **Large Suburban** and 6.9 for **Urban Suburb**. It is quite possible to conduct the majority of the required mandatory training in two or three days or less of in-service training, depending on an officer's assignment.

A follow-up question was asked of participants to inquire how often within the past 4 years had they received in-service training on domestic violence. Respondents were asked to circle all the years from 2005 to 2008 in which they had received this training, those responses can be seen in Appendix Table 4.13. All of the police agencies were asked if they had completed their training for 2008 before this questionnaire was distributed. In fact, this survey was distributed on the day of in-service training on domestic violence at three police agencies prior to the officers receiving this training. All of the other police departments in this study stated that they had in fact completed their training for the year.

The results of table Appendix 4.13 are perhaps the most disturbing and likely the most controversial of this entire research. Less than half of respondents (N=197/425) self-reported that they had received the state-mandated domestic violence training in each of the past four years. Over 35% (N=135) of all study participants had only received domestic violence training once in the past four years, with 19 police officers reporting having received no training at all over this period. There are issues that fall upon the responsibility of the police officer to remain current with the present state of the law. However, domestic violence training is a mandate that is the responsibility of the chain of command within the police department to insure compliance. There should not and cannot be any excuse for the failure of the departmental responsibility to properly train their police officers. Many of the major findings of Johnson (2010) concurred with the findings of this research in that officers who, resolved the largest proportion of domestic violence incidents with an arrest operated under a departmental mandatory arrest policy, had received specialized training in domestic violence investigations, and were patrol officers.

The success or failure of a law enforcement agency depends more on the quality of its first-level supervision than on the quality of supervision at any other managerial level (Schroeder et al, 1999). A supervisor's fundamental responsibility is to ensure that what needs to be accomplished during a given shift is accomplished effectively and according to a lawful manner. They are concerned with supervision of the day-to-day concerns of law enforcement officers (Bennett & Hess, 2007).

Appendix Table 4.14 displays officer perception of the support provided by the study subject's immediate supervisor for the strict enforcement of domestic violence laws. It is clear (94%) that there is widespread agreement among most the of the study participants that their immediate supervisor supports or strongly supports domestic violence enforcement. Police officers will often take their lead for their actions from their immediate supervisors. This is often termed " leading by example". This question will be further explored in part II of this research where participant's motivations for handling hypothetical domestic violence incidents are examined in detail.

The results of departmental support of strict enforcement of domestic violence laws are examined in Appendix Table 4.15. The findings are almost identical to those displayed in previous tables. It would appear from the results reported in Appendix Tables 4.14 and 4.15 that there is a fairly consistent and strong indication that participants of this study, feel that widespread organizational support exists for the enforcement of domestic violence laws. In order for any organizational goal to be realized over a long period, it is vital that it receive support and encouragement from the upper levels of management as well as first-level supervisors.

Appendix Table 4.16 represents the combination of actions in terms of the number of years that an officer was provided with the mandatory domestic violence in-service training over the past four years, along with participant's perceptions of both immediate and departmental support for domestic violence enforcement. It should not be surprising that the strong support as displayed in Appendix Tables 4.14 & 4.15 would translate into a similar result even when combined with the lower domestic violence training results of Appendix Table 4.13.

There is an overall 90% support or strong support across all settings. As seen in other tables by settings, the **Urban** reported the lowest (21.4%) level of "strong support" for domestic violence enforcement, with **Small Suburban** the second lowest percentage at 32.5%. The **Large Suburban** reported a considerable increase to 60.9% strong support for domestic violence enforcement and **Urban Suburb** reported the highest percentage at 75.9%.

What do police officers consider their primary motivation in the handling of domestic violence calls? Table Appendix 4.17 examines study participants' responses to this question. Across all four settings "situational characteristics" (N=209) was found to be the primary motivation for the handling of domestic violence calls; all groups displayed a response rate of about 50%. **Urban Suburb** was slightly higher than the rest at 55.2%, with **Urban** at 49%, **Small Suburban** at 48.1% and **Large Suburban** at 47.9%. "Legal constraints" was the next category with the most responses (N=157) across all four settings with 36.9% of all responses. Few study participants considered the other three alternative responses as primary motivations for their handling of domestic violence calls. Only 5% (N=23) of research subjects reported their primary motivation as "my individual characteristics," while 5% (N=20) considered "community characteristics," and 4% (N=16) reported "situational characteristics."

By setting, **Large Suburban** showed slightly higher percentage response with 39.6% of participants citing this reason followed by **Urban** officers at 38.8%, **Small Suburban** at 32.5% and **Urban Suburb** at 31%. Of the three remaining possible responses "my individual characteristics" was only cited by a total of 23 police officers (or 5.4%) of the sample followed by "community characteristics" with 20 officers, (or 4.7%) selecting this option and "organizational characteristics" the least cited response with only 16 officers (or 3.8 %) selecting this response.

This conclusion is further supported by the results of Appendix Table 4.18 in which officers were asked how often they feel that they personally try to enforce the Attorney General Guidelines on domestic violence. A large majority of 76.6% (N=326) of all respondents answered they "always" try to enforce the AG Guidelines, and 20.7% (N=88) gave the second most popular response "often." Only 2.4% of respondents answered "sometimes," and .2% (or 1) participant stated "never." There was an overall 90% support or strong support across all geographic settings. As seen in other tables presented by settings, the **Urban** respondents reported the lowest (21.4%) "strong support" of departmental support for domestic violence enforcement, with **Small Suburban** the second lowest percentage at 32.5%. The **Large Suburban** reported a considerable increase to 60.9% strong support for domestic violence enforcement and **Urban Suburb** reported the highest percentage at 75.9%.

By setting, the responses for Appendix Table 4.18 are similar to those found in Table 4.17. Police officer's opinions were grouped around those answers that support the enforcement of domestic violence laws. In the **Urban** setting, the highest percentage of survey participants responded they always try to enforce the domestic violence laws with 80.6%, the **Small Suburban** setting at 77.9%, the **Urban Suburb** at 75.9% and the **Large Suburban** at 74.5%. Of those officers who responded that they "often" try to enforce domestic violence laws the highest percentage was found in the **Large Suburban** setting at 23.4%, the **Urban** setting at 19.4%, the **Urban Suburb** at 19%, and the **Small Suburban** at 16.9%.

Appendix Table 4.19 displays the study participant's responses to their perception of how practical the domestic violence laws of New Jersey are to enforce. It is somewhat surprising that over one-third of all the respondents (35.3%) opinioned that the domestic violence laws were either "sometimes" or "never" practical to enforce. The most frequent response to this question was that the domestic violence laws were "often" practical to enforce (42.1%), while only 22.6% found that the laws were "always" practical to enforce. The responses by setting revealed somewhat more variance than the several previous ones concerning the New Jersey Attorney General Guidelines. For the category that the domestic violence laws are practical to enforce "always" the **Urban** survey participants were 30.6% (N=30), while the **Urban Suburb** participants were 27.6% (N=16), the **Small Suburban** setting were 26% (N=20) and the **Large Suburban** setting were only 15.6% (N=30) or just above half that of the **Urban** setting. For the category that the domestic violence laws are practical to enforce "often" the **Urban** survey participants were 46.9% (N=46), the **Large Suburban** setting participants were 44.8% (N=86), the **Urban Suburb** setting participants were 41.4% (N=24), and the **Small Suburban** setting participants were 29.9% (N=23).

For the category that the domestic violence laws are practical to enforce "sometimes" the **Small Suburban** setting respondents represented 42.9% (N=33) and the **Large Suburban** setting respondents were 39.1% (N=75). There was a sharp decline in the **Urban Suburb** setting reporting 31% (N=18) and the **Urban** setting respondents at 21.4% (N=21). The response that it was "never" practical to enforce the domestic violence laws only had three total respondents in the entire survey (N=425).

Appendix Table 4.20 exemplifies one of the difficulties in the enforcement of the domestic violence laws in New Jersey. This question goes to the heart of training and the practicality of domestic violence enforcement. The survey asked officers if and how often they had arrested both parties in a domestic violence incident in the last six months. This question will come up again in Part II of the survey when one of the scenarios will involve significant injuries to both parties. The training component is that the New Jersey Division of Criminal Justice *Domestic Legal Aspects of Domestic Violence Instructor Manual* (2003) states in this regard that:

> Where both parties in a domestic violence incident are injured, the officer should consider the following factors to determine which of the two should be arrested as the domestic violence assailant: the comparative extent of injuries suffered, the history of domestic violence between the parties, if any, or each person's fear of physical harm, if any, which resulted from the other person's threatened or actual use of force, and whether a person was acting in self defense and inflicted injuries upon the aggressor, other relevant factors.
>
> The officer should not automatically arrest both parties in a domestic violence incident. An officer should attempt to determine who was the victim and who was the assailant.

Where an officer is not able to determine who was the primary aggressor and arrests both parties, the officer should note in the incident report the reason for the dual arrest." (p. 2-12)

It is clear that the majority of police officers in the study (74.6%) have not reported making a dual arrest in a domestic violence incident within the last six months. However, it is unclear if that they were trying to follow the Attorney General Guidelines in regards to avoiding dual arrests or that the opportunity had just not presented itself within the relatively short time frame of this question. The majority of officers who reported making a dual arrest (20.9%) have only had one or two such encounters within the period. Only 4.5% (N=19) participants in this study reported having made more than two dual arrests in the previous six months. The officers' responses to this question will be again examined in part II of the scenarios where one of the situations could be interpreted as a potential dual arrest situation.

Participants were asked if police officers should be empowered by law to make warrantless arrests on probable cause for disorderly persons domestic assaults which the police do not witness. Currently under the law in New Jersey, if a victim exhibits signs of physical injury police officers are mandated to make an arrest and sign a criminal complaint. If the victim does not exhibit signs of injury police officers may make a discretionary arrest if the police officer has probable cause to believe an act of domestic violence has been committed (N.J.S.A. 2C:25-21b).

The results of Appendix Table 4.21 support widespread agreement on the concept of empowering police officers to make warrantless arrests on probable cause for disorderly person's domestic assaults that the police do not witness. There is greater "agreement" or "strong agreement" by setting among **Small Suburban** 80.5% (N=62) and **Urban Suburb** 70.7% (N=41) than among the larger departments in the study. There was 63.9% (N=142) support among **Large Suburban** police officers and 63.3% (N=62) among **Urban** police officers.

Only 20.9% (N=89) of the survey participants in Appendix Table 4.21 were found to "disagree' with the concept, and only 6.8% (N=29) that "strongly disagree" with the premise that the police should be empowered to make warrantless arrests on probable cause for disorderly person's domestic assaults that the police do not witness.

Appendix Table 4.22 examines the participating officer's opinion on one of the most difficult provisions of the New Jersey Domestic Violence Act, which inquires about the severe restrictions placed upon police discretion in the handling of domestic disputes that rise to the level of mandatory action under the Act. As previously discussed, an officer has no discretion in making an arrest by four mandatory criteria. He may not even take into consideration the desires of the victim. This removal of discretion has also come with a major protection for police officers who act in good faith to enforce the provisions of New Jersey Domestic Violence Act. Under 2C:25-24, police officers will not be held liable in a civil action for enforcing the domestic violence act by:

1. Making an arrest based on probable cause
2. Enforcing a court order in good faith, or
3. Any other act or omission in good faith under the domestic violence act.

Many situations do not fall neatly into the precise categories of mandatory or discretionary arrest in domestic violence situations. An example of this is that according to New Jersey Uniform Crime Report (2008), alcohol and/or drugs were involved in 28% (N= 19,691) of all the reported domestic violence offenses (N=70,613). The fact that one or both of the parties in a domestic violence incident may not be in full control of their mental faculties can complicate an already difficult situation. Another fact is that in 2008, fully 33% of all domestic violence offenses entailed either the presence of or the involvement of children in the domestic violence situations handled by police (NJ UCR, 2008). The need to provide and arrange for the continuing caregiver services of minor children at the scene of domestic violence incidents can cause acute complications to an already volatile and emotionally-charged environment. Yet another complication is the lack of both parties still at the scene of a domestic violence offense when the police arrive. This circumstance makes it difficult to obtain statements from both of the involved parties and to make it difficult to arrest the departed and often offending party. This set, of conditions can partially account for the fact that arrests are recorded in only 31% of reported domestic violence offenses (NJ UCR, 2008). The New Jersey Domestic Violence Offense reports are written shortly after the initial incident and do not take into account subsequent arrests for offenses where the offender has fled and is apprehended at a later date. It is for these and other complications that police officers at times feel hampered by the Attorney General Guidelines.

Appendix Table 4.22 examines the desire of police officers to have more discretion in the handling of domestic violence incidents involving simple assault. A majority of 66.8% of all study participants (N= 284) either "agree" or "strongly agree" with this concept. Of the **Urban Suburb** setting participants, 38% (N= 22) either "disagree" or "strongly disagree" with allowing police officers more discretion compared to 34.7% (N=34) of **Urban** setting participants. **Large Suburban** setting police officers opposed more discretion in 33.9% (N= 65) of those surveyed while **Small Suburban** participants disagreed 26% (N=20). It is apparent that a majority of police officers in the study would like more discretion in the handling of minor assaults in domestic violence incidents.

Appendix Table 4.23 shows the research subjects' opinions about the concept of enhanced victim empowerment in simple assault domestic violence offenses by geographical settings. Those officers who "strongly disagree" represent 18.6% (N=79) of study participants and 40.2% (N=171) of officers in the study were found to "disagree." Combined, these groups represented 58.8% of police officers in this study. Police officers who "agree" with the concept of enhanced victim empowerment represented 37.6% (N=160) of research subjects. Those participants who "strongly agree" with this concept represented 3.5% (N=15) of survey respondents. Police officers in this study were consistent in their opposition on this issue across all four settings. Police officers opposing the concept within the **Small Suburban** setting at 59.8% (N=46), **Urban** at 59.2% (N=58), **Urban Suburb** at 58.7% (N=34, and **Large Suburban** at 58.3% (N=112).

Chart 4.2 represents a scale of officer support for the Attorney General Guidelines for Domestic Violence. It is comprised of five previously asked questions which either indicate agreement or disagreement with the current domestic violence policies; these include the items displayed in Tables 4.18, 4.19, 4.21, 4.22 and 4.23. While the scale originally represented four potential levels of support, no participants of this study fell into the bottom category of "very weak support" for the Attorney General guidelines. The remaining three responses are "weak support," "support," and "strong support."

As seen in Chart 4.2, 70.6% of study participants (N=425) "support" the New Jersey Attorney General Guidelines on Domestic Violence. There was "weak support" reported by 15.3% of police officers in the study (N=65) and "strong support" by 14.1% of study participants (N=60). By setting, there was considerably more variance in the **Urban** setting when compared to the three other settings. There was greater percentage of "weak support" in the **Urban** setting 18.4% (N=18) than in the **Large Suburban** 15.1% (N=9), the **Urban Suburb** setting 13.8% (N=8), or the **Small Suburban** at 13.0% (N=10).

Chart 4.2: Scale of Officer Support Attorney General Guidelines

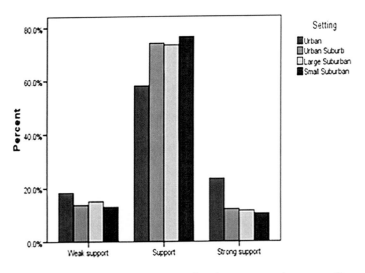

For the category of "support" for the current Attorney General Guidelines on Domestic Violence, the **Urban** setting displayed the lowest response rate at 58.2% (N=57) compared to the **Small Suburban** at 76.6% (N=43), **Urban Suburb** at 74.1% (N=43), and **Large Suburban** at 73.4% (N=141). The category "strong support" found greater support in the **Urban** setting at 23.1% or (N=23) compared to the **Small Suburban** at 10.4% (N=8), **Large Suburban** with 11.5% (N=22), and **Urban Suburb** at 12.1% (N=7).

Appendix Table 4.24 examines a basic concept of community policing in the domestic violence setting, that of empowering the public most directly affected by police policies with a voice in the enforcement of police activity. Study participants were asked if the current provisions of the New Jersey domestic violence laws regarding the mandatory arrest for offenses of disorderly person's simple assaults should be replaced by an option to allow the victim to decide if an immediate arrest is necessary.

Study participants either "strongly disagree or "disagree" with the concept of greater victim empowerment in simple assault domestic violence offenses 58.8% (N=250) of all respondents across all four settings. The **Large Suburban** setting was the category that had the largest percentage of "strongly disagree" responses with 20.8% (N=40), closely followed by the **Urban** setting with 20.4% (N=20). The **Small Suburban** setting was considerably lower at 15.6% (N=12) of study participants, and the **Urban Suburb** had the smallest percentage of respondents who "strongly disagreed" at 12.1% (N=7).

Appendix Table 4.24 investigates a concept that, although not part of the New Jersey domestic violence laws at present, has been successfully implemented in various jurisdictions within the United States- namely that of mandatory prosecutions. This concept is controversial for it diminishes the power of the victim, is costly not only to the police but to the courts as well, and is fraught with constitutional issues-most notably the right of a defendant to confront his/her accuser. It can also ultimately pit the police against the victim and increase the likelihood of the victim's support of their abuser in court.

Perhaps this can explain, in part, some of the frustration of police officers in the enforcement of domestic violence laws. The reluctance of many victims to seek legal sanctions against their abusers is well documented in the literature on domestic violence. Some of this reluctance is because of a desire by the victim to remain with the offender despite the abuse. Other reasons include a lack of alternatives-financial, emotional, and social which keep the victim clinging to the belief that conditions will improve at some juncture in the future. Police must return to the same location to intervene in domestic violence incidents between the same parties quite often.

Mandatory prosecution is an alternative that, as Appendix Table 4.24 displays, has a great deal of support from police officers across all settings. Officers in this study who "strongly agree" or "agree" with the concept comprise 69.9% of all respondents. The highest percentage positive response to this question came from the **Large Suburban** setting with 73.9% (N=142), followed by police officers in the **Urban** setting with 71.4%. (N=70). The **Urban Suburb** setting had a positive response rate of 63.8% (N=37), while the **Small Suburban** setting had the lowest positive percentage of 62.3% (N=48). Those officers who disagree with the concept of mandatory prosecution comprised 30.1% of all respondents. They were evenly distributed among all the four settings.

We have so far examined the officer's opinions regarding both the legislative and executive branches of government toward the enforcement of domestic violence. The final component will be to examine the study participants feeling regarding the judicial branch. Each officer was asked to evaluate their own municipal court system as to how domestic violence cases are handled. Many of the more serious offenses under domestic violence are indictable offenses that are handled by the Superior Court at the county level. This bifurcation of case assignment allowed the next series of questions to be focused on the most common offense under domestic violence handled at the local level by the municipal court system, that for the offense of simple assault, where the participating police officers would have greater interaction and direct knowledge of the outcomes. The most surprising issue with the next series of questions was that a few police officers declined to give any response to this set of questions. Since the number was statistically small, no attempt was made to substitute or average responses to compensate for the non-responses. The number of responses collected in the survey is given for each question.

Appendix Table 4.25 shows the responses to the question regarding the police officer's opinion on how strict the municipal judge(s) in their jurisdiction are in their application of domestic violence laws for the offense of simple assault (N=422). While few officers" strongly agreed" 8.8% (N=37) with this statement when combined with the respondents who "agreed" there was an overall positive response of 76.6% (N=323). Of those officers who "agreed" that their judge(s) strictly apply the domestic violence laws the **Small Suburban** setting had the largest percentage with 77.6% (N=59), next was the **Large Suburban** with a 67% (N=128), followed by the **Urban** with 66%. The lowest positive response rate of "agreed" was in the **Urban Suburb** setting with 60.3% (N=35); however, this result could have been due, in part, to the much greater "strongly agree" response rate of 20.7% (N=12) than were registered in the other three settings.

Appendix Table 4.26 examines study participants' opinions regarding simple assaults which occur within domestic violence cases in their local jurisdiction. Prosecutorial discretion is a factor that must be taken into consideration when investigating the entire dynamic of domestic violence enforcement. Municipal prosecutors in New Jersey are appointments made by the local legislative body for a specific term, often for 1 or 2 years. While a municipal prosecutor holds considerable discretion to prosecute, downgrade, or even dismiss cases involving domestic violence they are accountable at reappointment and to the Administrator of the Courts for any serious lapses of judgment.

Appendix Table 4.26 shows a clear division by setting on the subject of the aggressive prosecution of disorderly person offenses in domestic violence situation. By setting, **Urban** study participants "strongly disagree" with the concept of aggressive prosecutions in their jurisdiction 11.3% (N=11) of the group compared to the **Large Suburban** setting at 8% (N=15), the **Small Suburban** at 6.6% (N=5), and the **Urban Suburb** at 5.2% (N=3). The **Large Suburban** setting recorded the highest percentage of police officers who "disagree" with the concept of aggressive prosecutions of domestic violence simple assaults with 41% (N=77), **Urban Suburb** with 27.6% (N=16), **Small Suburban** with 22.4% (N=17) , and **Urban** with 21.6% (N=21). Combined, 39.4% of all respondents (N=419) either "disagree" or "strongly disagree" with the premise that their municipal prosecutor aggressively prosecutes simple assault domestic violence cases.

Of the 60.6% of participants in the study who agree that their local prosecutor is aggressive in the prosecution of simple assault domestic violence cases, the overwhelming majority "agree" with 56.8% with this concept. Meanwhile, only 3.8% of all participants "strongly agree." No setting recorded over a 2% response rate to the response "strongly agree." For the response "agree" all settings ranged from a high of 65.5% for **Urban Suburb** (N=38), to 61.8% for **Small Suburban** (N=47), to **Urban** with 60.8% (N=59), and **Large Suburban** at 50% (N=94). The total number of respondents used to collect the data for Table 4-26 is 419. It would appear from these results that while police officers report support for domestic violence prosecutions, very few feel their efforts receive strong support from prosecutors.

Appendix Table 4.27 examines a comparison between the court system's treatment of simple assaults that occur within and out of domestic violence situations. Participants were asked if they feel that domestic violence assaults are treated with the same degree of seriousness as assaults between strangers by the court system in their jurisdiction. It is an opportunity to examine the perceived outcome of the judicial process on the most common offense witnessed by the officers who regularly enforce mandatory arrests statutes.

The results of Appendix Table 4.27 show even more displeasure by police officers who participated in this study with the treatment of domestic violence assault offenses when compared with simple assaults between strangers in their local court system. Of 423 respondents, 47% (N=199) either "disagree" or "strongly disagree" with this concept of equal treatment for domestic violence offenses. While only 7.3% (N=31) "strongly disagree," a surprisingly high 39.7% (N=168) "disagree" with the concept. By setting **Large Suburban** participants for the "disagree" were 45.3% (N=86), **Urban Suburb** were 37.9% (N=22), **Small Suburban** 37.7% (N=29) and the setting with the lowest responses was **Urban** with 31.6% (N=31).

Officers surveyed who "agree" that their court takes domestic violence simple assaults as seriously as assaults between strangers were the largest group by setting at 48.5% (N=205). All settings were closely grouped on this answer, with the highest being the **Urban** setting at 53.1% (N=52), **Small Suburban** at 51.9% (N=40), **Urban Suburb** at 48.3% (N=28) and **Large Suburban** at 41.5% (N=85). Participants who responded "strongly agree" only comprised 4.5% of all officers, and no setting had a greater than 2% response rate by setting.

PART II SURVEY QUESTIONNAIRE SCENARIOS

The second part of this research was conducted by asking participants to respond to a series of six hypothetical domestic dispute scenarios. The stated purpose of this element of the research is to find out how the officers' would handle the situations as if they were occurring on their next tour of duty. The subjects were asked for their honest and forthright answers as to how they would respond to each situation.

Each survey first asked the participating officers to identify either the male or the female in the scenario as the offender. They were then asked to rank how often that they would take a particular course of action under the circumstances presented. The same twenty-five potential courses of action were presented for each scenario. Some of these actions were mandated under the Attorney General Guidelines, the New Jersey Criminal Code, and in one instance Federal law. Others actions were discretionary, and a few were inappropriate, given the specific nature of the scenario.

Study participants were asked to rate how often they would take a particular course of action under the presented circumstances. They were given five options: Always (A); Most of the time (M); About half the time (H); Some of the time (S); and Never (N). The research subjects were allowed to check off their responses for each question. A second follow-up question was then posed in which the police officer was asked to rank in order of importance, with 1 being the most important and 4 being the least important, why they had taken the actions they did in this particular scenario. Participants were asked to rank only four of seven potential responses, and to only use each number one time. The seven options were: a) Mandated under law; b) Discretionary under the law; c) Comply with the wishes of the victim; d) Based on my training as a police officer; e) Based on my experience as a police officer; f) Based on my departmental policy; and g) Based on my supervisor's preferences.

As each scenario varies in the requirements placed upon the officer by the applicable rules, regulations, guidelines and laws initially each scenario is displayed and then an analysis of the ideal response to the scenario are discussed and finally the survey participants' responses are displayed. As not all responses are appropriate in all situations, only those most appropriate in a given scenario are examined. The entire questionnaire is found in appendix "B".

Scenario 1

You respond to a call of a "noise complaint." Upon arriving, you find Billy Jean, standing in front of her home with a bleeding cut on her forehead. She is quite intoxicated and staggering around. She tells you that her husband Bob hit her during a fight over the remote control for the television. He left in his pickup truck to go out with the boys for the night. She does not want to make a complaint, since they are to go hunting in the morning. She only wants to go back inside and get some sleep. She states that her "nosey neighbors" called because of an ongoing dispute. What actions would you take?

Analysis: Scenario 1

In this situation, the officer is confronted by a number of issues. First, the female victim has sustained a visible head injury, is intoxicated, and she does not wish to make a complaint or pursue criminal charges. From her statement of "going hunting in the morning" it is safe to assume at least the possibility of weapons in the residence. She has identified her attacker as her husband and that he has left the scene for the evening.

First, there is an immediate need to[k] attend to the medical condition of the victim. While her staggering may be the result of the level of her intoxication, it could also be indicative of a more severe head injury than just the visible bleeding. In addition, her desire to go to sleep may be an indication of head trauma. Billy Jean qualifies as a victim of domestic violence as she was victim of a simple assault by her spouse, which resulted in a visible injury. Despite her desire not to pursue criminal charges, the officer **must** arrest and **must** sign [g] a criminal complaint against her husband and arrest him. If there is any indication that there are weapons in the house and that they pose a risk of serious bodily injury to the victim the officer should take all appropriate procedures to obtain a search warrant to [w] seize them. The officer **must** advise and explain to the victim [m] her rights under the domestic violence laws, including her right to obtain a Temporary Restraining Order. As an assault has occurred, the incident should be documented by the officer with: [t] an Investigation Report; [v] a Domestic Violence Offense form; and [x] a Victim Witness Notification form. As can be seen in Table 4.1, the overwhelming majority 95.1% (N= 404) correctly identified the husband of Billy Jean as the offender, in this scenario.

Appendix Table 4.29 displays how often participants of the study would make the mandatory advisement to the victim of her right to obtain a Temporary Restraining Order to seek relief from her abuser. The results show that the overwhelming majority of police officers who participated in the study, 89.9% (N=382), would comply with this provision of the Domestic Violence laws of New Jersey.

Table 4.5 Scenario 1 V: Document Incident with a "Domestic Violence Offense Report"

			Setting			
		Urban	Urban Suburb	Large Suburban	Small Suburban	Total
Always	Count	75	50	129	54	308
	% within Setting	76.5%	86.2%	67.2%	70.1%	72.5%
Most of the time	Count	18	4	33	10	65
	% within Setting	18.4%	6.9%	17.2%	13.0%	15.3%
About half the time	Count	2	1	17	2	22
	% within Setting	2.0%	1.7%	8.9%	2.6%	5.2%
Some of the time	Count	2	3	11	10	26
	% within Setting	2.0%	5.2%	5.7%	13.0%	6.1%
Never	Count	1	0	2	1	4
	% within Setting	1.0%	.0%	1.0%	1.3%	.9%
Total	Count	98	58	192	77	425

Appendix Table 4.30 displays study participants' frequency of completing the Victim Witness Notification form. This form allows law enforcement personnel to make mandatory notifications to a victim of domestic violence at specified times under the Domestic Violence Act. The fact that 95.6% (N=406) would "always" or "most of the time" complete the form is evidence of widespread knowledge of this mandatory element of domestic violence enforcement procedures and officer's willingness to comply with this provision of the law within the confines of this scenario.

Besides the mandatory requirements of the domestic violence laws of New Jersey, there are a number of possible actions in this research which are inappropriate and improper. They would be considered neglect of duty if police officers engaged in such activities. These actions could subject the officer up to departmental, civil or-in rare cases-criminal charges. It is important to repeat that police officers are only exempt from civil liability in the enforcement of domestic violence offenses when officers' act upon probable cause to make an arrest, commit an act in good faith to enforce a court order, or commit any other act or omission in good faith under the Domestic Violence Act. Given the facts of Scenario1, the following actions were deemed inappropriate and will be examined: Question 1 [a] "Take no police action, not a reportable offense"; Question 1 [n] "Advise victim to sign a complaint tomorrow"; and 1 [h] "Arrest the offender for an offense not under the domestic violence laws."

Appendix Table 4.31 is perhaps the most glaring example within Scenario 1 of an inappropriate response to an incident of domestic violence. The visible injury to Billy Jean, the statements of the victim and the surrounding circumstances all give rise to a presumption of sufficient evidence for a finding of probable cause that an act of domestic violence has occurred. With a fact pattern as described in Scenario 1, the responding police officer is mandated by law to sign a criminal complaint and made an arrest.

In this scenario the fact that 4.9% (N= 21) of officers would "always' take no police action and would not classify this incident as an offense (a disorderly persons offense, synonymous with a misdemeanor) or a crime (synonymous with a felony) is both surprising and disturbing. When combined with respondents that would not take any police action "most of the time" 5.2% (N=22), study participants who would take no action about half the time 4.2% (N=18), and police officers who would only act "some of the time" 16.7% (N=71), almost one-third of all respondents (N=132) would not consider this incident to be a criminal offense on at least an occasional basis. The denial of the protection of the Domestic Violence Act to a victim, even one that is intoxicated and uncooperative, is in direct contravention to both the spirit and letter of the law under the described circumstances. The results of Appendix Table 4.31 are very similar to those of Table 4.2 in that 68.9% of study participants would "never" refuse to take action and 63.9% would always arrest the offender in the circumstances of Scenario 1.

Appendix Table 4.31 is another example of an inappropriate action as police officers are required to sign a criminal complaint given the facts of Scenario 1 and to inform the victim that she should sign a complaint tomorrow is simply incorrect. The State of New Jersey, both through the legislature and the directives of the State Attorney General make it clear that there should be no delay in rendering assistance to victims of domestic violence. Protocols have been established and are well known to ensure 24/7 access to all police and judicial services for victims of domestic violence.

Appendix Table 4.32 shows how often participants would properly classify Scenario 1. This table is a combination of four questions 1p, 1q, 1r, and 1s. The "count" rows show how many participants per setting properly responded "never" to the various questions. The highest response rate was to "never document incident as unfounded" at 90% (N=381). The lowest response rate was to "never document incident as a verbal dispute" at just two-thirds or 67% (N=285) of participants. These numbers are again close to those produced in Table 4.33 where officers who "always" documented this incident with an Investigation Report 69.1% (N=293). They are also close to Table 4.32 where officers reported documenting the incident with a "Domestic Violence Offense Report" 72.5% (N=308) of the time. This table shows that slightly less than one-half or 48.3% (N= 205) of study participants would "never" improperly advise the victim to wait until the next day to sign a complaint against her attacker. It is extremely disheartening that in circumstances similar to Scenario 1 participants of this study would give victims of domestic violence erroneous information more than half the time.

Another alternative that can be employed by police officers when faced with a domestic violence situation is to make an arrest at the scene of a domestic disturbance, but not for a violation of an offense under the Domestic Violence laws. This alternative often satisfies the need to have an offender to be charged with an offense and removed from the scene of the domestic violence for the evening without triggering many of the time and work force consuming mandatory provisions of the Domestic Violence laws. Appendix Table 4.34 displays the frequency with which officers in this study were willing to employ such measures in Scenario 1.

The second question asked after scenario 1 examines the justification of why a study participant decided to take the particular course of actions under the specific circumstances. These results are found in Table 4.6. This question was asked after each scenario to explore if an officer's justifications may change with circumstances or if police officers consistently apply the same justifications regardless of the situational facts.

The responses were rank ordered to allow both the most important and least important justifications to be examined. Of the seven possible responses from which participants were given to choose, one justification had a response rate of 54% (N=357). This justification was "mandated under law." Three other possible responses had moderate response rates they are as follows: "based on my experience as a police officer" 13% (N=88); "based on my departmental policy" 11% (N=88); and "based on my training as a police officer" 11% (N=70). The final three responses were very low in Scenario 1 they are as follows: "based on my supervisor's preference" at 5% (N=30); "discretionary under law" 4% (N=28); and "comply with the wishes of the victim 2% (N=16).

Table 4.6 Scenario 1: Most Important Justification of Officer's Actions

	Urban 97 Subjects	Urban Suburb 58 Subjects	Large Suburban 192 Subjects	Small Suburban 76 Subjects	Total 423 Subjects
Mandated under law	87	48	159	63	357
Discretionary under the law	11	6	8	3	28
Comply with victim wishes	7	4	4	1	16
Training as a police officer	29	14	24	9	76
Experience as a police officer	31	9	36	12	88
Departmental policy	30	12	18	10	70
Supervisor's preferences	12	7	6	5	30
Total	207	100	255	103	665

Although participants were asked to rank and select each action only once, many officers decided to give multiple responses to this question; this resulted in more than 423 responses being recorded. If multiple responses were eliminated then the 357 responses of "Mandated under law" would represent the "most important" justification of 84% of all respondents in this study.

The high percentage of police officers in this study who base their actions on their knowledge of the law bodes well for the fact that the vast majority of police officers in this study believe that they are following the mandates of the Domestic Violence laws of New Jersey. The fact that a considerably lower number of officers complied with the mandated actions within the scenario may suggest issues concerning poor and insufficient training and inadequate understanding of the requirements for enforcing the requirements of Domestic Violence laws of New Jersey.

In Table 4.7 ranked the least important justification for the officer's actions in scenario 1. The response "mandated under law," which had the largest "most important" response, reported the smallest "least important justification" with only 4% (N=22) of all 504 responses.

The remaining five answers were all in a similar range of 12% to 17%. The responses in declining order were: "based on my supervisor's preferences" at 17% (N=88); the response "based on my experience as a police officer" at 15% (N=74); the response "discretionary under the law" at 15% (N=74); "based on my departmental policy" at 14% (N= 73); and "based on my training as a police officer" with 12% (N=58).

Scenario 2

You respond to the Jones residence where you find the Mrs. Jones in a disheveled state. She invites you in and you see an interior door smashed. She does not display any signs of injury, but she complains she had "the wind knocked out of her" and she is holding her ribs. She stated that her husband "just lost it" and threw her into the door. She doesn't know what to do. She states that she is in fear for the safety of her four children and herself. At this time, Mr. Jones comes back from Home Depot with a new door.

Table 4.7 Scenario 1: Least Important Justification of Officer's Actions

	Urban 97 Subjects	Urban Suburb 58 Subjects	Large Suburban 192 Subjects	Small Suburban 76 Subjects	Total 423 Subjects
Mandated under law	7	3	7	5	22
Discretionary under the law	22	12	30	10	74
Comply with victim wishes	35	18	45	17	115
Training as a police officer	12	2	29	15	58
Experience as police officer	16	16	29	13	74
Departmental policy	19	10	38	6	73
Supervisor's preferences	25	10	39	14	88
Total	136	71	217	80	504*

*Although participants were asked to rank and select each action only once, many officers decided to give multiple responses to this question. This resulted in more than 423 responses being recorded.

Analysis: Scenario 2

In this situation, the officer is confronted by a multitude of issues. Here the female victim Mrs. Jones is not exhibiting visible signs of an injury, but there is considerable evidence that an assault has taken place and that she has sustained internal injuries. Her complaint of "having the wind knocked out of her" and "holding her ribs" along with the physical evidence of the broken door are sufficient to establish probable cause that an assault has occurred. As this was caused by her husband it qualifies as an act of domestic violence under the New Jersey Criminal Code. The charges should include criminal mischief for the damaged door and assault for being thrown through the door.

Mrs. Jones' additional statements that she is in fear for her safety and that of her children trigger additional mandatory criteria. The fact that her husband has just returned with a new door should not influence the officer in the performance of his duty.

First, the police officer should dispatch the appropriate medical assistance for the victim. Second, Mr. Jones should be arrested for assault on his wife and the officer should sign the criminal complaint. Finally, the officer should assist the victim in applying for a temporary restraining order against her husband. As in Scenario 1, there are additional actions the officer must take. The officer **must** advise and explain to the victim [m] her rights under the domestic violence laws, including her right to obtain a Temporary Restraining Order. As an assault has occurred, the incident should be documented by the officer with: [t] an Investigation Report, [v] a Domestic Violence Offense form, and [x] a Victim Witness Notification form.

Table 4.8 displays the distribution of how officers identified the offender in Scenario 2. A total of 99.1% (N=421) of officers in the survey correctly identified the male, Mr. Jones, as the offender under the Domestic Violence laws in Scenario 2.

Table 4.8: Scenario 2: Identification of the Offender

		Setting				
		Urban	Urban Suburb	Large Suburban	Small Suburban	Total
Male	Count	98	58	191	74	421
	% within Setting	100.0%	100.0%	99.5%	96.1%	99.1%
Female	Count	0	0	0	1	1
	% within Setting	.0%	.0%	.0%	1.3%	.2%
Both	Count	0	0	0	1	1
	% within Setting	.0%	.0%	.0%	1.3%	.2%
Neither	Count	0	0	1	1	2
	% within Setting	.0%	.0%	.5%	1.3%	.5%
Total	Count	98	58	192	77	425

Table 4.9 displays the number of participants by setting that the police officers would arrest the male offender under the Domestic Violence laws of New Jersey in scenario 2. This scenario is clearly a mandatory arrest situation. A majority of 64.9% (N=276) of study participants would "always" arrest the offender under the Domestic Violence laws in Scenario 2, but this figure must be considered low. Even when added with the 17.2% (N=73) of participants who would arrest "most of the time" for a combined 82.1% (N=349), an arrest could be expected in only four out of five such incidents.

Table 4.9 Scenario 2 G: Arrest Offender Under Domestic Violence Laws

		Setting				
		Urban	Urban Suburb	Large Suburban	Small Suburban	Total
Always	Count	68	44	116	48	276
	% within Setting	69.4%	75.9%	60.4%	62.3%	64.9%
Most of the time	Count	15	8	36	14	73
	% within Setting	15.3%	13.8%	18.8%	18.2%	17.2%
About half the time	Count	9	1	16	5	31
	% within Setting	9.2%	1.7%	8.3%	6.5%	7.3%
Some of the time	Count	6	4	20	7	37
	% within Setting	6.1%	6.9%	10.4%	9.1%	8.7%
Never	Count	0	1	4	3	8
	% within Setting	.0%	1.7%	2.1%	3.9%	1.9%
Total	Count	98	58	192	77	425

Table 4.10 displays the frequency with which officers would undertake the mandatory action of personally signing a criminal complaint against the offender in Scenario 2. Similar to Scenario 1, in Scenario 2 less than half or 49.2 (N=208) of respondents would take this course of action mandated under the law. Even with the category "most of the time" combined, only 65.7%   (N=278) of police officers would take this action. The two **Urban** settings display higher rates of "always" making the mandatory arrest, but lower "most of the time" rates for Scenario 2.

Table 4.10 Scenario 2 J: Officer to Sign Complaint

				Setting		
		Urban	Urban Suburb	Large Suburban	Small Suburban	Total
Always	Count	56	34	85	33	208
	% within Setting	57.1%	58.6%	44.7%	42.9%	49.2%
Most of the time	Count	13	7	37	13	70
	% within Setting	13.3%	12.1%	19.5%	16.9%	16.5%
About half the time	Count	9	1	17	6	33
	% within Setting	9.2%	1.7%	8.9%	7.8%	7.8%
Some of the time	Count	13	10	31	10	64
	% within Setting	13.3%	17.2%	16.3%	13.0%	15.1%
Never	Count	7	6	20	15	48
	% within Setting	7.1%	10.3%	10.5%	19.5%	11.3%
Total	Count	98	58	190	77	423
	% within Setting	100.0%	100.0%	100.0%	100.0%	100.0%

Table 4.11 displays the findings in Scenario 2 that the study participants were slightly more willing to "always" document the incident with an "Investigation Report "76.9% (N=326) than officers

were in Scenario 1. When considered in combination with participants who would document this incident "most of the time," 9.9% (N=42) with an "Investigation Report" officers in this study group would correctly memorialize this act of domestic violence at least 77.8% (N=388) most of the time or more frequently.

Table 4.11 Scenario 2 U: Document Incident with an "Investigation Report"

		Setting				
		Urban	Urban Suburb	Large Suburban	Small Suburban	Total
Always	Count	72	49	137	68	326
	% within Setting	73.5%	84.5%	71.7%	88.3%	76.9%
Most of the time	Count	13	3	22	4	42
	% within Setting	13.3%	5.2%	11.5%	5.2%	9.9%
About half the time	Count	2	1	6	1	10
	% within Setting	2.0%	1.7%	3.1%	1.3%	2.4%
Some of the time	Count	3	2	9	3	17
	% within Setting	3.1%	3.4%	4.7%	3.9%	4.0%
Never	Count	8	3	17	1	29
	% within Setting	8.2%	5.2%	8.9%	1.3%	6.8%
Total	Count	98	58	191	77	424

Appendix Table 4.35 displays the frequency with which officers would dispatch medical assistance for a victim that is in obvious pain but exhibits only limited signs of physical injury as found in Scenario

2. This is a mandatory provision of the Domestic Violence laws with which officers are required to comply. Study participants responded that they would "always" dispatch medical assistance 77.6% of the time in Scenario 2. When combined with respondents who answered "Most of the time," victims would be dispatched medical assistance 90.1% (N=383) in such incidents.

In Scenario 2 the fact that Mrs. Jones has stated that she is in fear for her safety and that of her four children should trigger the responding officer's need to advise and assist the victim to obtain a Temporary Restraining Order (TRO). The Temporary Restraining Order is designed to prohibit contact between the victim and her attacker for a brief period, usually between a week and 10 days, in order to allow the victim time to rationally consider her/his situation and decide on how they wish to proceed in their relationship with their abuser.

There are, in addition to the no contact order, other provisions of the TRO for continued temporary financial support, and prohibiting the attacker from returning to the scene/ residence of the domestic violence without a police escort. This brief return is only for the removing of limited personal items, and represents a condition that can be imposed by the court. Anger management and an alcohol or drug treatment programs can also be imposed on the attacker if requested and warranted in the opinion of the judge. The victim will be required to appear in court to have a Superior Court judge at the County level decide to continue, modify or dismiss the TRO. The TRO can also be converted to a Final Restraining Order (FRO) which is permanent and remains in effect until such time as the victim wishes to rescind the FRO and goes before a judge, to have the order modified. Under no circumstances can the victim rescind or modify the restraining order by his/her own action or statement. Nor can the victim be held accountable if the offender violates a restraining order based on statements or actions of the victim. Violation of a TRO or FRO by the attacker provides grounds for a mandatory arrest under the Domestic Violence laws of New Jersey, based on probable cause.

Appendix Table 4.36 displays how often participants of the study would make the mandatory advisement to the victim of her right to obtain a Temporary Restraining Order to seek relief from her abuser. The results for survey question 2 [m] show that the overwhelming majority of police officers who participated in the study 90.4%

(N=384) would comply with this provision of the Domestic Violence laws of New Jersey. The category "most of the time" represented an additional 6.4% (N=27) of study participants. If combined, police officers in this study confronted with a similar scenario could be expected to advise victims of their rights to obtain a TRO under the provisions of the Domestic Violence laws of New Jersey 96.8% (N=411) of the time.

Appendix Table 4.37 shows the frequency for officers in this study that would have the victim of Scenario 2 sign the Victim Witness Notification form as required under the Domestic Violence laws of New Jersey. A total of 90.6% (N=385) of officers reported that they would "always" comply with this requirement. This is slightly higher than in Scenario 1 (85.9%). Another 5.4% (N= 23) would comply with this requirement "most of the time."

It is mandatory that for each domestic violence offense that occurs in New Jersey a Domestic Violence Offense report must be completed. In Table 4.12 found on the following page for Scenario 2, study participants reported that they would always" 83.8% (N= 356) document the incident with a Domestic Violence Offense report. Another 9.2% (N=39) would complete the Domestic Violence Offense report "most of the time." Combined, this would produce a compliance rate of 92% (N=395) for this scenario. This would represent over a 10% increase of study participants who would take this mandated action as compared to Scenario 1 despite both scenarios presenting conditions that would always require this action be taken by responding police officers.

In Scenario 2 there are specific actions that are inappropriate and constitute violations of the Domestic Violence laws of New Jersey. Among the list of possible courses of action the following would be inappropriate: [a] Take no police action, not a reportable offense; [e] Remove offender from household for night; [h] Arrest the offender for an offense not under the domestic violence laws; [n] Advise victim to sign a complaint tomorrow; [o] Make no written report of incident; [p] Document incident as "unfounded"; [q] Document incident as "Gone on Arrival"; [r] Document incident as "verbal dispute"; and [s] Document incident as "family problem."

Table 4.12 Scenario 2 V: Document with "Domestic Violence Offense Report"

| | | Setting | | | | |
		Urban	Urban Suburb	Large Suburban	Small Suburban	Total
Always	Count	82	53	156	65	356
	% within Setting	83.7%	91.4%	81.2%	84.4%	83.8%
Most of the time	Count	9	3	22	5	39
	% within Setting	9.2%	5.2%	11.5%	6.5%	9.2%
About half the time	Count	1	0	7	0	8
	% within Setting	1.0%	.0%	3.6%	.0%	1.9%
Some of the time	Count	4	2	5	7	18
	% within Setting	4.1%	3.4%	2.6%	9.1%	4.2%
Never	Count	2	0	2	0	4
	% within Setting	2.0%	.0%	1.0%	.0%	.9%
Total	Count	98	58	192	77	425

Appendix Table 4.38 depicts the most egregious of these transgressions in that the officers' report taking no police action in the circumstances and fact pattern of this situation. Fortunately, only 8.5% (N=36) of officers surveyed would "some of the time" or more frequently take no police action in Scenario 2. A total of 91.5% (N= 389) would take some form of police action in this situation.

Appendix Table 4.39 finds that slightly over one-half (or 50.6%) (N= 215) of study participants would "never" improperly advise the victim to wait until the next day to sign a complaint against her attacker. This is a mandatory arrest situation where the officer is required to sign the criminal complaint. While a slight improvement over Scenario 1, it is still disheartening that in circumstances similar to Scenario 2 participants of this study would give victims of domestic violence erroneous information almost half the time N= 210 of 425 (49.4%).

Appendix Table 4.40 shows how often participants would properly classify Scenario 2. This table is a combination of four questions-namely, 2p, 2q, 2r, and 2s. Each of these choices is improper as they would decriminalize the incident and attempt to minimize the facts of Scenario 2. The downgrading of the seriousness of a domestic violence incident is a major concern to all parties interested in the reduction of domestic violence. First, if the incident is not recorded as an act of domestic violence, the offender will not be discouraged from further acts of domestic violence, he/she will not be identified as a recidivist domestic violence offender, and the victim may feel that her abuse is not being treated with the degree of seriousness it deserves.

The "count" rows show how many participants per setting properly responded "never" to these particular questions. The highest response rate was to "never document incident as unfounded" at 98% (N=413). The answer "never document as gone on arrival" also received a very high response rate of 96% (N=408). The response "family problem" was used to define the facts of Scenario 2 by study participants 19% (N=81) of the time. The response "document incident as a verbal dispute" was used by 20% (N= 84) of study participants to improperly classify this scenario as something other than an act of domestic violence.

Although participants were asked to rank and select each action only once, many officers decided to give multiple responses to this question. This resulted in more than 422 responses being recorded. Of the seven possible responses from which participants were given to select, the justification "Mandated under Law" had the highest response rate of 51% (N=338). This was also the highest response in Scenario 1. Three other possible responses had moderate response rates in Scenario 2, and they are: "Based on my experience as a police officer" 12% (N=80); "Based on my training as a police officer" 11% (N=76); and "Based on my departmental policy" 10% (N=67). Again, the same categories were in the second tier of responses in Scenario 1. The final three responses were the lowest response rates in Scenario 2:

"Discretionary under law" 8% (N=50); "Based on my supervisor's preference" at 5% (N=36); and "Comply with the wishes of the victim 3% (N=19). If multiple responses are eliminated, then the 338 responses of "Mandated under law" would represent the "most important" justification of 80% of all respondents in this study. This is a lower statistic than found in the results of Scenario 1 by this measure.

Table 4.13 Scenario 2: Most Important Justification of Officer's Actions by Setting

	Urban 96 Subjects	Urban Suburb 58 Subjects	Large Suburban 192 Subjects	Small Suburban 76 Subjects	Total 422 Subjects
Mandated under law	79	46	155	58	338
Discretionary under the law	12	8	20	10	50
Comply with victim wishes	10	3	6	0	19
Training as a police officer	31	11	24	10	76
Experience as a police officer	28	13	27	12	80
Departmental policy	27	13	17	10	67
Supervisor's preferences	17	8	8	3	36
Total	204	102	257	103	666

Although participants were asked to rank and select each action only once, some officers decided to give multiple responses to this question. This resulted in more than 422 responses being recorded. In similar fashion, the study participants listed their least important justification for their actions within Scenario 2 in Table 4.14. The response "comply with the wishes of the victim" which had the smallest "most important" justification had the largest "least important" justification at 21% (N=105). If measured on the scale of possible study participants, the 105 would represent 25% of the 422 police officers who responded to this question. Research subjects considered the response "based on my experience as a police officer" next least important at 20% (N=97). The next tier of four responses was in the range of 16% to 11%. The greatest of these for "least important justification" was "based on my supervisor's preferences at 16% (N=77), the response "based on my departmental policy" was at 15% (N= 76), "Discretionary under the law" at 12% (N=61), and "based on my training as a police officer" with 11% (N=56). The response "mandated under law" which had the largest "most important" response reported the smallest "least important justification" with only 4% (N=21) of all 493 responses.

Table 4.14 Scenario 2 Least Important Justification of Officer's Actions by Setting

	Urban 96 Subjects	Urban Suburb 58 Subjects	Large Suburban 192 Subjects	Small Suburban 76 Subjects	Total 422 Subjects
Mandated under law	8	3	9	1	21
Discretionary under the law	19	9	24	9	61
Comply with victim wishes	33	14	40	18	105
Training as a police officer	12	7	28	9	56
Experience as a police officer	17	17	42	21	97
Departmental policy	17	13	37	9	76
Supervisor's preferences	19	10	33	15	77
Total	125	73	213	82	493

Appendix Table 4.41 examines an alternative to mandatory arrest under the Domestic Violence law. In these circumstances, the offender is arrested for a violation of the law, but not for a violation of the domestic violence laws. It may be a means to remove the offending party to allow the victim to collect her/his thoughts and make decisions without being influenced by their attacker. It may also allow for a cooling off period for both parties to deescalate the conflict. This alternative is now considered improper under current mandatory pro-arrest policies in New Jersey. Making an arrest for an offense other than an act domestic violence can also considerably reduce the paperwork the officer must complete than if the incident were treated under the provisions of the domestic violence laws. Considerably more officers were willing to employ this alternative to a mandatory arrest in Scenario 2 than in Scenario 1.

Scenario 3

You are cruising the parking lot of a popular nightclub just before closing time. You observe a female pulling away from her male companion. She is visibly upset. Upon investigation, you find that the two had been engaged, but that she broke it off. She just wants to be left alone; she has an hour ride back to the "City" to get home. While the ex-fiancé is telling you his sob story of female troubles, the female interrupts and states "Officer, I got a copy of my restraining order here from New York, he in not supposed to come within 100 feet of me. Can't you tell him just to leave me alone?" What actions do you take?

Analysis: Scenario 3

In this situation, the officer is again confronted by a victim, the female party in this scenario, who does not wish to press a criminal complaint but simply wants her attacker to stop harassing her. The female is a victim of domestic violence in that a valid court order protecting her has been violated. For the police officer, simply separating the parties and sending them on their way may have been possible if not for the out-of-state restraining order that the officer is made aware of in the course of his investigation. Despite the fact that the restraining order is not from a New Jersey court, it must be given full faith and credit. The facts of this scenario are clearly a violation of the terms of a *bona fide* restraining order. While there is no need for an additional domestic violence offense to occur for a violation of a restraining order to take place in this situation, just the mere presence of the offender in physical contact with the victim is sufficient to trigger the violation of the New York Court order.

It must be noted that a court order only prohibits the offender from having any contact with the victim. The victim cannot violate the terms of a restraining order in New Jersey. Even if the victim lures the defendant into a situation where the offender is in violation, with the implied or explicit consent of the victim, the offender is still the only one in violation of the court-imposed order. The restraining order can only be violated by the defendant, and any contact can subject him/her to a mandatory arrest in New Jersey.

Depending what the officer's investigation reveals, it may also trigger additional charges for harassment or stalking. The violation is witnessed by the officer, and this fact turns this ex-lovers spat into a **mandatory** arrest situation for the offender. The police officer also **must** sign the criminal complaint. The appropriate paperwork would include: [t] an Investigation Report, [v] a Domestic Violence Offense form, and [x] a Victim Witness Notification form. Among the list of possible courses of action, the following would be inappropriate are: [a] Take no police action, not a reportable offense, [e] Remove offender from household for night, [h] Arrest the offender for an offense not under the domestic violence laws, [n] Advise victim to sign a complaint tomorrow, [o] Make no written report of incident, [p] Document incident as "unfounded", [q] Document incident as "Gone on Arrival", [r] Document incident as "verbal dispute", s) Document incident as "family problem", and [t] Document the incident with an "Operations report."

Table 4.15 examines the ability of study participants to make a correct identification of the male as the offending party in Scenario 3. Police officers in this research correctly indentified the male as the offender in this situation 94.4% (N=401) of the time.

This situation is fraught with serious implications for the officer who fails to take the necessary actions. If the officer witnessing this offense were to do nothing, and if either later this date, or in the future, the male offender were to injure the victim or worse, the police officer could be held liable civilly for failing to protect the victim. Departmental discipline could also be imposed up to and including dismissal from the department. There would also be the potential for civil liability for the police department and the officer's supervisors under the theory of vicarious liability for failure to supervise and failure to train.

Table 4.15 Scenario 3: Identification of the Offender

		Setting				
		Urban	Urban Suburb	Large Suburban	Small Suburban	Total
Male	Count	90	56	185	70	401
	% within Setting	91.8%	96.6%	96.4%	90.9%	94.4%
Female	Count	1	1	4	0	6
	% within Setting	1.0%	1.7%	2.1%	.0%	1.4%
Both	Count	5	1	1	4	11
	% within Setting	5.1%	1.7%	.5%	5.2%	2.6%
Neither	Count	2	0	2	3	7
	% within Setting	2.0%	.0%	1.0%	3.9%	1.6%
Total	Count	98	58	192	77	425
	% within Setting	100.0%	100.0%	100.0%	100.0%	100.0%

Table 4.16 displays the number of study participants who would arrest the offender under the Domestic Violence laws and the frequency with which they would do so in each geographic setting. In this research, 70.7% of all study subjects would "always" make the mandatory arrest in the circumstances described in Scenario 3. When combined with the category "most of the time" 11.1% (N=47) a compliance rate of 81.8% is calculated. More officers in the study were reluctant to take the required action mandated by the Scenario 3 fact pattern than in either of the other scenarios thus far examined.

Table 4.16 Scenario 3 G: Arrest Offender Domestic Violence Laws

		Setting				
		Urban	Urban Suburb	Large Suburban	Small Suburban	Total
Always	Count	66	45	140	48	299
	% within Setting	68.0%	77.6%	73.3%	62.3%	70.7%
Most of the time	Count	15	3	23	6	47
	% within Setting	15.5%	5.2%	12.0%	7.8%	11.1%
About half the time	Count	4	2	9	2	17
	% within Setting	4.1%	3.4%	4.7%	2.6%	4.0%
Some of the time	Count	6	4	11	12	33
	% within Setting	6.2%	6.9%	5.8%	15.6%	7.8%
Never	Count	6	4	8	9	27
	% within Setting	6.2%	6.9%	4.2%	11.7%	6.4%
Total	Count	97	58	191	77	423

To examine this phenomenon more closely the responses to the option to arrest the offender not under the Domestic Violence laws will be examined to see how many study participants chose to select this alternative course of action to resolve Scenario 3. Appendix Table 4.42 reveals that almost one–half of all study participants or 49.5% (N=209) would arrest the offender, but not under the Domestic Violence laws "some the time" or more.

Appendix Table 4.43 examines the participant's responses to the issue if the Scenario 3 warrants' "no police action" at all. It is clear that the majority of police officers 85.4% (N=363) in this study report that they would not ignore the situation and take "no police action." This lends credibility to Table 4.16 & Appendix Table 4.41 in which most study subjects would take some police action to arrest the offender in Scenario 3. The results are slightly lower than in Scenario 2 (91.5%), but considerably higher than in Scenario 1 (68.9%) on this same question.

Table 4.17 displays the frequency with which officers would undertake the mandatory action of personally signing a criminal complaint against the offender in Scenario 3. As this is a violation of one of the mandatory arrest situations under the New Jersey Domestic Violence Act, police officers are required to sign the criminal complaint in this situation. Participants in this study were slightly more likely to take this action in Scenario 3, 52.4% (N=221) than in the two previous hypothetical scenarios.

Table 4.17 Scenario 3 J: Officer to Sign Complaint

		Setting				
		Urban	Urban Suburb	Large Suburban	Small Suburban	Total
Always	Count	50	35	101	35	221
	% within Setting	52.1%	60.3%	52.6%	46.1%	52.4%
Most of the time	Count	14	3	21	9	47
	% within Setting	14.6%	5.2%	10.9%	11.8%	11.1%
About half the time	Count	3	3	12	4	22
	% within Setting	3.1%	5.2%	6.2%	5.3%	5.2%
Some of the time	Count	16	7	28	10	61
	% within Setting	16.7%	12.1%	14.6%	13.2%	14.5%
Never	Count	13	10	30	18	71
	% within Setting	13.5%	17.2%	15.6%	23.7%	16.8%
Total	Count	96	58	192	76	422

The largest increase occurred in the **Large Suburban** setting which rose to 52.6% of respondents would "always" sign the complaint against the offender as compared to Scenario 2 where only 44.7% (N=85) would and Scenario 1 where only 40.8% (N=78) would.

Appendix Table 4.44 shows the results with respect to the frequency with which officers in this study would comply with the mandatory provisions of the Domestic Violence laws to advise the victim of her rights to obtain a Temporary Restraining Order. The relatively low number of officers who would advise the victim of her rights to a restraining order, 52.7% (N=216) may reflect the fact there is already a standing restraining order in effect. This may also explain a small number of study participants (N=15) who chose not to answer this particular question.

Table 4.18 Scenario 3 U: Document Incident with an "Investigation Report"

| | | Setting | | | | |
		Urban	Urban Suburb	Large Suburban	Small Suburban	Total
Always	Count	66	46	130	56	298
	% within Setting	68.0%	79.3%	67.7%	72.7%	70.3%
Most of the time	Count	9	3	16	5	33
	% within Setting	9.3%	5.2%	8.3%	6.5%	7.8%
About half the time	Count	5	0	14	3	22
	% within Setting	5.2%	.0%	7.3%	3.9%	5.2%
Some of the time	Count	6	4	8	5	23
	% within Setting	6.2%	6.9%	4.2%	6.5%	5.4%
Never	Count	11	5	24	8	48
	% within Setting	11.3%	8.6%	12.5%	10.4%	11.3%
Total	Count	97	58	192	77	424

Table 4.18 shows the frequency that police officers in the study were only willing to "always" document this incident with an "Investigation Report" 70.3% (N=298) of the time. This action is an indication of the seriousness with which the study participant is treating the incident as it generates a Uniform Crime Report statistic. The result for Scenario 3 was somewhat lower than in Scenario 2 (N=326) but marginally higher than in Scenario 1 (N=293). An additional 7.8%

(N=33) of study participants would document the incident "most of the time" with an Investigation Report.

The mandatory requirement in New Jersey for each domestic violence offense to be documented with a Domestic Violence Offense report is examined for Scenario 3 in Table 4.19. Study participants reported that, given the facts of Scenario, 3 they would "always" document the incident with a Domestic Violence Offense report 73.8% (N=313). This is, again, consistently similar to the "always" of Scenario 1 (72.5%) and is lower than was exhibited in Scenario 2 (83.8%). The combined results for the responses "most of the time" and "always" are similar with Scenario 3 recording a response rate of 81.6%, Scenario 1 with 81.4% and Scenario 2 at 93%.

Appendix Table 4.44 displays how often study participants would have the victim of Scenario 3 sign the Victim Witness Notification form as required under the Domestic Violence laws 80.1% (N=338). The results are the lowest percentage of officers complying with this mandatory requirement of the Domestic Violence laws so far seen in this study. Even when combined with the category "most of the time," Scenario 3 results 85.8% were considerably lower than Scenario 1 at 95.5% or Scenario 2 at 96%. This is consistent with the results of Table 4.16 where more police officers were reluctant to view this incident as a mandatory arrest under the Domestic Violence laws.

Scenario 3, as is the case for all the incidents hypothesized for participants in this research, contains questions about actions that are not only improper, but actually contrary to the legal requirements of the Domestic Violence laws of New Jersey. In Scenario 3, if the victim had simply made a complaint that a violation of the restraining order had occurred out of eyesight of the officers there may have been some doubt as to the establishment of the requirement of probable cause to make an arrest or sign a criminal complaint. Under those circumstances, it is then appropriate for the officers to document the incident. If the victim still wishes to pursue a civil or criminal complaint, then the officer should arrange transport to police headquarters for the victim to begin the complaint process on their own. If the victim is reluctant to or does not wish to begin the complaint process, and none of the four mandatory arrest criteria are met, it is proper to advise the victim/complainant of the complaint procedure to sign a criminal complaint the next day if she were to change her mind.

Table 4.19 Scenario 3 V: Document with "Domestic Violence Offense Report"

		Setting				
		Urban	Urban Suburb	Large Suburban	Small Suburban	Total
Always	Count	75	48	141	49	313
	% within Setting	77.3%	82.8%	73.4%	63.6%	73.8%
Most of the time	Count	8	2	20	3	33
	% within Setting	8.2%	3.4%	10.4%	3.9%	7.8%
About half the time	Count	3	0	9	2	14
	% within Setting	3.1%	.0%	4.7%	2.6%	3.3%
Some of the time	Count	6	3	10	12	31
	% within Setting	6.2%	5.2%	5.2%	15.6%	7.3%
Never	Count	5	5	12	11	33
	% within Setting	5.2%	8.6%	6.2%	14.3%	7.8%
Total	Count	97	58	192	77	424

However, in Scenario 3 the violation of a court order was witnessed by the police officers thereby establishing probable cause and escalating the incident to a mandatory arrest situation. The police officer **must** make an arrest and **must** sign a criminal complaint, even if the victim does not wish to press charges. Under the circumstances to advise the victim to sign a complaint tomorrow is incorrect and contrary to the spirit and letter of the criminal statutes of the State of New Jersey. The results of Appendix Table 4.46 show that 60% (N=252) of study participants would "never" improperly advise a victim, as was found in Scenario 3, to wait until the next day to sign a criminal complaint against the offender. Again, this is the first instance in this study where the officer observed the offense and did not have to rely on the statements of the victim to establish probable cause that an act of domestic violence with a mandatory arrest situation had occurred. While the results of Appendix Table 4.46 are encouraging, there is still considerable room for improvement in the 40% of study participants who would "some of the time" or more give the improper advice to the victim to wait until the next day (when she would be back in New York and out of the officer's jurisdiction) to sign a complaint against the offender.

Appendix Table 4.47 shows how often participants would properly classify Scenario 3. This table is a combination of four questions-3p, 3q, 3r, and 3s. Each of these choices is improper as they would decriminalize the incident and serve to minimize the facts of Scenario 3. The "count" rows show how many study participants in each setting properly responded "never" to the various questions, thereby refusing to improperly classify the criminal offense of this scenario. The highest response rate was to "never document incident as unfounded" at 94% (N=396). The response "never document as gone on arrival" also received a very high response rate of 93% (N=395). The other two responses enjoyed a greater usage and as such an improper selection as a classification for documenting scenario 3. The response "never document incident as a family problem" was used to define the facts of Scenario 3 in 87% (N=369) by study participants. The response "never document incident as a verbal dispute" was used by 74% (N=312) of study participants who would not attempt to diminish the severity of the offenses actions in Scenario 3 by misidentification of the incident.

These numbers again closely reflect those produced in Table 4.18 where study participants who "always" documented this incident with an Investigation Report 70.3% (N=298). They also closely reflect the study participants who "always arrested the offender under the Domestic Violence laws" at 70.7% (N=299). The fact that a considerable number of study participants on a regular basis would not classify Scenario 3 as a crime or an act of domestic violence, this finding is one of serious concern. Despite the fact that the victim does not wish to pursue the issue or file a criminal complaint, that both parties are from out-of-state, and that the court order is also from an out-of-state jurisdiction, a police officer must uphold the domestic violence laws without exception. In reality, a prosecution under the circumstances of Scenario 3 may be an exercise in futility. There is little chance of a successful prosecution for such a violation, wherein both parties reside out-of-state and there is a reluctant victim.

The second question asked after scenario 3 will allow for a more detailed exploration of the justification as to why study participants chose the particular course of action. The responses were ranked order to allow both the most important and least important justifications to be examined. Table 4.20 displays the most important justification for officers in this study of their actions in Scenario 3.

Table 4.20 Scenario 3: Most Important Justification of Officer's Actions by Setting

	Urban 96 Subjects	Urban Suburb 58 Subjects	Large Suburban 192 Subjects	Small Suburban 76 Subjects	Total 422 Subjects
Mandated under law	78	46	164	55	343
Discretionary under the law	17	8	11	9	45
Comply with victim wishes	9	3	6	4	22
Training as a police officer	30	12	21	9	72
Experience as a police officer	26	14	26	18	84
Departmental policy	30	12	20	11	73
Supervisor's preferences	16	8	10	5	39
Total	206	103	258	111	678

Although participants were asked to rank and select each action only once, many officers decided to give multiple responses to this question. This resulted in more than 422 responses being recorded. Of the seven possible responses from which participants were given to select from, the justification "Mandated under Law" had the highest response rate of 50% (N=343). This was also the highest response in Scenarios 1 and 2. Three other possible responses had moderate response rates in Scenario 3 and they are: "Based on my experience as a police officer" 12% (N=84); "Based on my departmental policy" 11% (N=73); and "Based on my training as a police officer" 11% (N=72).

Again, these same categories were the second tier of responses in Scenarios 1 and 2. The final three responses, which were the lowest response rates in Scenario 3 are: "Discretionary under law" 7% (N=45); "Based on my supervisor's preference" at 6% (N=39); and "Comply with the wishes of the victim 3% (N=22). If multiple responses were eliminated, then the 343 responses of "Mandated under law" would represent the "most important" justification of 81% of all respondents in this study. This is a slightly higher statistic than found in the results of Scenario 2 (80%) and lower than in Scenario 1 (84%) by this measure.

Study participants listed their least important justification for their actions within Scenario 3 in Table 4.21. The response "comply with the wishes of the victim" which had the smallest "most important" justification, had the largest "least important" justification at 21% (N=104). If measured on the scale of possible study participants, the 104 would represent 25% of the 422 police officers who responded to this question.

Although participants were asked to rank and select each action only once, many officers decided to give multiple responses to this question. This resulted in more than 422 responses being recorded. Where study participants could justify, in some ways, their frequent inaction in Scenarios 1& 2 on a lack of probable cause, Scenario 3 was designed to eliminate this obstacle by having the officer observe the violation of the Domestic Violence laws as it occurred. Even so, the analysis of each of the hypothetical situations on an identical series of questions resulted in very similar outcomes for all the scenarios that constituted mandatory arrest situations.

Research subjects considered the response "based on my experience as a police officer" next least important at 18% (N=87), followed by "based on my departmental policy" at 17% (N=86) and "based on my supervisor's preferences" at 17% (N=83). The final three responses recorded the following tallies for least important justifications: "discretionary under the law" at 12% (N=60); "based on my training as a police officer" with 11% (N=55); and "mandated under law" which had the largest "most important" response reported the smallest with only 4% (N=18) of all responses. It would appear that from the responses to Tables 4.20 and 4.21 the police officers in this study were inclined to disregard the wishes of the victim and to rely on the mandatory requirements of the law in determining the correct course of action to take, given the facts of Scenario 3. Yet, only 70.7% of police officers would "always" make the arrest under the circumstances (Table 4.16). While 81% of study participants list the justification "mandated under law" as their primary motivation in this scenario, many study participants either misunderstand or misapply the law.

Table 4.21 Scenario 3: Least Important Justification of Officer's Actions by Setting

	Urban 96 Subjects	Urban Suburb 58 Subjects	Large Suburban 192 Subjects	Small Suburban 76 Subjects	Total 422 Subjects
Mandated under the law	7	1	7	3	18
Discretionary under the law	17	8	22	13	60
Comply with victim wishes	35	10	40	19	104
Training as a police officer	10	5	30	10	55
Experience as a police officer	16	18	36	17	87
Departmental policy	18	15	42	11	86
Supervisor's preferences	25	10	37	11	83
Total	128	67	214	84	493

Scenario 4

You respond to a report of a "domestic in progress" where you are met by Mrs. Daniels. The complainant tells you that her husband Jack has violated a court order and she wants him removed and taken either to jail or to the hospital. You enter to find her husband passed out naked on the bedroom floor. He is highly intoxicated. There is a mess on the kitchen floor with milk dripping out of a container and several broken eggs. Mrs. Daniels goes on to say that she is very aware of her rights under domestic violence and insists that you arrest and remove her husband immediately. She tells you that a condition of his probation is that he not return to the household if he has been drinking. She goes on to say that Jack made the mess in the kitchen looking for more beer. There is no history of prior domestic violence between the parties or restraining orders in effect. What actions do you take?

Analysis: Scenario 4

In Scenario 4, the responding police officer is confronted by several issues that have a direct bearing on his or her handling of the situation. First, despite both the dispatch call and Mrs. Daniels assertion that this is an act of domestic violence, it is in reality a first aid call. There is no history of domestic violence between the parties. Nothing in the fact pattern can be construed as an act of domestic violence. The fact pattern in this scenario tells the officer that there are no restraining orders in effect. There are no violations of the Domestic Violence laws that would warrant a mandatory arrest. However, a highly intoxicated and unconscious Mr. Daniels is in need of medical assistance. Mr. Daniels should be taken to the nearest hospital for the appropriate medical treatment not under arrest, but rather for his own safety.

As to Mrs. Daniels' assertions that her husband is on probation and forbidden to return to the household if drinking may be true, but without actual proof that this is in fact the case the responding police officer would be irresponsible to arrest Mr. Daniels on the basis solely of the statements made by Mrs. Daniels. She is in no imminent danger as her husband will be under medical care and supervision. The officer should document the incident and advise Mrs. Daniels of her right to obtain a Temporary Restraining Order tomorrow. There is no need for a Domestic Violence Offense report as no crime has been committed. A Victim Witness Notification form may be completed as Mrs. Daniels will be advised of her rights, more as a courtesy than a necessity in this situation. Some form of documentation for the incident is appropriate, both for the medical treatment of Mr. Daniels, and to memorialize why this was not an act of domestic violence.

The actions that an officer would undertake in a situation, such as Scenario 4, are considerably different for the reasons previously explained. As such, several questions not previously examined will be explored in Scenario 4. This incident was included in this research, both as a control to see how officers would respond to a non-arrest situation and to explore officer's reactions when a complainant insists that an arrest be made but no probable cause exists to take such action.

Table 4.22 examines which party the study participants consider to be the offender in Scenario 4. A total of 70.1% (N=298) of the research subjects consider the male to be the offender, while 24.7% of the officers in the study found neither party to be considered an offender in Scenario 4. Meanwhile 4.2% (N=18) of respondents considered Mrs. Daniels to the offender under the circumstances.

Table 4.22 Scenario 4: Identification of the Offender

		Setting				
		Urban	Urban Suburb	Large Suburban	Small Suburban	Total
Male	Count	67	49	133	49	298
	% within Setting	68.4%	84.5%	69.3%	63.6%	70.1%
Female	Count	6	2	7	3	18
	% within Setting	6.1%	3.4%	3.6%	3.9%	4.2%
Both	Count	0	1	2	1	4
	% within Setting	.0%	1.7%	1.0%	1.3%	.9%
Neither	Count	25	6	50	24	105
	% within Setting	25.5%	10.3%	26.0%	31.2%	24.7%
Total	Count	98	58	192	77	425

Table 4.23 shows the research participant's responses to the statement "take no police action, not an offense or crime." While no crime or offense has taken place upon which the officer must or can make an arrest, he is still required to render first aid to the intoxicated and unconscious Mr. Daniels in this situation. It was surprising that

41.8% of officers surveyed stated that "some of the time" or more, they would take no police action under the circumstances of Scenario 4. Only in the setting **Urban Suburb** was there any relative variation in the percentage of officers who would "never take no police action" compared to the other three settings.

Table 4.23 Scenario 4 A: Take No Police Action

| | | Setting | | | | |
		Urban	Urban Suburb	Large Suburban	Small Suburban	Total
Always	Count	14	4	12	9	39
	% within Setting	14.3%	6.9%	6.3%	11.7%	9.2%
Most of the time	Count	15	2	21	10	48
	% within Setting	15.3%	3.4%	11.1%	13.0%	11.3%
About half the time	Count	4	4	16	8	32
	% within Setting	4.1%	6.9%	8.4%	10.4%	7.6%
Some of the time	Count	12	7	33	6	58
	% within Setting	12.2%	12.1%	17.4%	7.8%	13.7%
Never	Count	53	41	108	44	246
	% within Setting	54.1%	70.7%	56.8%	57.1%	58.2%
Total	Count	98	58	190	77	423

Table 4.24 shows the research subjects' ability to use the art of persuasion to diffuse the issues in Scenario 4. Mrs. Daniels is under the misimpression that the police are going to arrest her husband. The responding police officer is not able to accommodate the wishes of Mr. Daniels. They can remove him and get him the medical assistance he

requires. There is a need for the officer to show concern for the desire of Mrs. Daniels to see her husband incarcerated, but to convince her that his medical condition takes priority. In Scenario 4, 35.5% (N=151) of study participants would "always" try to 'deescalate, mediate and resolve the situation," 52% (N=221) would "some of the time" to "most of the time" try to deescalate this situation. Only 12.5% of those surveyed would not attempt to diffuse this situation through mediation.

Table 4.24 Scenario 4 B: Deescalate, Mediate, Resolve the Situation

		Setting				
		Urban	Urban Suburb	Large Suburban	Small Suburban	Total
Always	Count	34	22	70	25	151
	% within Setting	34.7%	37.9%	36.5%	32.5%	35.5%
Most of the time	Count	17	9	40	18	84
	% within Setting	17.3%	15.5%	20.8%	23.4%	19.8%
About half the time	Count	14	12	34	6	66
	% within Setting	14.3%	20.7%	17.7%	7.8%	15.5%
Some of the time	Count	16	9	29	17	71
	% within Setting	16.3%	15.5%	15.1%	22.1%	16.7%
Never	Count	17	6	19	11	53
	% within Setting	17.3%	10.3%	9.9%	14.3%	12.5%
Total	Count	98	58	192	77	425

Table 4.25 displays study participants who would take the action of removing the offender in order to obtain medical treatment for detoxification and/or counseling. Only 12.2% (N=51) of officers surveyed would "never" take this action under the specific hypothetical circumstances of Scenario 4. Of the 295 study participants who identified the male as the offender, only 47.5% (N=140) would

"always" remove the individual for detoxification and/or counseling. Another 43% (N=127) of respondents who identified Mr. Daniels as the offender would "some of the time" to "most of time" seek treatment for him.

Table 4.25 Scenario 4 F: Remove Offender for Detoxification /Counseling

		Remove offender for detox/counseling					
		Always	Most of the time	About half the time	Some of the time	Never	Total
Male as offender	Count	140	67	20	40	28	295
	% within row	47.5%	22.7%	6.8%	13.6%	9.5%	100.0%
Female as offender	Count	8	4	2	0	4	18
	% within row	44.4%	22.2%	11.1%	.0%	22.2%	100.0%
Both as offenders	Count	2	0	0	1	1	4
	% within row	50.0%	.0%	.0%	25.0%	25.0%	100.0%
Neither as offender	Count	35	22	12	13	18	100
	% within row	35.0%	22.0%	12.0%	13.0%	18.0%	100.0%
Total	Count	185	93	34	54	51	417

Table 4.26 displays the frequency with which study participants would arrest the individual, if any, whom they identified as the offender in Scenario 4. Of those study participants who identified the **male** as the offender (N=298,) over half 56% (N=167) would arrest Mr. Daniels for a violation of the Domestic Violence laws. Of the 102 officers in the study who identified neither party as the offender, 32 would arrest someone (who it is not clear) at "least some of the time" or more often in this scenario. Just under half, 49.2% (N=207), of all survey participants would "never" make an arrest.

Table 4.26 Scenario 4 G: Arrest Offender Under Domestic Violence Laws

| | | \multicolumn{6}{c}{Arrest offender under Domestic Violence laws} | | | | | |
		Always	Most of the time	About half the time	Some of the time	Never	Total
Male as offender	Count	49	25	27	66	131	298
	% within row	16.4%	8.4%	9.1%	22.1%	44.0%	100.0%
Female as offender	Count	4	3	2	4	4	17
	% within row	23.5%	17.6%	11.8%	23.5%	23.5%	100.0%
Both as offenders	Count	0	0	0	2	2	4
	% within row	.0%	.0%	.0%	50.0%	50.0%	100.0%
Neither as offender	Count	7	8	2	15	70	102
	% within row	6.9%	7.8%	2.0%	14.7%	68.6%	100.0%
Total	Count	60	36	31	87	207	421

Appendix Table 4.48 displays the frequency with which officers participating in this research would arrest the individual whom they identify as the offender for an offense not under the Domestic Violence laws. For this to occur the police officer would have made the determination that no act of domestic violence has transpired, but a criminal offense of some kind had taken place. In this scenario, it would be difficult for an officer to make an arrest for a disorderly person's offense as it would have had to occur in the presence of the officers, especially as the male in this scenario is unconscious.

It is somewhat surprising and disappointing that of the research subjects in this study who identify Mr. Daniels as the offender, 55.9% (N=166) would arrest him "some of the time" or more in Scenario 4 for an offense not under the Domestic Violence laws of New Jersey. However, there is no basis for a mandatory or even a discretionary arrest given the fact pattern of this scenario. It is also dismaying that over fifty percent (215 of 420) of police officers surveyed would find it necessary to arrest someone in this situation at least "some of the time."

Perhaps the silver lining in the data displayed in Appendix Table 4.48 is that only 8% (N=32) of the police officers in this study would "always" make an arrest for an offense other than the Domestic Violence laws given the facts of Scenario 4. Still, it is of some consolation that the arrest rates for Scenario 4 indicate that a sizable minority 49% (N=205) of police officers participating in this research would not arrest for a violation of the law not under the domestic violence laws and identical and similar number (N=207) would not arrest under the domestic violence laws.

Appendix Table 4.49 offers another indication that study subjects are not as likely to resolve Scenario 4 by making an arrest as in the other situations of this research. Only 11% (N=46) of police officers in this research would "always" sign a complaint against an individual given the facts of Scenario 4. Conversely, 53.6% (N=224) of all research subjects would "never" personally sign a complaint in this situation. Of those officers who determined Mr. Daniels to be the offender (N=295) in this scenario, almost half or 47.5% (N=140) would "never" sign a complaint against him. Of the officers who found neither party to be the offender (N=102,) still 26.5% (N=27) would personally sign a complaint in this situation. This table demonstrates the fact that many officers in this study are justifiably uneasy with making an arrest or personally signing a complaint given the circumstances in the fact pattern of this situation.

Appendix Table 4.50 examines the responses of police officers in this study as to the issue of advising the victim to seek counseling. This is an appropriate response as this is not an incident of domestic violence and there is a need for some form of intervention on what would appear to be an ongoing and growing problem between the parties. Only 7.8% (N=23) of all study participants who indentified the male as the offender would not advise Mrs. Daniels to seek counseling. Over half 52.7% of officers who identified Mr. Daniels as the offender would "always" offer this advice to his wife in the circumstances of Scenario 4. Where officers identified neither party as the offender, 83% still offered advice to the parties to seek counseling. As from the fact pattern Mr. Daniels is unconscious and highly intoxicated in Scenario 4, it is safe to assume that this advice would be given to his wife under the circumstances. The same will hold true for the advice that results in Appendix Table 4.51.

Appendix Table 4.51 displays how often research participants would advise Mrs. Daniels to obtain a restraining order under the circumstances of Scenario 4. Regardless of who was identified as the offender, 60.6% (N=255) of officers taking part in this study would "always" give the advise to one of the parties to seek a restraining order. Only 13.1% (N=55) would never make this suggestion under these circumstances. Mrs. Daniels would still have the option of seeking a restraining order in front of a judge if she so desired. It will be up to the judge to establish probable cause and issue a restraining order as he/she may deem necessary.

In scenario 4, as the fact pattern is not an incident which involves an act of domestic violence it is less important as to what type of report is generated to memorialize the incident just as long as some form of documentation is produced so that the officer's actions are recorded. Appendix Table 4.52 examines study participants' responses to the frequency with which they would not document Scenario 4 by generating a report on the incident. This need for documentation is evidenced by 80.5% (N=339) of study participants declining to select the option "make no written report" in this scenario. While the original call of a "domestic in progress" may be unfounded, Mrs. Daniels allegations of her husband violated a court order and the reason for taking no action warrant some paperwork and the justifications for the police not taking the requested action. The scenario states that a check was conducted and no record of a domestic violence restraining order could be found. This may be an important point if Mrs. Daniels makes a complaint in the future over the perceived inaction in this situation. The responding officer in Scenario 4 made a good faith effort to verify Mrs. Daniels allegations. He cannot act solely on her allegations; these allegations must be verified before any police action can be taken. There is also a need to render first aid and provide transportation for her husband to a medical facility, if deemed appropriate.

Appendix Table 4.53 displays study participants' responses to the frequency with which they would document Scenario 4 with a Domestic Violence Offense report. Generating this report would mean that the officer would have to document which of the fourteen crimes enumerated under the Domestic Violence Act the offender had committed. Given the facts of Scenario 4, it would be difficult to find any criminal act that has occurred. It is most curious that despite 103 officers in the study finding "neither" as an offender, 40.8% (N=42) of those officers chose to complete the Domestic Violence Offense Report. Most surprising in Table 4.53 is the fact that of the majority of police officers in the study would not "always" complete the required Domestic Violence Offense Report. Of the study participants who identified Mr. Daniels as the offender, 71% (N=298) over one–fourth 26.2% (N=78) would "never" document the offense with a Domestic Violence Offense report. Another 33.6% (N=100) of officers in this category would complete this required paperwork "some of the time" to "most of the time" in this scenario. In fact, only 40.3% (N=120) of police officers who determined (erroneously in this case) that an act of domestic violence had occurred would "always" file this mandatory paperwork.

Appendix Table 4.54 displays how often research participants in this study would have the victim sign the "Victim Witness Notification" form by whom they identified as the "offender" in Scenario 4. It is difficult to justify how those officers participating in this study who identified Mr. Daniels as the "offender" (N=297) failed to have his wife sign the "Victim Witness Notification" form. Only 56.9% (N=169) of this group would have "always" completed this form, while 17.2% (N=51) would "never" do so.

In Scenario 4 there was a considerable shift in the rationalization given by the research participants as to their "most important" justification for their actions. This is displayed in the study results reported in Table 4.27. Of the 666 responses, only 37% (N=245) of police officers in this study considered the option of "mandated by law" as one of their most important responses to this question. If duplicate responses are eliminated, the percentage rises to 48%. This is still well below the Scenario 1 response rate to this question of (84%), the Scenario 2 response rate of (80%), and the Scenario 3 response rate of 81%.

This shift is to be expected as Scenario 4 was not a mandatory arrest situation or one in which a criminal offense occurred. The response with the largest increase in Scenario 4 was the rationale "discretionary under law." Where this response had previously received "most important" justification in Scenario 1 of 4%, Scenario 2 of 8% and Scenario 3 of 7% in Scenario 4 this response rose to 16%. The attempts in the wording of Scenario 4 by Mrs. Daniels to influence the actions of responding officer had no influence on their justification in this situation. The justification to "comply with the wishes of the victim" received only 3% (N=22) of all responses. This was similar to Scenario 1 at 2% (N=16), Scenario 2 at 3% (N=19), and Scenario 3 at 3% (N=22).

Table 4.27 Scenario 4: Most Important Justification of Officer's Actions by Setting

	Urban 96 Subjects	Urban Suburb 58 Subjects	Large Suburban 192 Subjects	Small Suburban 76 Subjects	Total 422 Subjects
Mandated under law	64	29	108	44	245
Discretionary under the law	31	17	40	19	107
Comply with victim wishes	8	2	10	2	22
Training as a police officer	27	16	30	13	86
Experience as a police officer	31	13	37	17	98
Departmental policy	25	14	19	8	66
Supervisor's preferences	15	11	10	6	42
Total	201	102	254	109	666

Although participants were asked to rank and select each action only once, some officers decided to give multiple responses to this question. This resulted in more than 422 responses being recorded. In a similar fashion, survey respondents were not influenced by the words of Mrs. Daniels in determining their "least important" justification in Scenario 4 as seen in Table 4.28. As in the three previous scenarios, the justification to "comply with the wishes of the victim" was ranked first at 19% (N=95). This is similar to Scenario 1 at 23% (N=115), Scenario 2 at 21% (N=105), and Scenario 3 at 21% (N=104). The other six options for "least important justification were also all similar to the other three scenarios in their response rates, with minor variations.

Table 4.28 Scenario 4: Least Important Justification of Officer's Actions by Setting

	Urban 96 Subjects	Urban Suburb 58 Subjects	Large Suburban 192 Subjects	Small Suburban 76 Subjects	Total 422 Subjects
Mandated under law	15	3	12	3	33
Discretionary under the law	14	7	20	7	48
Comply with victim wishes	29	12	33	21	95
Training as a police officer	17	8	31	7	63
Experience as police officer	16	16	40	15	87
Departmental policy	19	12	40	9	80
Supervisor's preferences	23	7	36	16	82
Total	133	65	212	78	488*

* Although participants were asked to rank and select each action only once, many officers decided to give multiple responses to this question. This resulted in more than 422 responses being recorded.

Scenario 5

You respond to the Delta apartment complex at 11PM having received numerous complaints from neighbors of a domestic dispute in progress. Upon your arrival, angry neighbors swarm you. They tell you that action must be taken to arrest someone. The door to the apartment is wide open. Mrs. Coors is punching and kicking away at her husband. He is holding her off, but he has a bloody lip and a minor laceration from a kitchen knife wound inflicted by his wife. She has deep bruises on both arms that are already turning black, apparently from her husband trying to restrain her. Mr. Coors is somewhat intoxicated and belligerent towards you. Your supervisor is yelling over the radio that there is a serious accident on the other side of town where you needed to assist. What actions do you take?

Analysis: Scenario 5

Scenario 5 involves an altercation between a husband and wife where the female is the aggressor having used a weapon, a knife, to superficially cut her husband. While Mrs. Coors has also sustained bruises, the scenario makes clear that her husband inflicted these bruises in self-defense trying to restrain his wife from inflicting further injury. The New Jersey Criminal Code makes it clear that the investigating officer must insure that "no victim shall be denied relief or arrested or charged under this act with an offense because the victim used reasonable force in self-defense against domestic violence by an attacker" *N.J.S.A.* 2C:25-21c(3). In this situation, the officers also witnessed Mrs. Coors assaulting her husband as they approached the residence. Study participants have more than enough probable cause to establish that an act of domestic violence has occurred. This scenario is a **mandatory arrest** situation as a weapon was used to inflict an injury. Mrs. Coors should be arrested for the aggravated assault on her husband. First aid should be provided to both parties. Inquiries should be made if there are any weapons in the residence that may pose a threat to Mr. Coors. Obviously, the police would not confiscate every kitchen knife in the residence, but if there were firearms that belonged to Mrs. Coors or any other potentially dangerous weapons, the police are obligated to seize them. Mr. Coors' intoxication and belligerence is noted in the fact pattern, but as no criminal actions were placed in the scenario this should not have been a factor in deciding to arrest him.

The police officer also **must** sign the criminal complaint. The appropriate paperwork would include: [t] an Investigation Report, [v] a Domestic Violence Offense form, and [x] a Victim Witness Notification form. Among the list of possible courses of action the following would be inappropriate: [a] Take no police action, not a reportable offense; [e] Remove offender from household for night; [h] Arrest the offender for an offense not under the domestic violence laws;

[n] Advise victim to sign a complaint tomorrow; [o] Make no written report of incident; [p] Document incident as "unfounded"; [q] Document incident as "Gone on Arrival"; [r] Document incident as "verbal dispute"; [s] Document incident as "family problem"; and [t] Document the incident with an "Operations report."

Table 4.29 Scenario 5: Identification of the Offender

| | | Setting | | | | |
		Urban	Urban Suburb	Large Suburban	Small Suburban	Total
Male	Count	12	6	6	1	25
	% within Setting	12.2%	10.3%	3.1%	1.3%	5.9%
Female	Count	69	43	159	50	321
	% within Setting	70.4%	74.1%	82.8%	64.9%	75.5%
Both	Count	17	8	27	26	78
	% within Setting	17.3%	13.8%	14.1%	33.8%	18.4%
Neither	Count	0	1	0	0	1
	% within Setting	.0%	1.7%	.0%	.0%	.2%
Total	Count	98	58	192	77	425

The other external factors that the neighbors are demanding that someone be arrested, or that your supervisor is requesting your assistance at another call on the other side of town, are irrelevant. The police officer responding to a violent domestic dispute is obligated to handle the situation and make the arrest and process the crime scene.

As can be seen from Table 4.29, 75.5% (N=321) police officers who participated in this study correctly identified Mrs. Coors as the offender in Scenario 5. Only 5.9% identified Mr. Coors as the offender. Surprisingly, 18.4% of study participants came to the conclusion that both parties were offenders in this scenario. By combining the 'female and "both" categories, Mrs. Coors would have been correctly arrested by 93.9% of the officers in this study. Conversely, Mr. Coors would have been improperly arrested by 24.3% of the officers in this study for the facts as they were presented.

It is interesting to note that Mr. Coors was much more likely to be identified as the sole offender in the **Urban** and **Urban Suburb** settings, while both parties were much more likely to be identified as the offenders in the **Small Suburban** setting. The **Large Suburban** setting was more likely to correctly identify only Mrs. Coors as the offender.

Table 4.30 shows that the police officers in this study consider the facts of Scenario 5 to warrant an "always" arrest, with a rate of 89.2% (N=379). If this statistic is combined with the officers who selected "most of the time," the arrest rate jumps to 96% (N=408). It is clear that either the level of mutual violence or the fact that a weapon was used in this scenario caused the officers in the study to consider the need to make an arrest imperative under the circumstances presented.

Table 4.30 Scenario 5 G: Arrest Offender Under Domestic Violence Laws

| | | Setting | | | | |
		Urban	Urban Suburb	Large Suburban	Small Suburban	Total
Always	Count	84	53	169	73	379
	% within Setting	85.7%	91.4%	88.0%	94.8%	89.2%
Most of the time	Count	9	2	16	2	29
	% within Setting	9.2%	3.4%	8.3%	2.6%	6.8%
About half the time	Count	4	1	3	0	8
	% within Setting	4.1%	1.7%	1.6%	.0%	1.9%
Some of the time	Count	1	1	1	2	5
	% within Setting	1.0%	1.7%	.5%	2.6%	1.2%
Never	Count	0	1	3	0	4
	% within Setting	.0%	1.7%	1.6%	.0%	.9%
Total	Count	98	58	192	77	425

The data from Scenario 5 G will also be examined, by the identity of the offender, as there were such a large number of research subjects who elected to arrest both offenders in this circumstance. The findings reported in Table 4.31 would indicate that of those officers who determined that Mrs. Coors was the aggressor in this situation, 91% (N=292) would "always" arrest her in this situation. Of those officers who determined that "both" parties in Scenario 5 were the offenders, 88.5% (N=69) would "always" make the arrest. Only .9% (N=4) of all study participants would never make an arrest in this scenario. This scenario offers a good opportunity to examine the concept of dual arrest within the concept of domestic violence offenses. The male victim was incorrectly arrested by 24% of the study participants under the circumstances of this scenario.

Table 4.31 Scenario 5 G: Identify and Arrest Offender Under the Domestic Violence Laws

Identified as the offender		Arrest offender under DV laws					
		Always	Most of the time	About half the time	Some of the time	Never	Total
Male	Count	18	1	4	1	1	25
	% within row	72.0%	4.0%	16.0%	4.0%	4.0%	100.0%
Female	Count	292	22	2	3	2	321
	% within row	91.0%	6.9%	.6%	.9%	.6%	100.0%
Both	Count	69	6	2	0	1	78
	% within row	88.5%	7.7%	2.6%	.0%	1.3%	100.0%
Neither	Count	0	0	0	1	0	1
	% within row	.0%	.0%	.0%	100.0%	.0%	100.0%
Total	Count	379	29	8	5	4	425

Appendix Table 4.55 examines the frequency with which study subjects would make an arrest for an offense not under the Domestic Violence laws. This table reveals more than one–half of all study participants 56.2.5% (N=237) would select this option. This is less than in Scenarios 1 (N=223) & 3 (N=209), and the same as in Scenario 2 (N=185). Most surprising in Appendix Table 4.28 is that 54.4% (N=173) of study participants who correctly identified Mrs. Coors as the primary offender in Scenario 5 would "some of the time" or more often arrest Mrs. Coors not under the Domestic Violence laws but rather for another offense. The number of police officers in the study who would "always" arrest the offender, but not for an offense under the Domestic Violence laws, was also much higher for Scenario 5 (N=94) than in the other scenarios which also constituted mandatory arrest situations.

Since a large portion of the survey participants determined that both parties were offenders, the data in Scenario 5 G is presented in two forms. Appendix Table 4.56 displays how often study participants would arrest the individuals they deemed to be the offender in Scenario 5 under laws other than the Domestic Violence laws. The results of Appendix Table 5.57 show that almost all police officers in this study 95.5% (N=405) would take some form of police action in the conditions of Scenario 5. Only 1.6% (N=7) of all respondents reported that they would "always" take no police action. This is a good indication that most study subjects were able to identify the severity of the parties' actions in this scenario and take some action to intervene.

Table 4.32 displays the frequency with which officers would undertake the mandatory action of personally signing a criminal complaint against the offender in Scenario 5. Study participants were much more likely to sign the criminal complaint 73.8% (N=313) "always" than in the other three mandatory arrest scenarios examined. This was consistent across all four geographic settings in this scenario. Only 4.5% (N=19) of officers in this study would "never" personally sign the criminal complaint, a requirement under the Attorney General Guidelines and the Domestic Violence laws.

Table 4.33 shows the frequency that police officers in the study were only willing to "always" document this incident with an "Investigation Report" at 82.8% (N=351). The crime described in Scenario 5 was the most serious offense committed in this study. It is proper for this incident to receive an Investigation Report as documentation of the incident as it would be recorded for the Uniform Crime Report Statistics, for follow-up investigative services, and for potential court proceedings. The data for Scenario 5 support this supposition, as the documentation rates from the other scenarios were somewhat lower than was the case in this situation: Scenario 2, 76.9% (N=326); Scenario 3, 70.3% Scenario 1, 69.1% (N=293).

Table 4.32 Scenario 5 J: Officer to Sign Complaint

		Setting				
		Urban	Urban Suburb	Large Suburban	Small Suburban	Total
Always	Count	72	43	144	54	313
	% within Setting	73.5%	74.1%	75.4%	70.1%	73.8%
Most of the time	Count	16	4	19	9	48
	% within Setting	16.3%	6.9%	9.9%	11.7%	11.3%
About half the time	Count	5	1	8	5	19
	% within Setting	5.1%	1.7%	4.2%	6.5%	4.5%
Some of the time	Count	4	4	12	5	25
	% within Setting	4.1%	6.9%	6.3%	6.5%	5.9%
Never	Count	1	6	8	4	19
	% within Setting	1.0%	10.3%	4.2%	5.2%	4.5%
Total	Count	98	58	191	77	424

Appendix Table 4.58 shows the frequency with which officers in this study 90.7% (N=382) would "always" comply with the mandatory provisions of the Domestic Violence laws to advise the victim of his/her rights to obtain a Temporary Restraining Order. As Scenario 5 is the most serious of all the situations presented in this research, it was anticipated that a larger number of study subjects would take this action compared to the other situations. This was not substantiated by the data of Appendix Table 4.58, as the percentages for the other mandatory scenarios were Scenario 1, 89.9%; Scenario 2, 90.4%; Scenario 3, 52.7%. Perhaps the perception of mutual combat and the effect of dual arrests reduced the number of officers who would take this mandatory action under these circumstances.

Table 4.33 Scenario 5 U: Document with "Investigation Report"

		Setting				
		Urban	Urban Suburb	Large Suburban	Small Suburban	Total
Always	Count	76	51	153	71	351
	% within Setting	78.4%	87.9%	79.7%	92.2%	82.8%
Most of the time	Count	7	3	13	2	25
	% within Setting	7.2%	5.2%	6.8%	2.6%	5.9%
About half the time	Count	3	0	1	0	4
	% within Setting	3.1%	.0%	.5%	.0%	.9%
Some of the time	Count	2	1	7	0	10
	% within Setting	2.1%	1.7%	3.6%	.0%	2.4%
Never	Count	9	3	18	4	34
	% within Setting	9.3%	5.2%	9.4%	5.2%	8.0%
Total	Count	97	58	192	77	424

Appendix Table 4.59 examines the frequency with which study participants would "always" have the victim of Scenario 5 sign the Victim Witness Notification form 93.9% (N=399) as required under the Domestic Violence laws. The result for this scenario is the highest percentage of officers complying with this mandatory requirement. This is an indication that the officers in this study found the fact pattern of this situation sufficiently serious for reporting to the State Police for inclusion in the Uniform Crime Reports. The findings for the other scenarios are: Scenario 1, 85.9% (N=365); Scenario 2, 90.6% (N=385); and Scenario 3, 80.1% (N=338).

For Scenario 5, the mandatory requirement for each domestic violence offense that occurs in New Jersey must be documented with a Domestic Violence Offense report is examined in Table 4.34. Study subjects consistently recognized this fact across all settings for the serious nature of Scenario 5. Police officers in the study reported "always" documenting the incident with a Domestic Violence Offense report 91.1% (N=387) of the time. This was a higher percentage than for any other scenario with a mandatory arrest requirement: Scenario 1 (72.5%), Scenario 2 (83.8%), and Scenario 3 (76.9%). This willingness to document an act of domestic violence properly is a good indicator that police officers know the requirements of the law and will comply with the its provisions when the incident is sufficiently serious and action must be taken.

Table 4.34 Scenario 5 V: Document with "Domestic Violence Offense Report"

| | | Setting | | | | |
		Urban	Urban Suburb	Large Suburban	Small Suburban	Total
Always	Count	84	54	177	72	387
	% within Setting	85.7%	93.1%	92.2%	93.5%	91.1%
Most of the time	Count	5	2	6	5	18
	% within Setting	5.1%	3.4%	3.1%	6.5%	4.2%
About half the time	Count	4	1	2	0	7
	% within Setting	4.1%	1.7%	1.0%	.0%	1.6%
Some of the time	Count	3	1	4	0	8
	% within Setting	3.1%	1.7%	2.1%	.0%	1.9%
Never	Count	2	0	3	0	5
	% within Setting	2.0%	.0%	1.6%	.0%	1.2%
Total	Count	98	58	192	77	425

Scenario 5 is the one situation in this research where a typical weapon, in particular a knife, is used in the commission of an act of domestic violence. In Scenario 5, that weapon also caused an injury. Under the Attorney General Guidelines of New Jersey, this fact would trigger the need for further investigation by the responding police officer to determine if there were other weapons present that may pose a threat to the victim and require the need for seizure. As seen in Appendix Table 4.60, a high percentage of police officers in this study 88.4% (N=375) had knowledge of and would take the appropriate actions required to seize any additional weapons present in the household that may pose an ongoing threat to the victim.

In Scenario 5 the fact pattern left little doubt that an act of domestic violence had occurred, and the vast majority of police officers in this study concurred with this assessment and would take appropriate action to resolve this incident. Still a few of the inappropriate responses to the questions of Scenario 5 are worth examining individually. One of these actions [5H] "arrest the offender for an offense not under the domestic violence laws" has already been examined. Question [5A] "take no police action, not a reportable offense" demonstrates that the police officers in this study are aware of the proper response and under sufficiently serious conditions will enforce the laws of New Jersey to their fullest extent. Question [5N], "advise the victim to sign a complaint tomorrow" is more ambivalent as to strict enforcement. Finally, a table that combines questions [5P], [5Q], [5R], and [5S] and possible classifications of this incident as events other than a crime will be examined.

Appendix Table 4.61 stands as an example of the correct actions by the overwhelming majority of police officers studied in response to the facts of Scenario 5. It examines the frequency with which officers would take no police action under the described circumstances. Fully 95.5% (N=406) of study participants classified this situation as requiring some form of police action as a crime had been committed. Only 1.6% (N=7) of all research subjects were found to have elected to "always" fail to take any action under the circumstances of this scenario. The majority of police officers in this category (N=6) were from the **Urban** setting. The **Small Suburban** setting had the highest correct response rate of "never" at 98.7%, followed by the **Urban Suburb** at 98.3%, **Large Suburban** at 96.9, and **Urban** at 88.8%.

Appendix Table 4.62 displays the frequency with which police officers in this study would "advise the victim to sign a complaint tomorrow" in contravention of the New Jersey Attorney General Guidelines. The Guidelines require police officers to sign the criminal complaint when a mandatory arrest is required as by the fact pattern of the scenario. In Scenario 5, 61.2% (N=259) of study subjects would properly "never" give the advice to the victim to wait until the next day to file a criminal complaint. This is only slightly better than the 60% (N=252) response rate of Scenario 3, and somewhat better than the 50.6% (N=215) response rate of Scenario 2 or the 48.3% (N=205) of Scenario 1. In Scenario 5 the study participants reported a slightly higher percentage of officers who would "always" advise the victim to wait till the next day to sign a complaint [15.6% (N=66)] compared to the other mandatory arrest scenarios of Scenario 3 at 14.5% (N=61, Scenario 2 at 12.2% (N=52), and Scenario 1 at 11.3% (N=48). This finding is difficult to explain in as much as more officers in this scenario selected to both arrest the offender under the Domestic Violence laws and to personally sign the criminal complaint against the offender than in any other hypothetical situation posed in this research. Appendix Table 4.62 shows how often participants would properly classify Scenario 5. This table is a combination of four questions, 5p, 5q, 5r, and 5s. Each of these choices is improper as they would decriminalize the incident and attempt to minimize the facts of Scenario 5. The "count" rows show how many study participants in each setting properly responded "never" to the various questions, thereby refusing to improperly classify the criminal offense featured in this scenario.

Study participants were extremely adamant in their nearly universal rejection of misclassifying this incident especially as "unfounded" at 96.9% (N=410), "gone on arrival" at 96.7% (N=409), and "verbal dispute" at 93.4% (N=395). Only the response to classify the incident as "family problem" gained any limited traction with study participants in as much as 87% (N=368) rejected this option. This in an indication that the severity of the domestic violence incident portrayed in Scenario 5, including the use of a weapon and the injury sustained in this altercation.

These conclusions are in many ways confirmed by the results of Table 4.35, which examines the most important justification for the study participants' actions in the scenario. Consistent with the results of this question in the other scenarios, the response "mandated under law" was the most frequently given with 54% (N=372) of police officers in this study justifying their actions in Scenario 5. This was once again the highest of the seven possible selections and the highest percentage of responses to this question in the study. Excluding multiple responses of the 424 study participants, 88% of police officers in this research made this selection their top choice. This scenario produced the fewest officers that misunderstood or misapplied the prevailing criminal statutes.

Table 4.35 Scenario 5: Most Important Justification of Officer's Actions by Setting

	Urban 97 Subjects	Urban Suburb 58 Subjects	Large Suburban 192 Subjects	Small Suburban 77 Subjects	Total 424 Subjects
Mandated under law	83	46	174	69	372
Discretionary under the law	10	8	6	7	31
Comply with victim wishes	11	2	6	2	21
Training as a police officer	28	13	24	12	77
Experience as police officer	29	13	22	14	78
Departmental policy	32	14	19	10	75
Supervisor's preferences	14	6	10	3	33
Total	207	102	261	117	687*

* Although participants were asked to rank and select each action only once, many officers decided to give multiple responses to this question. This resulted in more than 424 responses being recorded.

The second tier of responses to the most important justification of the police officer's actions were "based on my experience" at 11% (N=78), "based on my training" at 11% (N=77), and 'based on departmental policy" 11% (N=75). The results for this category in Scenario 5 are consistent with the other mandatory arrest situations in scenarios 1, 2, and 3, both with respect to the responses selected and the percentages of those responses. The three least popular categorical responses 'based on my supervisor's preference" was at 5% (N=33), "discretionary under law" at 5% (N=31), and "comply with the wishes of the victim" at 3% (N=21).

In this scenario, the study participants were not given any facts or indication as to the wishes of either of the individuals involved in the altercation in regards to pursuing criminal complaints against the other. Table 4.36 explores study subjects' least important justification of officer's actions. This was, in part, due to the need to explore which party the police officer would identify as the victim and to preclude the fact pattern from giving any indication of who this may be. Still the response rate for "comply with the wishes of the victim" was as low here as when there was a clear indication that the victim did not wish to file charges against their attacker in Scenarios 1 and 3.

Table 4.36 Scenario 5 Least Important Justification of Officer's Actions by Setting

	Urban 97 Subjects	Urban Suburb 58 Subjects	Large Suburban 192 Subjects	Small Suburban 77 Subjects	Total 424 Subjects
Mandated under law	9	3	5	1	18
Discretionary under the law	21	7	21	9	58
Comply with victim wishes	26	15	29	12	82
Training as a police officer	20	7	31	10	68
Experience as police officer	13	20	37	22	92
Departmental policy	21	11	55	11	98
Supervisor's preferences	19	10	35	16	80
Total	129	73	213	81	496*

*Although participants were asked to rank and select each action only once, some officers decided to give multiple responses to this question. This resulted in more than 424 responses being recorded.

Four responses were found in the upper tier of answers to this question "based on my departmental policy" at 20% (N=98), "based on my experience as a police officer" 18% (N=92), "comply with the wishes of the victim" 16% (N=82) and "based on my supervisor's preferences" at 16% (N=80). Police officers in the study considered the following responses in the second tier of "least important" justifications: "based on my training as a police officer" at 14% (N=68), and "discretionary under the law" at 12% (N=58). The response with the lowest response to this question was again "mandated by law" at 4% (N=18).

Scenario 6

You respond to a 911 call for help at the Cleaver residence. They are "frequent flyers" in that this is at least the fourth time in the last year that your department has responded to domestic disturbances at this residence. On one prior occasion Mr. Cleaver was arrested for simple assault. You arrive to witness Mrs. Cleaver again being assaulted in your presence by her husband, there are signs of physical injury, but she is refusing to press charges and begs you not to arrest him since Mr. Cleaver only became more violent after his previous arrest. She just wants you to take her and their child to her mother's house in the next town. What action do you take?

Analysis: Scenario 6

This scenario involves a situation all too familiar to the members of law enforcement-namely, the presence of a recidivist abuser and the victim who cannot break the bonds with that abuser. Based on the fact pattern of this situation, an act of domestic violence has occurred in the presence of the responding police officer who has witnessed the assault upon Mrs. Cleaver by her husband. There is also a rich history of prior domestic disturbances between the parties, and at one incidence of domestic violence with Mr. Cleaver being arrested. Despite Mrs. Cleaver's pleas to be allowed to leave with the children and that no criminal charges be filed, the police officer responding to this situation has some very clear directives and standards that he or she must enforce.

As the police officer witnessed the act of domestic violence, which involved an assault with physical injuries, the responding officer **must** make an arrest of Mr. Cleaver and **must** sign a criminal complaint under the Domestic Violence laws. The offense should be documented with an "Investigation Report" as a criminal offense has occurred, the "Domestic Violence Offense Report" to document the act of domestic violence, and a "Victim Witness Notification Form" so that the appropriate notifications to the victim can be made in a timely manner. Medical assistance should be dispatched for the victim to care for her physical injuries. The victim must be advised of her right to obtain a Temporary Restraining Order. If there are any weapons that remain in the residence (those either new since the last offense or which were not confiscated at that time) that pose a threat to the victim or the children, the police officers should arrange to seize them at this time.

Table 4.37 Scenario 6: Identification of Offender

		Setting				
		Urban	Urban Suburb	Large Suburban	Small Suburban	Total
Male	Count	97	58	192	74	421
	% within Setting	99.0%	100.0%	100.0%	96.1%	99.1%
Female	Count	0	0	0	2	2
	% within Setting	.0%	.0%	.0%	2.6%	.5%
Both	Count	0	0	0	1	1
	% within Setting	.0%	.0%	.0%	1.3%	.2%
Neither	Count	1	0	0	0	1
	% within Setting	1.0%	.0%	.0%	.0%	.2%
Total	Count	98	58	192	77	425

Inappropriate actions in Scenario 6 would include taking no police action or not considering this incident to be an offense or a crime, to mislabel this incident as "unfounded", "gone on arrival," a verbal dispute, or as a "family problem." Other improper actions would include to advise the victim to sign a complaint the next day, arrest the offender for an offense not under the Domestic Violence laws, and to make no written report on the incident.

Police officers responding to a situation such as described in Scenario 6 must be keenly aware that victims of domestic violence are at their greatest risk when they attempt to leave their abuser. Every precaution should be taken to ensure that if the victim does wish to make a clean break from her abuser that her location remains confidential from her attacker. The fact pattern of Scenario 6 left little doubt as to the aggressor and attacker in the situation. With probable cause firmly established by observations of the officer and visible injuries to the victim being apparent, this situation was the clearest mandatory arrest of all the scenarios. Scenario 6 was presented as a situation in which the police officers would have little or no difficulty in distinguishing between the victim and the attacker. This question was intentionally included to give a gold standard base line against which the responses to the other scenarios could be measured. This is illustrated by Table 4.37 with 99.1% (N=421) of study participants.

The results of Table 4.38 show that under the facts given in Scenario 6, 91% (N=386) of the police officers, in the study would "always" arrest the offender. It is difficult to explain how the correctly 8.1% of officers, who in the previous Table 4.37 identified Mr. Cleaver as the offender, would not make the required arrest given the circumstances as explained in the scenario. The percentage of police officers who would "always" make the required arrest was consistent across all four settings. Of the respondents who would make the arrest "most of the time" the **Large Suburban** and **Urban** settings exhibited considerably larger percentages compared to other locations.

For **Urban** police officers only, 7% (N=9) of study participants would not "always" make an arrest in the facts of Scenario 6. The percentage of officers who regularly respond to domestic violence calls and would "always arrest' the offender in this scenario was 90.5% compared to 91.4% for those officers who do not respond to domestic violence calls on a regular basis. In the **Urban Suburb** setting, of those study participants who would "always" arrest the offender police officers with primary responsibility to domestic violence calls made the arrest in 94.3% of the time compared to 100% of officers who did not regularly answer domestic violence calls as part of their duties. For the **Large Suburban** setting in Scenario 6, officers who regularly responded to domestic calls would "always" make the arrest 88.6% of the time, while officers not assigned to do so would arrest the offender in 92.9% of such incidents. In the **Small Suburban** setting the officers in the study, who regularly respond to domestic calls, would "always" make the arrest 92% of the time while officers assigned to other responsibilities would make the arrest in 92.6% of such instances. This pattern was repeated in the category of arresting the offender "most of the time" with the exception of the **Small Suburban** setting where the numbers were so small as to be irrelevant. It is a reasonable assumption, from these findings, that assignment is not a factor in the determination to arrest the offender in this situation. It would also suggest that officer training of departmental attitudes should be examined more closely as a factor in determining the variations between settings found in Table 4.12.

Table 4.38 Scenario 6 G: Arrest Offender Under the Domestic Violence Laws

| | | Setting | | | | |
		Urban	Urban Suburb	Large Suburban	Small Suburban	Total
Always	Count	89	55	171	71	386
	% within Setting	90.8%	94.8%	89.5%	92.2%	91.0%
Most of the time	Count	7	1	15	3	26
	% within Setting	7.1%	1.7%	7.9%	3.9%	6.1%
About half he time	Count	1	0	0	2	3
	% within Setting	1.0%	.0%	.0%	2.6%	.7%
Some of the time	Count	1	1	3	0	5
	% within Setting	1.0%	1.7%	1.6%	.0%	1.2%
Never	Count	0	1	2	1	4
	% within Setting	.0%	1.7%	1.0%	1.3%	.9%
Total	Count	98	58	191	77	424

In Appendix Table 4.64 one of the improper actions that a study participant could take in Scenario 6 is examined. Of all survey participants, 49.2% (N=209) reported that they would "never" make an arrest of the offender that was not under the Domestic Violence laws. Police officers in the study reported that 22.3% (N=94) of the time that they would "always" arrest the offender for an offense other than under the Domestic Violence laws. This is improper as the only offense committed in the fact pattern of Scenario 6 is that of an assault which meets the criteria of a domestic violence offense.

Table 4.39 displays the frequency with which officers would undertake the mandatory action of personally signing a criminal complaint against the offender portrayed in Scenario 6. Study participants were most likely to sign the criminal complaint 81.2% (N=345) "always" than in the other four mandatory arrest scenarios featured in this survey.

Table 4.39 Scenario 6 J: Officer to Sign Complaint

| | | Setting | | | | |
		Urban	Urban Suburb	Large Suburban	Small Suburban	Total
Always	Count	78	49	159	59	345
	% within Setting	79.6%	84.5%	82.8%	76.6%	81.2%
Most of the time	Count	9	1	11	8	29
	% within Setting	9.2%	1.7%	5.7%	10.4%	6.8%
About half he time	Count	3	2	6	2	13
	% within Setting	3.1%	3.4%	3.1%	2.6%	3.1%
Some of the time	Count	7	4	11	1	23
	% within Setting	7.1%	6.9%	5.7%	1.3%	5.4%
Never	Count	1	2	5	7	15
	% within Setting	1.0%	3.4%	2.6%	9.1%	3.5%
Total	Count	98	58	192	77	425

When combined with the category "most of the time" 88% of police officers in the study would personally sign the criminal complaint given the fact pattern of this scenario. This is a further indication of the willingness of police officers to take the appropriate action when offenses under the domestic violence laws occur in their presence and are of a serious nature that requires immediate action.

Appendix Table 4.65 displays the frequency with which officers would dispatch medical assistance to the victim as found in scenario 6. This is a mandatory provision of the Domestic Violence laws component with which officers are required to comply. While more police officers would dispatch medical assistance for the victim in Scenario 6 at 81.6% (N=345,) it was not that much greater than in Scenario 1 where the victim was intoxicated and uncooperative 75.4% (N=318).

Still, there is considerable room for improvement at the other end of the spectrum of responses in Appendix Table 4.65. The fact that 7.8% (N=33) police officers would "never" document this incident with an Investigation Report, and that additionally 1.2 % (N=12) would "some of the time" or "about half the time" fail to properly document an incident with the fact pattern of Scenario 6 is disheartening. It shows that there is room for improvement in officers' response in situations similar to the one described.

In Appendix Table 4.66 are found the frequencies with which officers in this study 96% (N=408) would "always" comply with the mandatory provisions of the Domestic Violence laws to advise the victim of his/her rights to obtain a Temporary Restraining Order. As Scenario 6 is the most obvious domestic violence scenario presented in this research, it was anticipated that a larger number of study subjects would take this action and advise the victim to seek a temporary restraining order compared to the other situations. In addition, the fact that there is a history of domestic violence between the parties would make the responding police officers more likely to view this as a pattern of domestic violence and encourage the victim to go forward and seek the protection of the court. This expectation was substantiated, as the percentages for the other mandatory scenarios were: Scenario 5 90.7% (N=382); Scenario 1, 89.9%; Scenario 2, 90.4%; Scenario 3, 52.7%.

Table 4.40 shows the frequency that police officers in the study were inclined to memorialize this incident with an "Investigation Report." The study found 84.2% (N=356) of study participants would "always" correctly document this scenario. This crime was the most obvious offense committed in this study. The officers witnessed the assault as it occurred in their presence. It is logical for this incident to receive the appropriate documentation by a high percentage of study participants.

The statistics support this expectation, as the data for officer compliance was even marginally higher than the more serious Scenario 5 which involved an aggravated assault with a weapon 82.8% (N=351). This was considerably higher than the other scenarios where the fact patterns were less explicit while still featuring violations of the Domestic Violence laws: Scenario 2, simple assault with a fearful victim at 76.9% (N=326); Scenario 3, violation of a restraining order at 70.3%; and Scenario 1, simple assault with an uncooperative victim and a missing offender at 69.1% (N=293).

Table 4.40 Scenario 6 U: Document with "Investigation Report"

| | | Setting | | | |
		Urban	Urban Suburb	Large Suburban	Small Suburban	Total
Always	Count	78	53	153	72	356
	% within Setting	80.4%	91.4%	79.7%	94.7%	84.2%
Most of the time	Count	6	1	14	1	22
	% within Setting	6.2%	1.7%	7.3%	1.3%	5.2%
About half he time	Count	4	0	2	0	6
	% within Setting	4.1%	.0%	1.0%	.0%	1.4%
Some of the time	Count	1	0	5	0	6
	% within Setting	1.0%	.0%	2.6%	.0%	1.4%
Never	Count	8	4	18	3	33
	% within Setting	8.2%	6.9%	9.4%	3.9%	7.8%
Total	Count	97	58	192	76	423

Appendix Table 4.67 examines how often study participants in Scenario 6 would have the victim sign the "Victim Witness Notification form." It was found that police officers who would "always" meet this requirement comprised 94.3% (N=400) of the study, as required under the Domestic Violence laws. This result is the highest percentage of officers complying with this mandatory requirement in this study. The findings for the other mandatory arrest scenarios are: Scenario 1, 85.9% (N=365); Scenario 2, 90.6% (N=385); Scenario 3, 80.1% (N=338) and Scenario 5, 93.9% (N=399). The compliance ratio on this question was consistently above 90% across all four geographic settings.

Table 4.41 Scenario 6 U: Document with "Domestic Violence Offense Report"

| | | Setting | | | | |
		Urban	Urban Suburb	Large Suburban	Small Suburban	Total
Always	Count	89	56	174	75	394
	% within Setting	90.8%	96.6%	90.6%	97.4%	92.7%
Most of the time	Count	4	1	10	0	15
	% within Setting	4.1%	1.7%	5.2%	.0%	3.5%
About half he time	Count	4	0	3	0	7
	% within Setting	4.1%	.0%	1.6%	.0%	1.6%
Some of the time	Count	0	1	5	1	7
	% within Setting	.0%	1.7%	2.6%	1.3%	1.6%
Never	Count	1	0	0	1	2
	% within Setting	1.0%	.0%	.0%	1.3%	.5%
Total	Count	98	58	192	77	425

For Scenario 6, the mandatory requirement for each domestic violence offense to be documented with a Domestic Violence Offense report is examined in Table 4.41. Consistent with the previous results of this scenario, police officers in this study reported they would "always" document the incident with a Domestic Violence Offense report 92.7% (N=394) of the time. This was the highest rate of all the scenarios with a mandatory arrest requirement. This finding further supports the concept that police officers can and will comply with the statutory requirements in domestic violence situations when the facts clearly establish probable cause to take mandatory arrest actions.

Appendix Table 4.68 shows how often participants would properly classify Scenario 6. This table is a combination of four questions 6p, 6q, 6r, and 6s. Each of these choices is improper as they would decriminalize the incident and attempt to minimize the facts of Scenario 6. By examining the response "never" to this question, we obtain a good indication of the frequency with which officers in the study would not misclassify or misidentify the incident in an attempt to remove this scenario from the requirements of the Domestic Violence laws. It is clear, from this, that the only alternative classification that would gain any traction with study participants is the category "document as a family problem" which 13% (N=56) police officers would use to explain this incident "some of the time" or more often.

Table 4.42 examines the "most important" justification for the study participants' actions in Scenario 6. Consistent with the results of this question in the other scenarios, the response, "mandated under law" was the most frequently given with 54% (N=372) of police officers in this study justifying their actions thusly in this scenario. This was, once again, the highest of the seven possible selections and the exact same percentage of responses to this question in the study as in Scenario 5. Excluding multiple responses of the 424 study participants, 88% of police officers in this research made this selection their "most important" choice. It is reassuring to observe that the overwhelming majority of police officers in this study not only would initiate the proper course of action, but they cite the mandatory obligations of the law, as their primary motivation for their actions.

The second tier of responses to the "most important" justification of the police officer's actions were "based on my experience" at 12% (N=82), "based on my training" at 11% (N=77), and 'based on departmental policy" 10% (N=71). The results for this category in Scenario 6 are consistent with the other mandatory arrest situations in scenarios 1, 2, and 3 both in the responses selected and the percentages of those responses. The three least popular categorical responses 'based on my supervisor's preference" was at 5.5% (N=38), "discretionary under law" at 5.5% (N=38), and "comply with the wishes of the victim" at 2% (N=16).

In this scenario, the study participants were not given any indication as to the wishes of either of the participants in regards to pursuing criminal complaints against the other. This was, in part, due to the need to explore which party the police officer would identify as the victim and to preclude the fact pattern from giving any indication of who this may be. The study participants' low response rate for the justification "comply with the wishes of the victim" was a clear indication that this reasoning is not an important factor in determining the police officers' actions in domestic violence situations under the mandatory arrest circumstances of New Jersey law.

Table 4.42 Scenario 6: Most Important Justification of Officer's Actions

	Urban 97 Subjects	Urban Suburb 58 Subjects	Large Suburban 192 Subjects	Small Suburban 77 Subjects	Total 424 Subjects
Mandated under law	85	47	169	71	372
Discretionary under the law	15	7	9	7	38
Comply with victim wishes	6	4	5	1	16
Training as a police officer	31	14	21	11	77
Experience as a police officer	31	14	26	11	82
Departmental policy	30	13	19	9	71
Supervisor's preferences	16	8	8	6	38
Total	214	107	257	116	694*

*Although participants were asked to rank and select each action only once, many officers decided to give multiple responses to this question. This resulted in more than 424 responses being recorded.

By setting, the study participants in **Small Suburban** were most likely to justify their actions in Scenario 6 by "mandated by law" at 92% (N=71) of the time, followed by the **Urban** participants at 89% (N=85) and **Large Suburban** at 88% (N=169). The category in which police officers in the study with the least percentage justifying their actions in Scenario 6 as "mandated under law" was the **Urban Suburb** setting.

In Table 4.43 study participants listing their least important justification for their actions within Scenario 6 are displayed. Two responses were found in the upper tier of most frequent answers to this question-namely, "comply with the wishes of the victim" 21% (N=106), and "based on my departmental policy" at 19% (N=92). The next tier of responses included "based on my experience as a police officer" at 17% (N=85), based on my supervisor's preferences" at 16% (N=79), "discretionary under the law" at 12% (N=59), and "based on my training as a police officer" at 11% (N=53). The final response which has consistently had the fewest justifications in mandatory arrest situations is "mandated by law at 4% (N=20).

Responses to officer's least important justification in Table 4.43 show considerable variation as to study participants' reasoning. **Urban** (37%) and **Small Suburban** (25%) respondents chose "comply with the wishes of the victim" as their most popular "least important" justification. **Urban Suburb** police officers (33%) in the study chose "based on my experience as a police officer," while **Large Suburban** participants chose "based on my departmental policy" as their most frequent response for least important justification.

Table 4.43 Scenario 6: Least Important Justification of Officer's Actions

	Urban 97 Subjects	Urban Suburb 58 Subjects	Large Suburban 192 Subjects	Small Suburban 77 Subjects	Total 424 Subjects
Mandated under law	9	4	6	1	20
Discretionary under the law	18	7	21	13	59
Comply with victim wishes	36	14	37	19	106
Training as a police officer	12	5	27	9	53
Experience as a police officer	14	19	34	18	85
Departmental policy	19	11	54	8	92
Supervisor's preferences	22	7	36	14	79
Total	130	67	215	82	494*

* Although participants were asked to rank and select each action only once, some officers decided to give multiple responses to this question. This resulted in more than 424 responses being recorded.

CHAPTER 5

Discussion and Conclusions Regarding Domestic Violence

MAJOR FINDINGS

- Despite mandates for annual in-service training on domestic violence for all police officers, many officers do not receive this training as prescribed by law.
- Increased frequency of in-service training enhances enforcement of domestic violence laws even when that training is not directly related to domestic violence enforcement.
- Police officers in a mandatory arrest jurisdiction for the enforcement of domestic violence laws rely heavily on their perception of the law to justify their enforcement activities.
- There are significant correlations between a police officer's personal and professional positive opinions toward the enforcement of domestic violence legislation and his actions in mandatory arrest domestic violence situations.
- When police officers observe a domestic violence offense in a mandatory arrest jurisdiction, they are more likely to make an arrest than when they must rely on victim statements or physical evidence.
- Victim's wishes and opinions on the enforcement of domestic violence laws have little effect on the arrest outcome in mandatory arrest jurisdictions, according to both officer's opinions and their reactions to hypothetical situations.

RESEARCH QUESTIONS AND HYPOTHESES ADDRESSED

H 1 There are geographic determinants, which will influence the enforcement of domestic violence laws by police officers.

Research Question 1. Does the size and type of municipality where a police officer is employed affect his/hers enforcement of domestic violence laws? Do **Urban** and **Urban Suburb** police agencies take their responsibilities for the enforcement of domestic violence laws as seriously as **Suburban** departments? Are there differences in the enforcement of domestic violence laws by the Civil Service status of a police agency?

Table 5.1: Arrest Mean Scores by Geographic Work Setting

	Urban	Urban Suburb	Large Suburban	Small Suburban	Total
Mean	25.37	25.55	24.34	23.56	24.61
Std. Deviation	4.599	4.650	4.414	4.467	4.538
N	97	58	188	75	418

Table 5.1 displays the analysis of variance across the four setting groups for the combined scores of the five mandatory arrest scenarios (1, 2, 3, 5, & 6). The ratio of mean squares, the F statistic is 3.358 with observed significance level of .019. It is unlikely that the means of the arrest summary scores for the four settings featured in this study are the same. The **Urban Suburb** setting had the highest mean arrest summary score at 25.55, followed by the **Urban** setting at 25.37. The next highest score was for the **Large Urban** setting at 24.34 with the **Small Suburban** ranking last in mean arrest summary score at 24.61.

Using the Bonferroni procedure for multiple comparisons of the four settings in the study produces Appendix Table 5.1. While none of the results are significant at the .05 level the table does show that the greatest variance differences are between the **Small Suburban** and the **Urban** (.055) and **Urban Suburb** (.07) settings.

A geographic determinant beyond the control of the police officer is the Civil Service status of the police department. This factor is determined at the municipal level and controls many factors of police agencies' operations relating to hiring, promotions, and discipline. Table 5.2 displays the arrest mean for police departments participating in this study by Civil Service status. The ANOVA findings for this table are an F statistic of 5.529 and a significance of 0.019. This observed significance level is small, so it is possible to reject the null hypothesis that the means of the two groups based on their department's participation in Civil Service are unequal. The arrest mean is lower for the Civil Service police agencies participating in this study.

Table 5.2: Arrest Mean Scores by Civil Service Status

Civil Service Agency	N	Mean	Std. Deviation
Yes	263	24.21	4.601
No	155	25.28	4.362
Total	418	24.61	4.538

Research Question 2. Do police officers in urban settings focus more on violent felony domestic violence offenses than on misdemeanor domestic violence crimes? Do higher crime rates and the need to deal with more serious crimes than misdemeanor domestic violence offenses translate into attitudes which foster less enforcement?

Scenario 5 is the only scenario that involves a violent felony crime, an aggravated assault with a weapon resulting in injury. Scenario 6 is the most serious misdemeanor domestic violence assault observed by the participants in the study. Scenario 1 is the situation with the lowest mandatory arrest response rate involving an assault in this study.

Table 5.3 examines the research question that police officers in urban settings are more likely to focus on violent felony domestic violence offenses than on misdemeanor domestic violence crimes. All of these scenarios are mandatory arrest situations under the Domestic Violence laws of New Jersey with a maximum score of six. While there would appear to be a minor variance in Scenario 5 for the **Urban** setting, the Analysis of Variance produces an *F* ratio of 1.056 and a significance of

.368. It is not possible to reject the null hypothesis that the arrest means are the same for all four settings.

Table 5.3: Arrest Mean Scores by Felony vs. Misdemeanor Domestic Violence Crimes

	Urban	Urban Suburb	Large Suburban	Small Suburban	Total
Scenario 5 Arrest Mean	5.65	5.81	5.76	5.84	5.76
N	98	58	192	77	425
Scenario 6 Arrest Mean	5.79	5.81	5.73	5.78	5.76
N	98	58	191	77	424
Scenario 1 Arrest Mean	5.16	5.25	4.91	4.81	5.00
N	98	58	190	75	421

In Scenario 6, the **Urban** setting displays the second highest arrest mean in the study. The Analysis of Variance examination produces an F ratio of .214 and a significance of .887. It is not possible to reject the null hypothesis that the arrest means are the same for all four settings. In Scenario 1, the **Urban** setting again produces the second highest arrest mean. The ANOVA analysis results in an F ratio of 1.65 and a significance of .176, failing to reject the null hypothesis that the means of the four setting are the same. From these results, it is clear that the **Urban** setting police officers in this study cannot be found to vary from police officers in the three other settings when dealing with felony domestic violence offenses, as compared to misdemeanor domestic violence offenses.

Research Question 3. Do a larger number of police officers assigned to a shift or squad have a positive effect on a police officer's enforcement of domestic violence laws within a specific geographical setting?

Crank and Wells (1991) and Weiseheit, Wells & Falcone (1999) found that officers from larger, more urban police departments spend more time on the crime control functions than officers in smaller agencies. Conversely, it was found that officers in smaller police agencies expended significantly more resources providing services than did their counterparts in larger agencies.   Meager (1985) found significant variation in police activities by city size in a national study of 249 municipal agencies. How does this translate into the actions of the police in domestic violence situations involving the implementation of mandatory arrest? Does the working environment of the individual police officer have a direct effect on the enforcement of mandatory arrest domestic violence situations?

   Table 5.4 displays the ANOVA results across the four groups for the size of the shift that a police officer is assigned to by the combined scores of the five mandatory arrest scenarios (1, 2, 3, 5, & 6). The ratio of mean squares, the F statistic is 5.51 with observed significance level of .001. It is unlikely that the means of the arrest summary scores for the four shift size categories in this study are the same. The 1-3 officer shift size (N=30) had the highest mean arrest summary score at 27.03, followed by the more than 9 officer shift size (N=77) at 25.47. The next highest score was for the 3-6 officer shift size (N=209) at 24.39 with the 7-9 officer shift size (N=102) recorded the smallest mean arrest rate of 23.69.

Table 5.4: Arrest Mean Scores by Shift Size in Mandatory Arrest Scenarios

	1-3 Officers	3-6 Officers	7-9 Officers	More than 9 Officers	Total
Mean	27.03	24.39	23.69	25.47	24.61
Std. Deviation	4.038	4.598	4.383	4.364	4.538
N	30	209	102	77	418

   From the data displayed in Tables 5.3 and 5.4, there do appear to be significant differences in the handling of domestic violence incidents when the working environment of the police officer is measured by the number of officers assigned to a specific shift in mandatory arrest domestic violence situations. Shifts with a small number of police officers (N=1-3) and large number of officers (N = more than 9) display higher mean arrest scores.

Using paired comparisons of the Bonferroni procedure, this study found significant differences (p<.05) in the mean scores for several of the pairwise comparisons. These are displayed in Appendix Table 5.2. The arrest mean of the smallest shift size of 1-3 police officers was found to be significantly different from the means for both the groups of 4-6 officers (.016) and with the 7-9 officers (.002) categories. The more than 9 officers per shift group failed to achieve significance with any of the other three shift compliments although; it did come close with the 7-9 officers per shift group at .051.

Research Question 4.   Do police officers working in urban areas display an adverse desire to the strict enforcement of misdemeanor domestic violence crimes compared to officers in either urban suburb or suburban municipalities?

This question will be examined by combing the arrest mean scores for the four misdemeanor crimes (disorderly person offenses in New Jersey criminal code language) from Scenarios 1 (assault), Scenario 2 (assault), Scenario 3 (violation of a restraining order), and Scenario 6 (assault) and comparing study participants by the geographical setting where they work. The results will be examined by the use of ANOVA and the Bonferroni test procedure for significance.

Table 5.5: Misdemeanor DV Crimes Arrest Mean Scores by Geographic Setting

	Urban	Urban Suburb	Large Suburban	Small Suburban	Total
Mean	20.91	21.14	20.35	19.58	20.45
Std. Deviation	3.231	3.332	3.293	3.515	3.351
N	97	58	187	74	416

Table 5.5 displays the Analysis of Variance across the four geographic groups of the study, by the study participants combined arrest scores of the four disorderly persons mandatory arrest scenarios (1, 2, 3, & 6). The ratio of mean squares (the F statistic) is 3.184 with an observed significance level of .024. It is unlikely that the means of the arrest summary scores for the four shift size categories in this study

are the same. The **Urban** setting recorded the second highest mean arrest score and the smallest standard deviation of all four settings. Using paired comparisons of the Bonferroni test procedure, this study did not find any significant differences ($p < .05$) in the mean scores of the pairwise comparisons for the **Urban** setting against the other three settings. The results of these analyses are displayed in Appendix Table 5.3. The only statistically significant pairwise arrest mean by setting was between the **Urban Suburb** and the **Small Suburban** settings at 0.047.

From this analysis, it would appear that police officers in **Urban** settings take their responsibilities concerning domestic violence enforcement of disorderly person offenses just as seriously as those in the other geographic settings of this research. If there is any indication by the arrest mean of study participants, **Urban** police officers are above the average of two of the other settings in this study.

H 2 There are variances in the enforcement of domestic violence laws by police   officers based on the level of in-service training and self-motivated learning to which   officers are exposed.

Research Question 5. Does the frequency of in-service training positively affect an officer's attitude toward the enforcement of domestic violence laws?

Breci, (1989) conducted studies in four police agencies, two in the Southeast and two in the Midwest, where 242 respondents completed questionnaires that measured police training and attitudes regarding domestic disturbances. The findings of this research concluded that trained officers were more likely to have a service-oriented perspective on their role in handling domestic disputes. Officers with little training, on the other hand, were more likely to view their role in terms of enforcing the law. This research concluded that the more training the officers received, the more likely they were to resent guidelines and policies that limit their ability to use alternative interventions to resolve domestic disputes. This research runs counter to the express intent of the State of New Jersey mandating four hours of annual training in domestic violence. The current research study hypothesizes that training will have a positive effect on an officer's attitudes and actions toward adherence to and enforcement of domestic violence laws.

Table 5.6 examines the research question if and how training affects an officer's performance under domestic violence mandatory arrest situations. Police officers were asked how often within the past four years had they received their mandatory domestic violence training. Responses could range from no in-service training (none) to training in all four years (4). This information was then compared to the first three scenarios in the study.

These situations were selected because in the first two scenarios the officers had to rely on the statements of the victims and the fact present upon their arrival to make a determination if the facts warranted a mandatory arrest situation. The third scenario tested officers' knowledge of seldom-used clause of the Attorney General Guidelines, which concerns the full faith and credit requirement of out-of-state restraining orders. The scores on the arrest factor received a maximum score of 18 and a minimum of 3.

Table 5.6: Arrest Mean Scores of Scenarios 1, 2, & 3 by Years of Domestic Violence Training

	Years of Domestic Violence Training in Past Four Years					
	None	1	2	3	4	Total
Mean	14.00	14.28	13.89	14.43	15.14	14.65
Std. Deviation	3.448	3.295	3.675	3.165	2.997	3.212
N	19	130	38	35	196	418

The analysis of variance examination produces an *F* ratio of 2.366 and a significance of .052. An analysis using the Bonferroni test procedure found no significant differences in the pairwise comparisons of the five levels of training in domestic violence by the arrest means for officers in this research. However, it is worth noting that those officers who had received the most training with three or all four years did score above the mean of arrest scores, while those officers who reported no training or just one or two years within the past four all scored below the arrest mean in this table. The two groups receiving the most training also displayed the smallest standard deviation within their respective groups of all those found in this study. While the differences are not significantly different at the .05 level, they do merit discussion. Furthermore, it is beyond the limits of this study to determine the effectiveness of the present in-service training that is provided at the local police agency level.

Research Question 6. Do police officers who have recently studied for a promotional exam with a formal study group show an increased arrest mean scores in his/hers enforcement of domestic violence laws?

Table 5.7 displays the analysis of variance for officers who have studied for a promotional exam within the last three years against the officer's responses to the five mandatory arrest scenarios (1, 2, 3, 5, & 6). Three years was selected as a period to examine this question, as this is the standard cycle for promotional exams on Civil Service police agencies. Non-Civil Service police agencies are free to hold promotional exams as needed on no particular cycle. The promotional exams process is one of the best examples of self-motivated learning directly related to the law enforcement profession and the advancement of a police officer's career that is available to most police officers. Civil Service police agencies exam notices are usually posted about six months prior to the test date. Usually, a suggested reading list of books, along with the criminal code and the Attorney General Guidelines are used to form the basis for many of the test questions.

The promotional exam testing process is a brief, and if done properly for success, an intense learning procedure that exposes the student/police officer to a broad range of subjects that he or she must master for promotion. There is a percentage of officers, at all ranks, that are simply content with their present position in law enforcement and do not either study for or even take promotional exams. Other officers may miss eligibility due to lack of time in a current position to qualify for promotional exams and have to wait for the next exam cycle. This may explain why such a high number of police officers (N=217) in this study have not taken a promotional exam within the last three years.

The ratio of mean squares, the F statistic, is 6.327 with observed significance level of .012 for Table 5.7. It is unlikely that the means of the arrest summary scores for those officers who did study for a promotional exam within the past three years is the same as for those officers who did not study for promotion. Police officers who studied for a promotional exam were found to achieve a statistically significantly higher arrest mean score than officers who had not. It should also be noted that the standard deviation for officers participating in study groups is also smaller.

Table 5.7: Arrest Mean Scores by Promotional Exam Studying

Study for Promotional Exam	N	Mean	Std. Deviation	Std. Error
Yes	201	25.18	4.36	.308
No	217	24.07	4.64	.315
Total	418	24.61	4.53	.222

Table 5.8 displays the ANOVA results for officers who have studied for a promotional exam within the last three years with a study group against the officer's responses to the five mandatory arrest scenarios (1, 2, 3, 5, & 6). The ratio of mean squares, the F statistic, is 2.536 with observed significance level of 0.112. From the results of this research question it is not possible to reject the hypothesis that the two population variances are equal. This is surprising based on the results of Table 5.9, where studying for a promotional exam was found to be significant. Therefore, while studying for a promotional exam is significant when measured by the mean arrest score, participation in a study group is not a significant factor in predicting how police officers would react given the domestic violence scenarios of this study.

Table 5.8: Arrest Mean Scores by Study Group Participation

Study for Promotional Exam with Study Group	N	Mean	Std. Deviation
Yes	127	25.14	4.182
No	291	24.37	4.673
Total	418	24.61	4.538

Table 5.9 displays the results of the level of a police officer's education by the arrest mean of the five mandatory arrest scenarios (1, 2, 3, 5, & 6) featured in this study. Several of the levels of education have been merged for this table from those previously displayed in this study. The Analysis of Variance examination produces an F ratio of .520 and a significance level of .669. It is not possible to reject the null hypothesis that the arrest means are the same for all four levels of education. No conclusions can be reached by this research concerning the effect of higher education on a police officer's enforcement of domestic violence laws.

Table 5.9: Arrest Mean Scores by Educational Level

Educational Level	N	Mean	Std. Deviation
High School	71	24.04	4.686
Up to 60 College Credits or Associates Degree	173	24.69	4.632
More than 60 College Credits up to College Degree	153	24.69	4.456
Some Masters Credits up to a Ph.D.	21	25.19	3.932
Total	418	24.61	4.538

H 3 There are social determinants which influence and effect the enforcement of domestic violence laws by police officers.

Research Question 8. Does the impression given by a police agency on strict adherence to the letter of the law affect an officer's attitude toward the enforcement of domestic violence laws?

Department leadership, attitudes of direct supervisors, and the work environment of the various police agencies will all affect how police officers perform their duties in domestic violence situations. Herbert (1998) found that formal and informal regulations commingle in ways that merit investigation. Legal and bureaucratic rules partially determine police activity; however, officers have the ability to interpret these rules in different ways. There is a need to examine how formal rules become real in daily practice. Table 5.10 displays study participants' self-report compliance with the Attorney General Guidelines for the enforcement of the domestic violence laws by the arrest mean for the five mandatory arrest scenarios featured in this research. While four responses were available to study participants, no police officer in the study selected the "never" response and was therefore not reported in this table. There is a clear linear relationship between the arrest mean and the degree of positive support for Attorney General Guidelines.

Table 5.10: Arrest Mean Scores by Self-Report Compliance with Attorney General Guidelines

	Sometimes	Often	Always	Total
Mean	18.82	22.86	25.29	24.61
Std. Deviation	2.714	4.032	4.456	4.538

It is also clear that domestic violence enforcement has widespread support among officers in this study given that over 75% of participants responded that they 'always" try to comply with the Guidelines. The ANOVA f statistic of 20.852 and a significance of .000 further support and confirm this conclusion. Using paired comparisons of the Bonferroni procedure, as shown in Appendix Table 5.4, this study found significant differences ($p < .05$) in the mean scores for all of the pairwise comparisons for arrest means by compliance with the Attorney General Guidelines for Domestic Violence. There is a positive correlation between study participant's self-report compliance with the Attorney General Guidelines and their arrest means in mandatory arrest scenarios of this study.

While police officers in this study attempt to comply with the Attorney General Guidelines for the most part, there is considerably less support on officer's opinions concerning the practicality of enforcing the Domestic Violence Laws of New Jersey. This may be because much of the discretionary powers usually reserved to allow law enforcement to informally handle situations have been removed from the arsenal of options available to police officers. It could also be a reaction to the very specific and complicated nature of the New Jersey

Domestic Violence laws. It may also indicate a level of frustration with the eventual adjudication of the vast majority of domestic violence offenses, namely dismissal of the charges, and the dropping of restraining orders, especially in cases involving misdemeanor assaults (simple assaults in New Jersey). It was not unusual to hear officers speaking of incidents where victims of domestic violence want to post bail for their attacker, even before the paperwork and processing are completed.

Appendix Table 5.5 examines the pairwise comparison of the four responses using the Bonferroni procedure that were examined in Table 5.11. There were significant differences in the means of the groups between the response "always" and both the "sometimes" (.000) and the "often" (.045) groups. The only pairwise comparison that did not achieve significance was between the "always" and the "never" responses; this was in large part due to the extremely small size of the "never" category which had only 3 responses in the survey. These results only reinforce the conclusions of the next table.

Table 5.11 displays study participants arrest mean by the practicality of enforcing domestic violence laws. The ANOVA procedure produced an *f* statistic of 8.313 and a significance of .000 resulting in a significant difference between the groups at the .01 confidence level. There is a clear linear correlation between officer's perception of how practical the domestic violence laws are to enforce and their willingness to arrest domestic violence offenders in the five mandatory arrest scenarios featured in this research.

Table 5.11: Arrest Mean Scores by Practicality of DV Enforcement

	Never	Sometimes	Often	Always	Total
Mean	21.67	23.42	24.74	26.25	24.61
Std. Deviation	7.638	4.389	4.214	4.749	4.538
N	3	144	176	95	418

Does the overall discipline of a police agency have an effect on police officers' actions in domestic violence situations? Study participants were asked their opinion and given a choice of four options. This response was then compared to the arrest mean of the five mandatory arrest situations to examine if any relationship could be found. The results were displayed in Table 5.12. The ANOVA procedure found an f statistic of 1.807 and a significance of .145. It is not possible to reject the null hypothesis that the arrest means are the same for all four levels of departmental discipline. No conclusions can be reached by this research concerning the effect of departmental discipline on a police officer's enforcement of domestic violence laws. This was further confirmed by the pairwise comparisons using the Bonferroni test procedure, which produced no significant mean differences at the .05 level.

Table 5.12: Arrest Mean Scores by Officer's Opinion of Departmental Discipline

	Very Strict	Somewhat Strict	Somewhat Loose	Very Loose	Total
Mean	25.77	24.32	24.39	24.97	24.61
Std. Deviation	4.870	4.400	4.385	5.096	4.538
N	62	207	116	33	418

Another measure of departmental support for the enforcement of domestic violence enforcement is displayed in Table 5.13. To arrive at a statistic for the overall departmental support, responses to several questions including frequency of domestic violence in-service training, administrative support for strict enforcement of domestic violence laws, immediate supervisor's support for strict enforcement of domestic violence laws and overall departmental discipline were combined into a single variable. The ANOVA statistical procedure across all four levels of support produced an f statistic of 2.804 and a significance of .040 resulting in a significant difference between the groups at the .05 confidence level. Using the Bonferroni test procedure for paired comparisons, statistically significant differences were found between the "strong support" and the "weak support" groups at the $p < .05$ on the mean arrest scores.

Table 5.13: Arrest Mean Scores by Departmental Support of DV Enforcement

	Very weak support	Weak support	Support	Strong support	Total
Mean	23.50	23.98	24.65	25.76	24.61
Std. Deviation	5.757	4.526	4.451	4.487	4.538
N	8	142	189	79	418

The data presented here supports the hypothesis that the impression given by a police agency on strict adherence to the letter of the law does have a positive effect an officer's attitude toward the enforcement of domestic violence laws when measured by the arrest mean scores in mandatory arrest situations.

Research Question 9. Does a police officer's years of service have a negative effect his/hers attitudes toward the enforcement of domestic violence laws?

Police cynicism is a concept which has been examined by several authors (Niederhoffer, 1969, Wilt & Bannon, 1976, Crank, 2004). In the context of this research, this concept is applied to both officer's attitudes and actions regarding domestic violence enforcement. Do police officers become less likely to enforce domestic violence laws as their years of service increase? Table 5.14 examines this question by exploring the study participants' self-report compliance with the Attorney General Guidelines on Domestic Violence arrayed by their years of police service. The years of service were compressed from previous tables in this study. The greater the mean for the years of service the greater the reported compliance with the Attorney General Guidelines.

The ANOVA statistical procedure across all four levels of compliance produced an f statistic of 2.447 and a significance of .033, resulting in a statistically significant difference between the groups at the .05 confidence level. The categories of "more than 24 years, but 30 or less" and "more than 30 years" recorded the highest mean self-reported compliance scores of the six categories. Whereas Table 5.14 examined officers' attitudes Appendix Table 5.6 and Appendix Table 5.7 examine officers' actions by their arrest means in the scenarios of this research to also assess if police cynicism affects the outcome of acts of domestic violence. For Appendix Table 5.6 the ANOVA procedure across all four levels of arrest mean produced an f statistic of 2.968 and a significance of .012. This result indicates a significant difference between the years of service groups at the .05 confidence level.

Table 5.14: Mean Scores for Compliance with DV Laws by Years of Police Service

Years of Police Service	N	Mean	Std. Deviation
6 years or less	100	3.62	.546
More than 6 years, but 12 or less	123	3.80	.418
More than 12 years, but 18 or less	75	3.76	.489
More than 18 years, but 24 or less	87	3.71	.569
More than 24 years, but 30 or less	32	3.84	.369
More than 30 years	8	4.00	.000
Total	425	3.74	.494

The lowest mean arrest score was recorded by study participants with the group "6 years or less" of service a finding which is surprising in as much as these officers are the most recent graduates from the police academy and would have been expected to exhibit the "romantic cynicism" of Neiderhoffer's (1968) typology and exhibit greater compliance and a higher arrest mean. Meanwhile, the "more than 24 years, but 30 or less" group recorded the second highest arrest mean in the study. The "more than 30 years" group recorded the fourth highest, ahead of the "more than 12 years, but 18 years or less" and the "6 years or less" groups. Using the Bonferroni test procedure for paired comparisons, a statistically significant difference between the years of service of "6 years or less" (sig .010) and the "more than 6 years, but 12 or less" and the "more than 18, but 24 or less" (sig .034) groups at the p <.05 on the mean arrest scores was found

.

H 4 There are variances in the enforcement of domestic violence laws based primarily on a police officer's justification for initiating and sustaining a specific course of action.

The subculture of normative orders, as described by Herbert (1998) based on the works of Parsons (1951), attempts to capture the importance of internalized values for structuring individual behavior. This concept will be examined for police officers participating in this study. This hypothesis is tested by officers' actual responses in a given scenario and their rationalization to justify actions in the second question for each scenario. Here officers must give some insight as to their reasoning for their chosen course of action. It is one thing for an officer to say that he or she abides by the law and another to do so in practice and be able to justify and articulate it. This examination will allow an investigation to examine police officer training and the connection between a participant's attitudes against his/her actions and justifications.

Research Question 10. Do the justifications given by a police officer for the actions he/she takes to resolve domestic violence situations explain their enforcement actions under State and Federal law?

To explore the question that represents various aspects of acts involving domestic violence three of the hypothetical scenarios will be examined. First, Scenario 1 will be analyzed since this had the lowest arrest rate of the mandatory arrest scenarios set forth in this study. Scenario 4 will be the second situation examined. This was the only non-mandatory arrest scenario included in the study. In fact, no criminal offense was committed in this situation. Never less, over twenty percent of all study participants identified and arrested the male participant either "always' or "most of the time." The last incident to be examined will be Scenario 6, the situation that recorded the highest arrest percentage of all the scenarios in the study.

Table 5.15 displays the arrest mean for Scenario 1 by the most popular justification given by study participants which was "mandated by law" for their actions given the facts of this situation. Eighty-four percent of study participants justified their actions as mandatory under the law. The arrest mean of officers who cited this justification as "most important" was understandably the highest of the five possible responses (5.19).

The ANOVA procedure across all five levels of importance produced an f statistic of 13.067 and a significance of 0.000. This result indicates a significant difference between the groups at the .001 confidence level. For the most important justification in Scenario 1 it would appear that officer's justifications for their arrest of the defendant do explain and in fact cite the mandatory provisions of the law as the reason for their actions.

Table 5.15: Arrest Mean Scores for Scenario 1 by Most Popular Justification: Mandated by Law

Justification: Mandated by law	N	Mean	Std. Deviation
Most Important	353	5.19	1.344
Important	13	4.85	1.405
Somewhat Important	12	3.92	1.564
Least Important	22	4.27	1.778
Not Ranked	19	3.21	1.357
Total	419	5.00	1.455

Table 5.16 displays the arrest mean for Scenario 1 by the least popular justification given by study participants which was "comply with the wishes of the victim" for their actions given the facts of this scenario. Twenty-seven percent of study participants considered the need to comply with the victims' wishes as their least important justification for their actions.

The arrest mean of officers who cited this justification as "least important" was the second lowest of the five possible responses at (4.88). The ANOVA procedure across all five levels of importance produced an f statistic of 4.501 and a significance of 0.001. This result indicates a significant difference between the groups at the .001 confidence level. For the least important justification in Scenario 1 it would appear that officer's justifications for the arrest the defendant was in part explained by their decision not to abide by the victim's wishes and to make an arrest under the circumstances presented despite the wishes and actions of the victim. Conversely, those study participants who responded that they considered the victims' wishes "important" or "most important" under the scenario circumstances were found to have statistically significant lower arrest mean scores.

Table 5.16: Arrest Mean Scores for Scenario 1 by Comply with Wishes of Victim

Justification: Comply with wishes of victim	N	Mean	Std. Deviation
Most Important	16	4.69	1.662
Important	20	3.85	1.387
Somewhat Important	31	5.00	1.592
Least Important	113	4.88	1.568
Not Ranked	239	5.18	1.326
Total	419	5.00	1.455

Table 5.17 displays the arrest mean for Scenario 4 by the most popular justification given by study participants which was "mandated by law" for their actions given the facts of this situation. Fifty-eight percent of study participants justified their actions as mandatory under the law.

The arrest mean of officers who cited this justification as "most important" was understandably the lowest of the five possible responses (3.86) as this scenario was not a mandatory arrest situation. In fact, in this situation no arrest was warranted or justifiable. The ANOVA procedure across all five levels of importance produced an f statistic of 11.543 and a significance of 0.000. This result indicates a significant difference between the groups at the .001 confidence level. For the most important justification in Scenario 4 it would appear that officer's justifications for not arresting the defendant explain and in fact cite the mandatory provisions of the law as the reason for their not effecting an arrest as frequently as officers who cited this justification as less than "most important ."

Table 5.17: Arrest Mean Scores for Scenario 4 by Most Popular Justification: Mandated by Law

Justification: Mandated by law	N	Mean	Std. Deviation
Most Important	245	3.86	2.010
Important	18	3.89	1.875
Somewhat Important	10	5.30	1.160
Least Important	33	4.88	1.746
Not Ranked	113	5.13	1.313
Total	419	4.32	1.894

Table 5.18 displays the arrest mean for Scenario 4 by the least popular justification given by study participants which was "comply with the wishes of the victim" for their actions given the facts of this scenario. Twenty-two percent of study participants considered the need to comply with the victims wishes as their least important justification for their actions.

The arrest mean of officers who cited this justification as "least important" was the highest of the five possible responses at (4.44). This is somewhat of a surprise, as the "complainant" Mrs. Coors wanted her husband arrested in this incident although no violation of the Domestic Violence laws had occurred in the fact pattern. The ANOVA procedure across all five levels of importance produced an f statistic of 1.980 and a significance of 0.097. It is not possible to reject the null hypothesis that the arrest means are the same for all five levels of least important justification in Scenario 4. No conclusions can be reached regarding officers' actions for their least important justification by the arrest means of this scenario.

Table 5.18: Arrest Mean Scores for Scenario 4 by Least Popular
Justification: Comply with Wishes of Victim

Justification: Comply with wishes of victim	N	Mean	Std. Deviation
Most Important	22	3.77	2.245
Important	22	3.91	2.068
Somewhat Important	35	3.71	1.808
Least Important	92	4.43	1.900
Not Ranked	248	4.44	1.839
Total	419	4.32	1.894

Table 5.19 displays the arrest mean for Scenario 6 by the most popular justification given by study participants which was "mandated by law" for their actions given the facts of this situation. Eighty-eight percent of study participants (N=371) justified their actions as mandatory under the law in this scenario. The arrest mean of officers who cited this justification as "most important" was understandably the highest of the five possible responses (5.84). The ANOVA procedure across all five levels of importance produced an f statistic of 12.798 and a significance of 0.000. This result indicates a significant difference between the groups at the .001 confidence level. For the most important justification in Scenario 6, it would appear that officer's justifications for their arrest of the defendant explain and cite the mandatory provisions of the law as the reason for their actions. Scenario 6 is the clearest example in this survey of an incident where the police officer can rely on his or her own observations to establish the requisite probable cause to make an arrest and take the case forward for prosecution without relying on statements of the victim or third parties. From both study participants' selection of the most important justification in Scenario 6 and the statistical analysis of their actions it would appear that based on the mean arrest scores, that police officers' justifications do explain their enforcement actions under the law.

Table 5.19: Arrest Mean Scores for Scenario 6 by Most Popular Justification: Mandated by Law

Justification: Mandated by law	N	Mean	Std. Deviation
Most Important	371	5.84	.680
Important	9	5.11	1.453
Somewhat Important	12	5.67	.778
Least Important	20	5.35	1.309
Not Ranked	11	4.36	1.690
Total	423	5.76	.825

Table 5.20 displays the arrest mean for Scenario 6 by the least popular justification given by study participants, which was "comply with the wishes of the victim" for their actions given the facts of this scenario. Twenty-five percent of study participants (N=105) considered the need to comply with the victims' wishes as their least important justification for their actions in this situation. The arrest mean of officers who cited this justification as "least important" was the squarely in the middle of the five possible responses at 5.70. The ANOVA procedure across all five levels of importance produced an *f* statistic of 4.015 and a significance of 0.003. This result indicates a significant difference between the responses at the $p < .05$ confidence level. Still as the arrest mean for the least important justification fell directly in the middle of the five responses and just below the overall mean, it would be difficult to draw any significant conclusions from these results.

The most significant relationships between study participants' compliance with the mandatory arrest provisions of New Jersey's Domestic Violence laws and the social and legal determinates which influence their decisions are found in Table 5.21. The most significant positive relationship was found between those officers who self-reported that they "always try to enforce" the domestic violence laws and arrest decisions. It is only logical that officers that make a conscious effort to properly enforce domestic violence laws would be able to correctly identify and take the necessary appropriate actions when confronted with various domestic violence scenarios. The converse of this result is an important factor that must also be stressed. Police officers who do not have a positive attitude toward the enforcement of domestic violence laws have been found to be less likely to correctly apply the law when confronted by incidents of domestic violence. This conclusion is of special importance to frontline supervisors and police administrators who must oversee officer and departmental adherence with the provisions of domestic violence laws. Personal attitudes cannot be allowed to interfere or obstruct the lawful professional responsibilities of law enforcement personnel in the performance of their sworn duties.

Table 5.20: Arrest Mean Scores for Scenario 6 by Least Popular Justification: Comply with Wishes of Victim

Justification: Comply with wishes of victim	N	Mean	Std. Deviation
Most Important	16	5.50	.894
Important	13	5.00	1.732
Somewhat Important	22	5.82	.853
Least Important	105	5.70	.982
Not Ranked	267	5.84	.651
Total	423	5.76	.825

The next most significant finding was the factor of departmental participation in the Civil Service process. As earlier discussed in Table 5.21, non-Civil Service police agencies in this study exhibited higher Arrest Mean Scores than Civil Service agencies. The fact that this was found to be such a significant factor in the multiple regression analysis was not anticipated.

Table 5.21: Summary Arrest Score as a Function of Social and Legal Determinants of Domestic Violence Enforcement By a Sample of New Jersey Police Officers

Predictor variables	Regression Coefficient	Significance
Police Officer Support for the Enforcement of Domestic Violence Laws	1.899	.000
Civil Service Agency	1.817	.000
Police Officer Support of Attorney General Guidelines	1.043	.009
Municipal Violent Crime Rate per 1,000 (2008)	.463	.000
Domestic Violence Training last 4 years	.388	.009
In-Service Training Days within last year	.230	.003
Constant	7.822	$R^2=.197$ (F=16.843) (n= 417)

Positive support for the Attorney General Guidelines by study participants translated into officer compliance with the law when measured by the summary arrest score. This is consistent with the earlier findings of this table. Police supervisors and administrators could utilize this conclusion to assess departmental needs and increase compliance with the mandatory provisions of the domestic violence laws.

Another surprising factor uncovered by this research is that officers who work in agencies that reported a higher violent crime rate per 1,000 residents displayed a more positive mean arrest summary score than officers who were employed by agencies with lower violent crime rates. This research only involved one scenario in which the actions of the offending party could be construed as a felony (scenario 5, an assault with a knife). It is also somewhat counterintuitive that officers in the busiest jurisdictions with the most serious crime would also adhere to the provisions of the domestic violence laws more stringently. This is another indication that high incidence of serious crime did not detract from domestic violence enforcement by officers in this study.

The final two significant factors in the multiple regression analysis of Table 5.21 involve training. Greater adherence with the mandatory provisions the Attorney General Guidelines for annual domestic violence training over the past four years was a significant factor in better mean arrest scores in the mandatory arrest scenarios of the research study subjects. This is again a compelling justification for annual training, something that over half of all study participants did not receive. The last significant relationship is that of the total number of training days a study participant received over the last year excluding firearms training. It is apparent that officers who are placed in a positive training environment not only for domestic violence training but for other programs as well, performed better than less well-trained officers when measured by the mean arrest scores of the mandatory arrest scenarios of this research. This further supports the positive influence of enhanced training program on the overall performance of police officers.

CONCLUSION

A wealth of information was gained from the compilation and analysis of this research, but much was also learned in the impromptu and informal discussions held with many of the police officers who participated in this project. Many police officers were surprised by the fact that the primary focus of this research was to learn their honest opinions on the enforcement of the Domestic Violence laws in New Jersey. One incident stood out above all the rest and needs to be retold. Two superior officers of a police agency were both participating in the study. I have personally known both officers for many years from the time when we were patrol officer with different agencies. After the completion of the surveys in general conversation I commented that their department had over the course of the past few years experienced a sharp decline in the number of reported domestic violence cases. The higher-ranking officer made a logical explanation that a large family had accounted for an unusually high number of domestic violence incidents and had relocated to another municipality, hence the drop in reported domestic violence incidents. It was a logical and on the surface a completely plausible explanation. It would have ended my inquiry, but then the subordinate, also a high-ranking officer in charge of the road patrol officers decided to add this comment. "Well, you know the guys on the road, they do what they have to do, but all that paperwork, sometimes it's just too much." While doing my best not to show too much reaction, I looked over at the superior officer, whose face registered shock. The subordinate left the room a moment later, while the superior officer, still in shock at the admission of his subordinate, just looked at me and said, "Do you believe it? What do I do now?" My only response was "Training, training, more training, and then more accountability." Somewhere along the way, the train had slipped off the tracks and no one seemed to have told the man at the controls.

This ties in directly to the first conclusion of my findings: Police officers are not receiving the training they need or are required to have under the law. Table 4.13 was something of a shock as it will be for any police chief, administrator, County Prosecutor, of member of the New Jersey Attorney General's office who may learn of its surprising statistic. Less than half of all officers, 197 of 425 in the study, had received all four years of mandatory domestic violence training. One hundred and fifty-four of this same population of police officers had received either none or only 1 year of training over the course of past four years. Who is to blame? Certainly, there is responsibility to be shared by many individuals.

While there are mandates under the law, there is very little enforcement and it all relies on voluntary compliance with minimal accountability being required. This research has shown that officers who are exposed to a greater number of training days on an annual basis translate that training into stricter enforcement of domestic violence laws. It would also be logical to assume that additional training would improve performance in other areas of law enforcement both directly and indirectly.

It is apparent that a severe disconnect has occurred between the desired goals of domestic violence training and the reality of its application. It is clear that for whatever reason local police agencies are often unable or unwilling to make the scheduling allowances that are required to comply with mandatory domestic violence training. Almost every county in New Jersey has, or is in association with, a police-training academy. To ensure consistent training not just within a police agency, but also over a wider jurisdictional area such as a county it would be beneficial from several aspects for regional training to become the standard for all mandatory training. If the County Prosecutor, the chief law enforcement officer in his jurisdiction, were responsible to oversee all training within his or her geographical area a clear chain of command and responsibility would be established. A typical county in this study had approximately 1,500 police officers. Discounting July and August, the two months of heaviest vacations, domestic violence training 150 officers per month over the course of a year could easily be accomplished in groups of 40-50 officers a week. Training could be undertaken by a designated representative of the Prosecutor to ensure consistent standards of training and proficiency in learning the material.

The third major finding which was also somewhat of a surprise to the principal investigator was the reluctance of police officers to make an arrest for disorderly person offenses when they do not personally observe the act of domestic violence. Only 156 of 418 valid respondents (37.3%) correctly arrested the defendant in all five of the mandatory arrest scenarios featured in this study. Many officers who informally talked with the principal investigator after the questionnaire was completed cited, as their primary reasoning for not making a mandatory arrest, was a perception of a lack of probable cause to make the arrest. This is even more disturbing when considering the fact that the overwhelming majority of study participants believed they were complying with the mandates of the law even when failing to make a mandatory arrest. This is ironic as part of the primary reason for the domestic violence legislation was to empower the police to stop incidents of assaults and other offenses that resulted from domestic situations which they did not witness. This remains the primary rationale why the New Jersey legislature granted limited immunity to police officers who act in good faith and upon probable cause to enforce the domestic violence laws. Each of the scenarios in this research demonstrate how the New Jersey Legislature and the Attorney General's Guidelines would appear to define bright line, black and white rules for the enforcement of domestic violence laws. Yet, much of the definition of just when an incident falls into a mandatory arrest situation lies within the purview of the responding officer. His or her perception, attitude, understanding of the law, and what he or she reports of the incident will be the primary determination of how the event is handled by the criminal justice system. This is, of course, monitored with limited oversight by his supervisors who, for the most part only see what the officer files in his report of the incident.

Take Scenario 1 as a hypothetical example. If, after being apprised of the consequences of her allegations, including the arrest of her husband, the probable seizure of any weapons that pose a threat to her and the loss of the hunting trip planned for the morning, the victim decides to recant her original statement. She now says that the gash on her forehead was the result of her falling while trying to grab the remote from her husband with no intent by her husband to injure her or cause her harm. She agrees to allow the EMS to dress her wound and evaluate her for a concussion. Upon medical clearance, she returns to her home to sleep off her intoxication. Based on her revised version of events, there is no longer any probable cause to believe that an act of domestic violence has occurred. There is no longer any need to conduct an investigation report, file the domestic violence paperwork, wake up the on-call judge to have him approve an arrest warrant, or for the police to track down the offender and conduct a search of the couple's residence for weapons under a domestic violence search warrant. The incident is written up as a first aid call of an intoxicated female and the officer resumes patrol. The officer's report will reflect the victim's revised statement; the EMS report will show that an intoxicated female sustained a minor laceration, showed no sign of a concussion, and refused further medical treatment. Provided no one is shot on the hunting trip the next day, the entire incident becomes a non-event and a non-issue. Of course, this is all a hypothetical example of how a domestic violence situation could turn into a few lines on a nondescript form suitable only for filing, at least until the next more serious domestic violence incident occurs a few months later between the same parties and the police took "no action" on a previous domestic violence situation.

The simple fact is that better and more consistent training will lead police officers to have a better understanding of what is expected and required of them when responding to domestic violence situations. It will remove, or at least diminish, the "probable cause gap" as a justification for failing to act when action is what is needed to protect victims of domestic violence.

The fourth major conclusion, which comes as no surprise, is the finding of significant correlations between a police officer's personal and professional positive opinions toward the enforcement of domestic violence legislation and his or her actions in mandatory arrest domestic violence situations. When police officers stop seeing the enforcement of domestic violence laws as an extraneous burden and perceive of domestic violence laws as a core value to protect the physically and psychologically abused from further attacks, then domestic violence laws will be enforced with the same motivation as drug law violations or other serious criminal activity. The day is near, but law enforcement is not there yet. I hope that it will come sooner rather than later.

SCOPE AND LIMITATIONS

This research is based a non-probability sample. During 2008, there were just under 26,000 municipal police officers employed in the State of New Jersey. There are 21 counties within the State, of which two were selected to participate in this study. Over 3,000 police officers from a two-county area were eligible for inclusion in this research. Fourteen Chiefs of Police agreed to allow the principal investigator to solicit volunteers for participation in the study. These departments represented 1,061 of the potential universe of participants. From this universe 425 police officers agreed and participated.

All New Jersey police officers operate under the same state laws and Attorney General Guidelines for the handling of domestic violence laws. While there is the possibility that a County Prosecutor could impose even more restrictive guidelines if he or she chose to do so, neither of the counties in this study have chosen do so. Likewise, none of the police agencies participating in this research had more restrictive policies than those of the Attorney General Guidelines for Domestic Violence. This eliminated the possibility of conflicting and confounding policies.

Self-administered questionnaires are found to have higher rates of return when a researcher delivers and picks up the completed questionnaires. Since the principal investigator was present at all sessions at which the questionnaires were distributed the process allowed for a consistent response to any questions or contingencies that may arise in the course of this research. This also enhanced the security of the data collected and confidentiality of the survey responses as only the principal investigator had access to the raw data and was able to monitor all the security protocols of this research.

As a precondition of the research design, complete anonymity was a primary consideration of this research at the county, municipal, and individual police officer levels. This component was an essential factor in gaining the confidence of so many police agencies and their officers to participate and give their honest responses. No one, at any level, was eager to participate if there was going to be any comparing and contrasting of identifiable entities.

Another factor at play was trust. Could the principal investigator be relied upon to keep his word and keep all responses and identities confidential? In this regard, I was able to exploit both my 26 years of law enforcement background, and point to family full of police officers. They permitted me access to those in law enforcement that could make this study happen, and literally open doors not usually available to academic researchers.

Yet the need for confidentiality has imposed some restrictions on this research including limiting analysis to geographical settings used in this research. It would have been fascinating to perform analysis of factors such as crime rates and actual domestic violence offenses with the results collected in this research. However, the wealth of information collected outweighs the limited possibilities; confidentiality was quite understandably an essential component on this research.

Some of the implications of this research could give one a reason to cheer and cry at the same time. Should we cheer that the vast majority of police officers in this study believe that their primary motivation in mandatory arrest domestic violence situations is to enforce the law? Alternatively, should we cry that so many officers with good intentions do not perform up to some very high standards society has set for them? Should we cheer that the official statistics for domestic violence in New Jersey show a steady decline for the last decade? On the other hand, should we cry that perhaps police officers are only completing the mandated domestic violence forms "most" or "some" of the time, as in this research and "doing what they have to do" the rest of the time? Do we condemn those administrators who do not provide the required training for the officers under their command? What of those officials who have the power to insure proper training programs are established and maintained, but instead just allow the status quo of poor or no training to be perpetuated with a wink and a nod? There is no doubt that the enforcement of the domestic violence laws has taken tremendous steps toward providing protection for many of the victims of domestic violence. It is the hope that this research can is some way advance the cause for the enforcement of domestic violence legislation for all victims of domestic violence.

CONTRIBUTIONS TO THE LITERATURE

Few studies of police response to domestic violence have included either characteristics or attitudes of responding officers as potential predictors of arrest decisions (Breci,1989; Robinson & Chandek, 2000; Hall, 2005). One study that was conducted (Robinson & Chandek, 2000) found no correlation between those attitudes and the decision to arrest. This study examines arrests for domestic violence in a state which imposes uniform mandatory arrest policies on all police officers. One of the primary dependent variables examined is the type of municipality in which the officer works.

The enforcement of domestic violence laws has been estimated to consume as much as one-third of police activity, yet little is known if the pro-arrest and mandatory arrest policies implemented over the last quarter century are actually working as designed. While official statistics from New Jersey would tend to suggest a steady slight decline in simple assaults in domestic violence situations over the last ten years, the data show no such decline in homicide or other serious offenses over the same time in domestic violence offenses. This research has explored and expands the knowledge of which social and legal factors are important in the enforcement of domestic violence laws in a mandatory arrest environment. It has examined this issue from the perspective of the police officer who is the gatekeeper and enforcer of these policies.

It is hoped that this research will lead to a better understanding of the dynamics of the decision making process that is involved when police officers respond to domestic violence situations. This research is designed to bridge the gap between the theory of mandatory arrest for crimes of domestic violence and the realities of the interrelated practical dynamics of enforcement by the police in the real world. It is not easy to ask anyone, even the police, to intrude into the private and personal lives of individuals often in the heat of emotional and physical assaults, betrayals, or worse. The least we as a society can do is to give law enforcement the training and every legal tool possible so they can protect the victims of domestic abuse.

FUTURE RESEARCH

Some of the findings of this research project have led to more questions and areas of examination that should be further examined by future research. An area of potential future research includes the need to examine the effect of an officers' justification for inaction in domestic violence crimes based on a lack of probable cause. Police officers are often criticized for exceeding constitutional limitations and making unwarranted arrests. However, when it comes to domestic violence enforcement police officers at times err on the side of caution and do not make an arrest even in mandatory arrest situations where they are required to do so.

Another area of potential future research would be to examine those factors that formulate and reinforce the attitudes and determinants that police officers hold prior to and during their career concerning domestic violence enforcement. It would be very interesting to examine if officers' attitudes change over the life course of their careers, or rather remain consistent with those held before socialization into police culture and training. This would be best carried through a longitudinal study of perhaps a large cohort of recruits at intervals of their law enforcement careers.

Appendices

Consent Form

My name is John Waldron and I am a doctoral student in the Criminal Justice Dept. at the Graduate School and University Center at the City University of New York (CUNY) located at John Jay College of Criminal Justice, and principal investigator of this project, entitled "Social and Legal Determinants on the Enforcement of Domestic Violence Laws by the Police: A Study of New Jersey Police Officers." This is a research study of police officers' attitudes and actions regarding hypothetical incidents of domestic violence. It will investigate how police officers respond to acts of domestic violence under current New Jersey laws and Attorney General Guidelines. I would like you to complete a 10-page questionnaire.

You are invited to participate in this research by completing a questionnaire. This should take approximately 45 minutes to one hour to finish. We plan to enroll between 400 and 600 participants into this study. Your participation in this study is strictly voluntary. You have the right to refuse to participate without consequences. If you decide not to participate, your decision will not affect your relationship with your department or with John Jay College.

The potential harm to subjects in this research project is minimal. It is a routine activity for police officers to respond to domestic disputes and violations of the domestic violence laws of the State of New Jersey. The questions focus on either hypothetical situations, questions about the officer's opinions toward domestic violence, or general questions regarding the police agency by which the officer is employed.

At any time, you can refuse to answer any question or to terminate your participation in the questionnaire without penalty. The questionnaire is completely anonymous. I do not want your name, badge number, department or any personalized identifying information on the survey. Only information directly related to the research will be asked. This is for your protection and privacy and to ensure your anonymity. This will also help to ensure that no individual can be identified by their responses. No one besides the principal investigator will see the original questionnaires. They will be kept under lock and shredded and destroyed after 5 years.

I plan to publish the results of the study, but the names of participants or any individual identifying characteristics will not be used in any form for the publications. If you would like a copy of the study, please provide your name and address on the list at the front of the room, and I will ensure that it is made available to you upon completion of the project.

If you have any questions about this research, you can contact me at home at (xxx-xxx-xxxx) or by email at xxxxxxxxxxxxx@aol.com. or my advisor Dr. Maria Haberfeld, Law and Police Science Department John Jay College of Criminal Justice/ City University of New York, 899 Tenth Avenue, #422. T Building/ New York, New York (xxx-xxx-xxxx) or xxxxxxxxxx @jjay.cuny.edu. If you have any questions about your rights as a research participant please feel free to contact the John Jay Institutional Review Board at jj-irb@jjay.cuny.edu, or (xxx) xxx-xxxx

Your signature below means that you have read this consent form, that you fully understand the nature and consequences of participation and that you have had all questions regarding participation in this study answered satisfactorily.

Appendix A

If you agree to participate and complete the questionnaire, please sign below.

_____   _____
Participants Name (PLEASE PRINT)   Participant Signature

_____   Date_____
Principal Investigator's signature

Thank you for your participation in the study. I will give you a copy of this form to take with you.

APPENDIX B

Data Collection Instrument:
The Waldron Domestic Violence Questionnaire 08

This survey was distributed on legal size 8.5 x 14 papers in New Roman Times 10 font to study participants. It has been reformatted to conform to the requirements of this format in 8 font.

The Waldron Domestic Violence Questionnaire 08 frev 073008

Directions: This questionnaire is completely anonymous; no one from your agency will see or know your responses. Please do not put your name, badge number, or department anywhere on the questionnaire. Please read each question carefully. Please answer the following questions completely and to the best of your ability. There is no right or wrong answer, only what you think and how feel and how you would honestly **react to the various situations. Answer each question** by circling the letter of the answer that best describes your response.

1. Are you a full time sworn law enforcement officer?
    a) Yes   b) No
2. In the course of your normal police duties, do you regularly respond to domestic disturbance calls?
    a) Yes   b) No
3. What is your current assignment?
    a)   Patrol   d)   Traffic
    b)   Detective   e)   Juvenile
    c)   Administration   f)Other(specify)_____
4. What is your current rank?
    a)   Police officer   d)   Other (specify)_____
    b)   Sergeant   e)   Captain/ Chief
    c)   Lieutenant
5. How many years have you been a Police Officer?
    a) 3 years or less.   g) More than 18 years, but 21 or less.
    b) More than 3 years, but 6 or less.   h) More than 21 years, but 24 or less.
    c) More than 6 years, but 9 or less.   i) More than 24 years, but 27 or less.
    d)   More than 9 years, but 12 or less. j) More than 27 years, but 30 or less.
    e)   More than 12 years, but 15 or less. k) More than 30 years
    f)   More than 15 years, but 18 or less.
6. What is the last grade of education you have completed?
    a)   High School   e)   College Degree
    b)   Some college   f)   Masters Degree
    c)   Associates degree   g)   Masters plus 30
    d)   More than 60 college credits,   h)   Doctoral Degree
                                         but less than 120

7. In the last six months, how many domestic calls have you responded to?
   a) less than 10
   b) 10 or more less than 20
   c) 20 or more less than 30
   d) 30 or more less than 40
   e) 40 or more less than 50
   f) 50 or more

8. Have you studied for a promotional exam within the last three years?
   a) Yes   b) No

9. Have you attended a formal study group for your last promotional exam?
   a) Yes   b) No

10. Is your department covered by Civil Service regulations?
    a) Yes   b) No

11. Please circle which description that best defines you own personal style of policing?
    a) Avoider (inclined to avoid conflict through inaction or persuasion.
    b) Reciprocator (inclined to trade services for self-interest.)
    c) Enforcer (inclined toward quick moral judgments and the use of force.)
    d. Professional (inclined toward flexibility and persuasion with minimal use   of force.)

12 Please circle your primary motivation in handling domestic violence incidents.
    a) My individual characteristics
    b) Situational characteristics
    c) Organizational characteristics
    d) Community characteristics
    e) Legal constraints

13. Please circle which definition best describes to organizational structure of your police department?
    a) Traditional Policing: Bureaucratic: rigid, formalized –paper based, rule oriented   "by the book policing," standardized. Centralization of all management, support, operational and authority functions.
    b) Community Policing: Non-bureaucratic: Corporate flexible- rules fit situation-paper where necessary, collegial atmosphere. Decentralization of authority and management function to meet operational requirements. Organization driven by front end and community-based needs.

14. What is the normal compliment of officers assigned to your squad or shift?
    1   2   3   4   5   6   7   8   9   10   11   12   13   14
    15   More than 15

15. I feel that I try to enforce the Attorney General Guidelines on Domestic Violence.
    a) never
    b) sometimes
    c) often
    d) always

16. I find that the Domestic Violence laws are practical to enforce
    a) never
    b) sometimes
    c) often
    d) always

17. How many times in the six months have you arrested both parties in a domestic violence incident?
    a) never
    b) one time
    c) two times
    d) three times
    e) four times
    f) five times or more

18. Police officers should be empowered by law to make warrantless arrests on probable   cause for disorderly persons domestic assaults which the police do not witness.
    a) strongly disagree
    b) disagree
    c) agree
    d) strongly agree

19. Police officers should have more discretion in the handling of domestic violence incidents involving a disorderly person's assault rather than a mandatory arrest policy.
    a) strongly disagree
    b) disagree
    c) agree
    d) strongly agree

20. On the replacement of mandatory arrest for domestic violence offenses involving disorderly persons simple assaults with an option to allow the victim to decide if an immediate arrest is necessary. I would
    a) strongly disagree
    b) disagree
    c) agree
    d) strongly agree

21. Once an arrest is made in a domestic violence incident there should be a no-drop policy and a mandatory prosecution even if the victim refuses to testify.
    a) strongly disagree
    b) disagree
    c) agree
    d) strongly agree

22. I am regularly kept abreast of changes in the law by my department.
    a) never
    b) sometimes always
    c) often
    d) always

23. How many days a year do you have programs of in-service training excluding firearms?
    a) None
    b) 1
    c) 2
    d) 3
    e) 4
    f) 5
    g) 6
    h) 7
    i) 8
    j) 9
    k) 10
    l) more than 10

24. In which years have you received in-service training on domestic violence?
    (Please circle all that apply)
    a) 2005   c) 2007
    b) 2006   d) 2008

25. I feel that the administration of my department supports the strict enforcement of the Domestic Violence laws.
    a) strongly disagree   c) agree
    b) strongly agree   d) disagree

26. I feel that my immediate supervisors support the strict enforcement of the Domestic Violence laws
    a) strongly disagree   c) agree
    b) strongly agree   d) disagree

27 I would consider the overall discipline of my department to be
    a) very strict
    b) somewhat strict

28. I feel that the municipal judge(s) in my jurisdiction are strict in their application of domestic violence laws for the offense of simple assault.
    a) strongly disagree   c) agree
    b) disagree   d) disagree

29. I feel that the municipal prosecutor in my jurisdiction aggressively prosecutes domestic violence cases for simple assault.
    a) strongly disagree   c) agree
    b) disagree   d) disagree

30. I feel that overall, incidents of domestic violence simple assault are treated with the same seriousness as incidents of simple assault between strangers by the court system in my jurisdiction.
    a) strongly disagree   c) agree
    b) disagree   d) disagree

On the following pages will be a series of hypothetical domestic dispute scenarios. The object is to find out how you would handle these incidents as if they were happening to you on your next tour of duty. This project is not looking for anything more than your honest and forthright answers to the situations presented to you. Thank you.

Appendix B

31. You respond to a call of a "noise complaint." Upon arriving, you find Billy Jean, standing in front of her home with a bleeding cut on her forehead. She is quite intoxicated and staggering around. She tells you that her husband Bob hit her during a fight over the remote control for the television. He left in his pickup truck to go out with the boys for the night. She does not want to make a complaint, since they are to go hunting in the morning. She only wants to go back inside and get some sleep. She states that her "nosey neighbors" called because of an ongoing dispute. What actions would you take? Identify the   [ ] Female as the offender?   [ ] Male as the offender?   Beside each of the statements presented below, please indicate how often you would take the action under the circumstances presented.

Always (A),   Most of the time (M),   About half the time (H).   Some of the time (S),   Never (N).

		A	M	H	S	N
a)	Take no police action, not an offense or crime.	[ ]	[ ]	[ ]	[ ]	[ ]
b)	Deescalate, mediate and resolve situation.	[ ]	[ ]	[ ]	[ ]	[ ]
c)	Issue verbal warning to offender.	[ ]	[ ]	[ ]	[ ]	[ ]
d)	Issue verbal warning to both parties.	[ ]	[ ]	[ ]	[ ]	[ ]
e)	Remove offender from household for night.	[ ]	[ ]	[ ]	[ ]	[ ]
f)	Remove offender for detox/ counseling.	[ ]	[ ]	[ ]	[ ]	[ ]
g)	Arrest the offender for an offense under the domestic violence laws.	[ ]	[ ]	[ ]	[ ]	[ ]
h)	Arrest the offender for an offense not under the domestic violence laws.	[ ]	[ ]	[ ]	[ ]	[ ]
i)	Obtain a warrant for the arrest of the offender.	[ ]	[ ]	[ ]	[ ]	[ ]
j)	Personally sign criminal complaint against defendant	[ ]	[ ]	[ ]	[ ]	[ ]
k)	Dispatch medical assistance for victim.	[ ]	[ ]	[ ]	[ ]	[ ]
l)	Advise victim to seek counseling.	[ ]	[ ]	[ ]	[ ]	[ ]
m)	Advise victim of right to obtain TRO.	[ ]	[ ]	[ ]	[ ]	[ ]
n)	Advise victim to sign a complaint tomorrow.	[ ]	[ ]	[ ]	[ ]	[ ]
o)	Make no written report of incident	[ ]	[ ]	[ ]	[ ]	[ ]
p)	Document incident as "unfounded."	[ ]	[ ]	[ ]	[ ]	[ ]
q)	Document incident as "Gone on Arrival."	[ ]	[ ]	[ ]	[ ]	[ ]
r)	Document incident as "verbal dispute."	[ ]	[ ]	[ ]	[ ]	[ ]
s)	Document incident as "family problem."	[ ]	[ ]	[ ]	[ ]	[ ]
t)	Document incident with "Operations report."	[ ]	[ ]	[ ]	[ ]	[ ]
u)	Document incident with "Investigation report."	[ ]	[ ]	[ ]	[ ]	[ ]

v)	Document incident with a "Domestic Violence Offense Report."	[ ]	[ ]	[ ]	[ ]	[ ]
w)	Seize any weapons that might pose a threat to victim.	[ ]	[ ]	[ ]	[ ]	[ ]
x)	Have victim sign "Victim witness notification form."	[ ]	[ ]	[ ]	[ ]	[ ]

32. Please rank in order of importance from 1 to 4 why you took the actions you listed in this situation with 1 being the most important and 4 being the least important. **You must rank at least four responses. Each number can only be used only one time.**

 a) Mandated under law. ____

 b) Discretionary under the law. ____

 c) Comply with the wishes of the victim. ____

 d) Based on my training as a police officer. ____

 e) Based on my experience as a police officer. ____

 f) Based on my departmental policies. ____

 g) Based on my supervisor's preferences. ____

33. You respond to the Jones residence where you find the Mrs. Jones in a disheveled state. She invites you in and you see an interior door smashed. She does not display any signs of injury but she complains she had "the wind knocked out of her" and she is holding her ribs. She stated that her husband "just lost it" and threw her into the door. She doesn't know what to do. She states that she is in fear for the safety of her four children and herself. At this time, Mr. Smith comes back from Home Depot with a new door. What actions do you take? Identify the [ ] Female as the offender [ ] Male as the offender Beside each of the statements presented below, please indicate how often you would take the action under the circumstances presented.

Always (A), Most of the time (M), About half the time (H). Some of the time (S), Never (N).

		A	M	H	S	N
a)	Take no police action, not an offense or crime.	[ ]	[ ]	[ ]	[ ]	[ ]
b)	Deescalate, mediate and resolve situation.	[ ]	[ ]	[ ]	[ ]	[ ]
c)	Issue verbal warning to offender.	[ ]	[ ]	[ ]	[ ]	[ ]
d)	Issue verbal warning to both parties.	[ ]	[ ]	[ ]	[ ]	[ ]
e)	Remove offender from household for night.	[ ]	[ ]	[ ]	[ ]	[ ]
f)	Remove offender for detox/ counseling.	[ ]	[ ]	[ ]	[ ]	[ ]
g)	Arrest the offender for an offense under the domestic violence laws.	[ ]	[ ]	[ ]	[ ]	[ ]
h)	Arrest the offender for an offense not under the	[ ]	[ ]	[ ]	[ ]	[ ]

domestic violence laws.

i)	Obtain a warrant for the arrest of the offender.	[ ]	[ ]	[ ]	[ ]	[ ]
j)	Personally sign criminal complaint against defendant	[ ]	[ ]	[ ]	[ ]	[ ]
k)	Dispatch medical assistance for victim.	[ ]	[ ]	[ ]	[ ]	[ ]
l)	Advise victim to seek counseling.	[ ]	[ ]	[ ]	[ ]	[ ]
m)	Advise victim of right to obtain TRO.	[ ]	[ ]	[ ]	[ ]	[ ]
n)	Advise victim to sign a complaint tomorrow.	[ ]	[ ]	[ ]	[ ]	[ ]
o)	Make no written report of incident	[ ]	[ ]	[ ]	[ ]	[ ]
p)	Document incident as "unfounded."	[ ]	[ ]	[ ]	[ ]	[ ]
q)	Document incident as "Gone on Arrival."	[ ]	[ ]	[ ]	[ ]	[ ]
r)	Document incident as "verbal dispute."	[ ]	[ ]	[ ]	[ ]	[ ]
s)	Document incident as "family problem."	[ ]	[ ]	[ ]	[ ]	[ ]
t)	Document incident with "Operations report."	[ ]	[ ]	[ ]	[ ]	[ ]
u)	Document incident with "Investigation report."	[ ]	[ ]	[ ]	[ ]	[ ]
v)	Document incident with a "Domestic Violence Offense Report."	[ ]	[ ]	[ ]	[ ]	[ ]
w)	Seize any weapons that might pose a threat to victim.	[ ]	[ ]	[ ]	[ ]	[ ]
x)	Have victim sign "Victim witness notification form."	[ ]	[ ]	[ ]	[ ]	[ ]

34 .Please rank in order of importance from 1 to 4 why you took the actions you listed in this situation with 1 being the most important and 4 being the least important. **You must rank at least four responses. Each number can only be used only one time.**

    a)   Mandated under law.   ____

    b)   Discretionary under the law.   ____

    c)   Comply with the wishes of the victim.   ____

    d)   Based on my training as a police officer.   ____

    e)   Based on my experience as a police officer. ____

    f)   Based on my departmental policies.   ____

    g)   Based on my supervisor's preferences.   ____

35.   You are cruising the parking lot of a popular night club just before closing time. You observe a
female pulling away from her male companion. She is visibly upset. Upon investigation, you find that
the two had been engaged, but that she broke it off. She just wants to be left alone, she has an hour
ride back to the "City," to get home. While the ex-fiancé is telling you his sob story of female
troubles, the female interrupts and states "Officer, I got a copy of my restraining order here from New
York, he in not suppose to come within 100 feet of me. Can't you tell him just to leave me alone?"
What actions do you take? Identify the [   ] Female as the offender? [   ] Male as the offender?
Beside each of the statements presented below, please indicate how often you would take the action
under the circumstances presented. Always (A),   Most of the time (M),   About half the time (H).
Some of the time (S),   Never (N).

		A	M	H	S	N
a)	Take no police action, not an offense or crime.	[ ]	[ ]	[ ]	[ ]	[ ]
b)	Deescalate, mediate and resolve situation.	[ ]	[ ]	[ ]	[ ]	[ ]
c)	Issue verbal warning to offender.	[ ]	[ ]	[ ]	[ ]	[ ]
d)	Issue verbal warning to both parties.	[ ]	[ ]	[ ]	[ ]	[ ]
e)	Remove offender from household for night.	[ ]	[ ]	[ ]	[ ]	[ ]
f)	Remove offender for detox/ counseling.	[ ]	[ ]	[ ]	[ ]	[ ]
g)	Arrest the offender for an offense under the domestic violence laws.	[ ]	[ ]	[ ]	[ ]	[ ]
h)	Arrest the offender for an offense not under the domestic violence laws.	[ ]	[ ]	[ ]	[ ]	[ ]
i)	Obtain a warrant for the arrest of the offender.	[ ]	[ ]	[ ]	[ ]	[ ]
j)	Personally sign criminal complaint against defendant	[ ]	[ ]	[ ]	[ ]	[ ]
k)	Dispatch medical assistance for victim.	[ ]	[ ]	[ ]	[ ]	[ ]
l)	Advise victim to seek counseling.	[ ]	[ ]	[ ]	[ ]	[ ]
m)	Advise victim of right to obtain TRO.	[ ]	[ ]	[ ]	[ ]	[ ]
n)	Advise victim to sign a complaint tomorrow.	[ ]	[ ]	[ ]	[ ]	[ ]
o)	Make no written report of incident	[ ]	[ ]	[ ]	[ ]	[ ]
p)	Document incident as "unfounded."	[ ]	[ ]	[ ]	[ ]	[ ]
q)	Document incident as "Gone on Arrival."	[ ]	[ ]	[ ]	[ ]	[ ]
r)	Document incident as "verbal dispute."	[ ]	[ ]	[ ]	[ ]	[ ]
s)	Document incident as "family problem."	[ ]	[ ]	[ ]	[ ]	[ ]
t)	Document incident with "Operations report."	[ ]	[ ]	[ ]	[ ]	[ ]
u)	Document incident with "Investigation report."	[ ]	[ ]	[ ]	[ ]	[ ]
v)	Document incident with a "Domestic Violence Offense Report."	[ ]	[ ]	[ ]	[ ]	[ ]

w)   Seize any weapons that might pose a threat
to victim.   [ ]   [ ]   [ ]   [ ]   [ ]

x)   Have victim sign "Victim witness   [ ]   [ ]   [ ]   [ ]   [ ]
notification form."

36.   Please rank in order of importance from 1 to 4 why you took the actions you listed in this
situation with 1 being the most important and 4 being the least important. **You must rank at
least four responses. Each number can only be used only one time.**

   a)   Mandated under law.   ____
   b)   Discretionary under the law.   ____
   c)   Comply with the wishes of the victim. ____
   d)   Based on my training as a police officer. ____
   e)   Based on my experience as a police officer. ____
   f)   Based on my departmental policies.   ____
   g)   Based on my supervisor's preferences. ____

37.   You respond to a report of a "domestic in progress" where you are met by Mrs. Daniels. The
complainant tells you that her husband Jack has violated a court order and she wants him removed and
taken either to jail or to the hospital. You enter to find her husband passed out naked on the bedroom
floor. He is highly intoxicated. There is a mess on the kitchen floor with milk dripping out of a
container and several broken eggs. Mrs. Daniels goes on to say that she is very aware of her rights
under domestic violence and insists that you arrest and remove her husband immediately. She tells
you that a condition of his probation is that he not return to the household if he has been drinking. She
goes on to say that Jack made the mess in the kitchen looking for more beer. There is no history of
prior domestic violence between the parties or restraining orders in effect. What actions do you take?
Identify the [ ] Female as the offender [ ] Male as the offender? Beside each of the statements
presented below, please indicate how often you would take the action under the circumstances
presented. Always (A), Most of the time (M), About half the time (H), Some of the time (S),Never(N)

		A	M	H	S	N
a)	Take no police action, not an offense or crime.	[ ]	[ ]	[ ]	[ ]	[ ]
b)	Deescalate, mediate and resolve situation.	[ ]	[ ]	[ ]	[ ]	[ ]
c)	Issue verbal warning to offender.	[ ]	[ ]	[ ]	[ ]	[ ]
d)	Issue verbal warning to both parties.	[ ]	[ ]	[ ]	[ ]	[ ]
e)	Remove offender from household for night.	[ ]	[ ]	[ ]	[ ]	[ ]
f)	Remove offender for detox/ counseling.	[ ]	[ ]	[ ]	[ ]	[ ]
g)	Arrest the offender for an offense under the domestic violence laws.	[ ]	[ ]	[ ]	[ ]	[ ]

h)	Arrest the offender for an offense not under the domestic violence laws.	[ ]	[ ]	[ ]	[ ]	[ ]
i)	Obtain a warrant for the arrest of the offender.	[ ]	[ ]	[ ]	[ ]	[ ]
j)	Personally sign criminal complaint against defendant	[ ]	[ ]	[ ]	[ ]	[ ]
k)	Dispatch medical assistance for victim.	[ ]	[ ]	[ ]	[ ]	[ ]
l)	Advise victim to seek counseling.	[ ]	[ ]	[ ]	[ ]	[ ]
m)	Advise victim of right to obtain TRO.	[ ]	[ ]	[ ]	[ ]	[ ]
n)	Advise victim to sign a complaint tomorrow.	[ ]	[ ]	[ ]	[ ]	[ ]
o)	Make no written report of incident	[ ]	[ ]	[ ]	[ ]	[ ]
p)	Document incident as "unfounded."	[ ]	[ ]	[ ]	[ ]	[ ]
q)	Document incident as "Gone on Arrival."	[ ]	[ ]	[ ]	[ ]	[ ]
r)	Document incident as "verbal dispute."	[ ]	[ ]	[ ]	[ ]	[ ]
s)	Document incident as "family problem."	[ ]	[ ]	[ ]	[ ]	[ ]
t)	Document incident with "Operations report."	[ ]	[ ]	[ ]	[ ]	[ ]
u)	Document incident with "Investigation report."	[ ]	[ ]	[ ]	[ ]	[ ]
v)	Document incident with a "Domestic Violence Offense Report."	[ ]	[ ]	[ ]	[ ]	[ ]
w)	Seize any weapons that might pose a threat to victim.	[ ]	[ ]	[ ]	[ ]	[ ]
x)	Have victim sign "Victim witness notification form."	[ ]	[ ]	[ ]	[ ]	[ ]

38. Please rank in order of importance from 1 to 4 why you took the actions you listed in this situation with 1 being the most important and 4 being the least important. **You must rank at least four responses. Each number can only be used only one time.**

    a) Mandated under law. ___

    b) Discretionary under the law. ___

    c) Comply with the wishes of the victim. ___

    d) Based on my training as a police officer. ___

    e) Based on my experience as a police officer. ___

    f) Based on my departmental policies. ___

    g) Based on my supervisor's preferences. ___

39.   You respond to the Delta apartment complex at 11PM having received on numerous complaints from neighbors, of a domestic dispute in progress. Upon your arrival, angry neighbors swarm you. They tell you that action must be taken to arrest someone. The door to the apartment is wide open. Mrs. Coors is punching and kicking away at her husband. He is holding her off but he has a bloody lip and a minor laceration from a kitchen knife wound inflicted by his wife. She has deep bruises on both arms that are already turning black, apparently from her husband trying to restrain her. Mr. Coors is somewhat intoxicated and belligerent towards you. Your supervisor is yelling over the radio that there is a serious accident on the other side of town that you needed to assist at. What actions do you take? Identify the [   ] Female as the offender? [   ] Male as the offender?

Beside each of the statements presented below, please indicate how often you would take the action under the circumstances presented. Always (A),   Most of the time (M),   About half the time (H), Some of the time (S),

		A	M	H	S	N
a)	Take no police action, not an offense or crime.	[ ]	[ ]	[ ]	[ ]	[ ]
b)	Deescalate, mediate and resolve situation.	[ ]	[ ]	[ ]	[ ]	[ ]
c)	Issue verbal warning to offender.	[ ]	[ ]	[ ]	[ ]	[ ]
d)	Issue verbal warning to both parties.	[ ]	[ ]	[ ]	[ ]	[ ]
e)	Remove offender from household for night.	[ ]	[ ]	[ ]	[ ]	[ ]
f)	Remove offender for detox/ counseling.	[ ]	[ ]	[ ]	[ ]	[ ]
g)	Arrest the offender for an offense under the domestic violence laws.	[ ]	[ ]	[ ]	[ ]	[ ]
h)	Arrest the offender for an offense not under the domestic violence laws.	[ ]	[ ]	[ ]	[ ]	[ ]
i)	Obtain a warrant for the arrest of the offender.	[ ]	[ ]	[ ]	[ ]	[ ]
j)	Personally sign criminal complaint against defendant	[ ]	[ ]	[ ]	[ ]	[ ]
k)	Dispatch medical assistance for victim.	[ ]	[ ]	[ ]	[ ]	[ ]
l)	Advise victim to seek counseling.	[ ]	[ ]	[ ]	[ ]	[ ]
m)	Advise victim of right to obtain TRO.	[ ]	[ ]	[ ]	[ ]	[ ]
n)	Advise victim to sign a complaint tomorrow.	[ ]	[ ]	[ ]	[ ]	[ ]
o)	Make no written report of incident	[ ]	[ ]	[ ]	[ ]	[ ]
p)	Document incident as "unfounded."	[ ]	[ ]	[ ]	[ ]	[ ]
q)	Document incident as "Gone on Arrival."	[ ]	[ ]	[ ]	[ ]	[ ]
r)	Document incident as "verbal dispute."	[ ]	[ ]	[ ]	[ ]	[ ]
s)	Document incident as "family problem."	[ ]	[ ]	[ ]	[ ]	[ ]
t)	Document incident with "Operations report."	[ ]	[ ]	[ ]	[ ]	[ ]
u)	Document incident with "Investigation report."	[ ]	[ ]	[ ]	[ ]	[ ]

		A	M	H	S	N
v)	Document incident with a "Domestic Violence Offense Report."	[ ]	[ ]	[ ]	[ ]	[ ]
w)	Seize any weapons that might pose a threat to victim.	[ ]	[ ]	[ ]	[ ]	[ ]
x)	Have victim sign "Victim witness notification form."	[ ]	[ ]	[ ]	[ ]	[ ]

40. Please rank in order of importance from 1 to 4 why you took the actions you listed in this situation with 1 being the most important and 4 being the least important. **You must rank at least four responses. Each number can only be used only one time.**

   a)   Mandated under law.   ___

   b)   Discretionary under the law.   ___

   c)   Comply with the wishes of the victim.   ___

   d)   Based on my training as a police officer.   ___

   e)   Based on my experience as a police officer.   ___

   f)   Based on my departmental policies.   ___

   g)   Based on my supervisor's preferences.   ___

41. You respond to a 911 call for help at the Cleaver residence. They are "frequent flyers" in that this is at least the fourth time in the last year that your department has responded to domestic disturbances at this residence. On one prior occasion Mr. Cleaver was arrested for simple assault. You arrive to witness Mrs. Cleaver again being assaulted in your presence by her husband, there are signs of physical injury, but she is refusing to press charges and begs you not to arrest him, since after his previous arrest Mr. Cleaver only became more violent. She just wants you to take her and their child to her mother's house in the next town. What action do you take? Identify the [ ] Female as the offender? [ ] Male as the offender? Beside each of the statements presented below, please indicate how often you would take the action under the circumstances presented. Always (A), Most of the time (M), About half the time (H), Some of the time (S), Never (N).

		A	M	H	S	N
a)	Take no police action, not an offense or crime.	[ ]	[ ]	[ ]	[ ]	[ ]
b)	Deescalate, mediate and resolve situation.	[ ]	[ ]	[ ]	[ ]	[ ]
c)	Issue verbal warning to offender.	[ ]	[ ]	[ ]	[ ]	[ ]
d)	Issue verbal warning to both parties.	[ ]	[ ]	[ ]	[ ]	[ ]
e)	Remove offender from household for night.	[ ]	[ ]	[ ]	[ ]	[ ]
f)	Remove offender for detox/ counseling.	[ ]	[ ]	[ ]	[ ]	[ ]
g)	Arrest the offender for an offense under the	[ ]	[ ]	[ ]	[ ]	[ ]

     domestic violence laws.

h)   Arrest the offender for an offense not under the   [ ]   [ ]   [ ]   [ ]   [ ]

     domestic violence laws.

i)   Obtain a warrant for the arrest of the offender.   [ ]   [ ]   [ ]   [ ]   [ ]

j)   Personally sign criminal complaint against   [ ]   [ ]   [ ]   [ ]   [ ]

     defendant

k)   Dispatch medical assistance for victim.   [ ]   [ ]   [ ]   [ ]   [ ]

l)   Advise victim to seek counseling.   [ ]   [ ]   [ ]   [ ]   [ ]

m) Advise victim of right to obtain TRO.   [ ]   [ ]   [ ]   [ ]   [ ]

n)   Advise victim to sign a complaint tomorrow.   [ ]   [ ]   [ ]   [ ]   [ ]

o)   Make no written report of incident   [ ]   [ ]   [ ]   [ ]   [ ]

p)   Document incident as "unfounded."   [ ]   [ ]   [ ]   [ ]   [ ]

q)   Document incident as "Gone on Arrival."   [ ]   [ ]   [ ]   [ ]   [ ]

r)   Document incident as "verbal dispute."   [ ]   [ ]   [ ]   [ ]   [ ]

s)   Document incident as "family problem."   [ ]   [ ]   [ ]   [ ]   [ ]

t)   Document incident with "Operations report."   [ ]   [ ]   [ ]   [ ]   [ ]

u)   Document incident with "Investigation report." [ ]   [ ]   [ ]   [ ]   [ ]

v)   Document incident with a "Domestic   [ ]   [ ]   [ ]   [ ]   [ ]

     Violence Offense Report."

w) Seize any weapons that might pose a threat

     to victim.   [ ]   [ ]   [ ]   [ ]   [ ]

x)   Have victim sign "Victim witness   [ ]   [ ]   [ ]   [ ]   [ ]

     notification form."

42.   Please rank in order of importance from 1 to 4 why you took the actions you listed in this
      situation with 1 being the most important and 4 being the least important. **You must rank at
      least four responses. Each number can only be used only one time.**

     a)   Mandated under law.   ____

     b)   Discretionary under the law.   ____

     c)   Comply with the wishes of the victim.   ____

     d)   Based on my training as a police officer. ____

     e)   Based on my experience as a police officer. ____

     f)   Based on my departmental policies.   ____

     g)   Based on my supervisor's preferences.   ____

APPENDIX C SUPPLEMENTAL TABLES CHAPTER 4

Appendix C Table 4.1: Police Officer's Rank

	Setting				
	Urban	Urban Suburb	Large Suburban	Small Suburban	Total
Police Officer	57	42	142	50	291
Detective	11	0	3	1	15
Corporal	0	1	0	3	4
Sergeant	20	12	30	11	73
Lieutenant	6	3	15	9	33
Captain/Chief	4	0	2	3	9
Total	98	58	192	77	425

Appendix C Table 4.2: Officer's Current Assignment

	Setting				
	Urban	Urban Suburb	Large Suburban	Small Suburban	Total
Patrol	59	49	153	64	325
Detective	20	4	20	4	48
Administration	7	2	10	8	27
Traffic	1	3	5	1	10
Juvenile	2	0	2	0	4
Narcotics	6	0	0	0	6
Internal Affairs	2	0	0	0	2
Domestic Violence	1	0	0	0	1
Community Policing	0	0	2	0	2
Total	98	58	192	77	425

Appendix C Table 4.3: Number of Officers Assigned to Shift

| | Setting | | | | |
	Urban	Urban Suburb	Large Suburban	Small Suburban	Total
1	1	0	3	2	6
2	1	0	3	0	4
3	5	9	3	3	20
4	8	26	12	29	75
5	2	7	20	16	45
6	12	1	67	14	94
7	18	3	19	2	42
8	12	3	17	4	36
9	11	3	9	2	25
10 or more	28	6	39	5	78
Total	98	58	192	77	425

Appendix C Table 4.4: Number of Domestic Calls Officer Responded to in Past Six Months

| Respond to Domestic Disturbances Calls as part of routine duties | Number of calls last 6 months | Setting | | | | |
		Urban	Urban Suburb	Large Suburban	Small Suburban	Total
Yes	Less than 10	14	11	38	38	101
	10 -19	16	15	44	8	83
	20-29	16	12	31	2	61
	30 or more	17	15	37	2	71
	Total	63	53	150	50	316
No	less than 10	34	5	40	27	106
	10 -19	0	0	1	0	1
	20-29	0	0	1	0	1
	30 or more	1	0	0	0	1
	Total	35	5	42	27	109

Appendix C Table 4.5: Officer's Years of Police Service

	Setting				
	Urban	Urban Suburb	Large Suburban	Small Suburban	Total
3 years or less	3	12	23	9	47
More than 3, but 6 or less	6	8	29	10	53
More than 6, but 9 or less	18	5	22	7	52
More than 9, but 12 or less	12	9	34	16	71
More than 12, but 15 or less	4	5	23	9	41
More than 15, but 18 or less	16	4	10	4	34
More than 18, but 21 or less	13	9	16	5	43
More than 21, but 24 or less	14	5	18	7	44
More than 24, but 27 or less	6	1	6	5	18
More than 27, but 30 or less	4	0	8	2	14
More than 30 years	2	0	3	3	8
Total	98	58	192	77	425

Appendix C Table 4.6: Police Officer's Level of Education

	Setting				
	Urban	Urban Suburb	Large Suburban	Small Suburban	Total
High School	22	6	24	19	71
Some College	44	24	45	19	132
Associates Degree	11	6	19	8	44
More than 60 credits, but less than 120	10	5	27	3	45
College Degree	10	15	60	27	112
Masters Degree	0	2	12	1	15
Masters Degree plus 30	1	0	2	0	3
Doctoral Degree	0	0	3	0	3
Total	98	58	192	77	425

Appendix C Table 4.7: Officer's Covered by Civil Service Regulations

Civil Service Agency	Setting				Total
	Urban	Urban Suburb	Large Suburban	Small Suburban	
Yes	98	20	99	49	266
No	0	38	93	28	159
Total	98	58	192	77	425

Appendix C Table 4.8: Civil Service Status and Studying for Promotional Exam by Group Study Participation

Civil Service Agency			Study Promotional Exam		
			Yes	No	Total
Yes	Study Group Participation	Yes	87	11	98
		No	63	105	168
		Total	150	116	266
No	Study Group Participation	Yes	24	7	31
		No	30	98	128
		Total	54	105	159

Appendix C Table 4.9: Officer's Opinion of Departmental Policing Style

	Setting				Total
	Urban	Urban Suburb	Large Suburban	Small Suburban	
Traditional Policing	65	34	109	28	236
Community Policing	33	24	83	49	189
Total	98	58	192	77	425

Appendix C Table 4-12: In-Service Training Days

		Setting			
		Urban	Urban Suburb	Large Suburban	Small Suburban	Total
In-Service Training Days per year	0	12	1	6	3	22
	1	10	0	7	5	22
	2	49	8	52	11	120
	3	13	9	17	33	72
	4	7	9	13	12	41
	5	1	2	11	3	17
	6	3	1	49	2	55
	7	1	5	6	2	14
	8	1	6	18	0	25
	9	0	5	1	0	6
	10	1	12	4	0	17
	11or more	0	0	8	6	14
	Total	98	58	192	77	425

Appendix C Table 4.13: Domestic Violence Training in Last 4 years

Years of Training	Setting				
	Urban	Urban Suburb	Large Suburban	Small Suburban	Total
None	14	0	2	3	19
1	51	12	35	37	135
2	8	3	12	15	38
3	7	5	20	4	36
4	18	38	123	18	197
Total	98	58	192	77	425

Appendix C Table 4.14: Supervisor's Support of Strict Enforcement of Domestic Violence Laws

	Setting				
	Urban	Urban Suburb	Large Suburban	Small Suburban	Total
Strongly Disagree	3	1	7	1	12
Disagree	1	2	9	0	12
Agree	65	26	127	54	272
Strongly Agree	29	29	49	22	129
Total	98	58	192	77	425

Appendix C Table 4.15: Departmental Support for Strict Enforcement of Domestic Violence Laws

	Setting				
	Urban	Urban Suburb	Large Suburban	Small Suburban	Total
Strongly Disagree	1	2	7	1	11
Disagree	3	2	6	0	11
Agree	65	22	134	57	278
Strongly Agree	29	32	45	19	125
Total	98	58	192	77	425

Appendix C Table 4.16: Scale of Departmental Support for Domestic Violence Enforcement

	Setting				
	Urban	Urban Suburb	Large Suburban	Small Suburban	Total
Very weak support	1	0	0	1	2
Weak support	17	3	12	2	34
Support	59	11	63	49	182
Strong support	21	44	117	25	207
Total	98	58	192	77	425

Appendix C Table 4.17: Motivation in Handling Domestic Violence Calls

	Setting				
	Urban	Urban Suburb	Large Suburban	Small Suburban	Total
My individual characteristics	3	2	11	7	23
Situational Characteristics	48	32	92	37	209
Organizational Characteristics	4	2	3	7	16
Community Characteristics	5	4	10	1	20
Legal Constraints	38	18	76	25	157
Total	98	58	192	77	425

Appendix C Table 4-18: Compliance with the Enforcement of Attorney General Guidelines

Domestic Violence Enforcement	Setting				
	Urban	Urban Suburb	Large Suburban	Small Suburban	Total
Never	0	0	0	1	1
Sometimes	0	3	4	3	10
Often	19	11	45	13	88
Always	79	44	143	60	326
Total	98	58	192	77	425

Appendix C Table 4.19: Practicality of Domestic Violence Enforcement

Practicality of Domestic Violence Enforcement	Setting				
	Urban	Urban Suburb	Large Suburban	Small Suburban	Total
Never	1	0	1	1	3
Sometimes	21	18	75	33	147
Often	46	24	86	23	179
Always	30	16	30	20	96
Total	98	58	192	77	425

Appendix C Table 4.20: Dual Arrest for Domestic Violence within Last Six Months

Dual arrest in last 6 months	Setting				
	Urban	Urban Suburb	Large Suburban	Small Suburban	Total
0	62	44	152	59	317
1	13	7	23	11	54
2	13	3	15	4	35
3	4	1	1	2	8
4	0	2	0	1	3
5 or more	6	1	1	0	8
Total	98	58	192	77	425

Appendix C Table 4.21: Officer Support of Warrantless Arrest for Disorderly Persons Assaults

Warrantless Arrest	Setting				
	Urban	Urban Suburb	Large Suburban	Small Suburban	Total
Strongly Disagree	10	3	13	3	29
Disagree	26	14	37	12	89
Agree	44	34	122	46	246
Strongly Agree	18	7	20	16	61
Total	98	58	192	77	425

Appendix C Table 4.22: Officer Support for More Discretion in Handling Domestic Violence

More Discretion Handling Domestic Violence	Setting				
	Urban	Urban Suburb	Large Suburban	Small Suburban	Total
Strongly Disagree	9	3	9	4	25
Disagree	25	19	56	16	116
Agree	43	27	99	40	209
Strongly Agree	21	9	28	17	75
Total	98	58	192	77	425

Appendix C Table 4.23: Victim Empowerment in Simple Assault Domestic Violence Offenses

	Setting				
	Urban	Urban Suburb	Large Suburban	Small Suburban	Total
Strongly Disagree	20	7	40	12	79
Disagree	38	27	72	34	171
Agree	34	21	75	30	160
Strongly Agree	6	3	5	1	15
Total	98	58	192	77	425

Appendix C Table 4.24: Officers' Opinion on Mandatory Prosecution

	Setting				
	Urban	Urban Suburb	Large Suburban	Small Suburban	Total
Strongly Disagree	7	4	9	4	24
Disagree	21	17	41	25	104
Agree	49	29	93	41	212
Strongly Agree	21	8	49	7	85
Total	98	58	192	77	425

Appendix C Table 4.25: Municipal Judges Strict Application of Domestic Violence Laws

	Setting				
	Urban	Urban Suburb	Large Suburban	Small Suburban	Total
Strongly Disagree	11	2	6	2	21
Disagree	17	9	44	8	78
Agree	64	35	128	59	286
Strongly Agree	5	12	13	7	37
Total	97	58	191	76	422

Appendix C Table 4.26: Aggressive Prosecution of Domestic Violence Simple Assault Cases

| | Setting | | | | |
	Urban	Urban Suburb	Large Suburban	Small Suburban	Total
Strongly Disagree	11	3	15	5	34
Disagree	21	16	77	17	131
Agree	59	38	94	47	238
Strongly Agree	6	1	2	7	16
Total	97	58	188	76	419

Appendix C Table 4.27: Municipal Court System Treatment of Domestic Violence Assaults

| Domestic Violence Assault Treatment | Setting | | | | |
	Urban	Urban Suburb	Large Suburban	Small Suburban	Total
Strongly Disagree	7	5	14	5	31
Disagree	31	22	86	29	168
Agree	52	28	85	40	205
Strongly Agree	8	3	5	3	19
Total	98	58	190	77	423

Appendix C Table 4.28 Scenario 1 K: Dispatch Medical Assistance for Victim

		Setting				
		Urban	Urban Suburb	Large Suburban	Small Suburban	Total
Always	Count	74	51	139	54	318
	% within Setting	77.1%	87.9%	72.8%	70.1%	75.4%
Most of the time	Count	16	5	27	16	64
	% within Setting	16.7%	8.6%	14.1%	20.8%	15.2%
About half the time	Count	1	0	8	3	12
	% within Setting	1.0%	.0%	4.2%	3.9%	2.8%
Some of the time	Count	4	2	16	4	26
	% within Setting	4.2%	3.4%	8.4%	5.2%	6.2%
Never	Count	1	0	1	0	2
	% within Setting	1.0%	.0%	.5%	.0%	.5%
Total	Count	96	58	191	77	422

Appendix C Table 4.29 Scenario 1 M: Advise Victim of Right to Obtain Temporary Restraining Order

		Setting				
		Urban	Urban Suburb	Large Suburban	Small Suburban	Total
Always	Count	87	54	169	72	382
	% within Setting	88.8%	93.1%	88.0%	93.5%	89.9%
Most of the time	Count	10	0	12	4	26
	% within Setting	10.2%	.0%	6.2%	5.2%	6.1%
About half the time	Count	0	2	5	1	8
	% within Setting	.0%	3.4%	2.6%	1.3%	1.9%
Some of the time	Count	0	2	5	0	7
	% within Setting	.0%	3.4%	2.6%	.0%	1.6%
Never	Count	1	0	1	0	2
	% within Setting	1.0%	.0%	.5%	.0%	.5%
Total	Count	98	58	192	77	425

Appendix C Table 4.30 Scenario 1 X: Victim to Sign "Victim Witness Notification Form"

		Setting				
		Urban	Urban Suburb	Large Suburban	Small Suburban	Total
Always	Count	84	56	159	66	365
	% within Setting	85.7%	96.6%	82.8%	85.7%	85.9%
Most of the time	Count	12	1	21	7	41
	% within Setting	12.2%	1.7%	10.9%	9.1%	9.6%
About half the time	Count	1	0	7	2	10
	% within Setting	1.0%	.0%	3.6%	2.6%	2.4%
Some of the time	Count	1	1	4	2	8
	% within Setting	1.0%	1.7%	2.1%	2.6%	1.9%
Never	Count	0	0	1	0	1
	% within Setting	.0%	.0%	.5%	.0%	.2%
Total	Count	98	58	192	77	425

Appendix C Table 4.31 Scenario 1 A: Take No Police Action No Offense or Crime Committed

		Setting				
		Urban	Urban Suburb	Large Suburban	Small Suburban	Total
Always	Count	6	4	6	5	21
	% within Setting	6.1%	6.9%	3.1%	6.5%	4.9%
Most of the time	Count	7	0	6	9	22
	% within Setting	7.1%	.0%	3.1%	11.7%	5.2%
About half the time	Count	2	1	13	2	18
	% within Setting	2.0%	1.7%	6.8%	2.6%	4.2%
Some of the time	Count	20	5	35	11	71
	% within Setting	20.4%	8.6%	18.2%	14.3%	16.7%
Never	Count	63	48	132	50	293
	% within Setting	64.3%	82.8%	68.8%	64.9%	68.9%
Total	Count	98	58	192	77	425

Appendix C Table 4.32 Scenario 1 N: Advise Victim to Sign Complaint Tomorrow

		Setting				
		Urban	Urban Suburb	Large Suburban	Small Suburban	Total
Always	Count	5	7	19	17	48
	% within Setting	5.1%	12.1%	9.9%	22.1%	11.3%
Most of the time	Count	17	4	19	8	48
	% within Setting	17.3%	6.9%	9.9%	10.4%	11.3%
About half the time	Count	3	4	22	5	34
	% within Setting	3.1%	6.9%	11.5%	6.5%	8.0%
Some of the time	Count	21	11	40	17	89
	% within Setting	21.4%	19.0%	20.9%	22.1%	21.0%
Never	Count	52	32	91	30	205
	% within Setting	53.1%	55.2%	47.6%	39.0%	48.3%
Total	Count	98	58	191	77	424

Appendix C Table 4.33 Scenario 1: Proper Classification to Document Incident

		Setting				
		Urban 98 Subjects	Urban Suburb 58 Subjects	Large Suburban 192 Subjects	Small Suburban 77 Subjects	Total 423 Subjects
Never document as "family problem"	Count	72	45	134	52	303
	% of subjects	73%	78%	70%	68%	71%
Never document as "Verbal Dispute"	Count	69	40	126	50	285
	% of subjects	70%	69%	66%	65%	67%
Never document as "Gone on Arrival"	Count	81	50	176	68	375
	% of subjects	83%	86%	92%	88%	88%
Never document as "Unfounded"	Count	85	51	178	67	381
	% of subjects	87%	88%	93%	87%	90%

Appendix C Table 4.34 Scenario 1 H: Arrest offender not Under Domestic Violence Laws

		Setting				
		Urban	Urban Suburb	Large Suburban	Small Suburban	Total
Always	Count	4	4	3	3	14
	% within Setting	4.1%	6.9%	1.6%	3.9%	3.3%
Most of the time	Count	2	2	8	4	16
	% within Setting	2.0%	3.4%	4.2%	5.3%	3.8%
About half the time	Count	6	5	13	9	33
	% within Setting	6.1%	8.6%	6.8%	11.8%	7.8%
Some of he time	Count	21	18	90	31	160
	% within Setting	21.4%	31.0%	46.9%	40.8%	37.7%
Never	Count	65	29	78	29	201
	% within Setting	66.3%	50.0%	40.6%	38.2%	47.4%
Total	Count	98	58	192	76	424

Appendix C Table 4.35 Scenario 2 K: Dispatch Medical Assistance for Victim

		Setting				
		Urban	Urban Suburb	Large Suburban	Small Suburban	Total
Always	Count	76	50	144	60	330
	% within Setting	77.6%	86.2%	75.0%	77.9%	77.6%
Most of the time	Count	14	5	24	10	53
	% within Setting	14.3%	8.6%	12.5%	13.0%	12.5%
About half the time	Count	3	1	10	3	17
	% within Setting	3.1%	1.7%	5.2%	3.9%	4.0%
Some of the time	Count	4	2	12	3	21
	% within Setting	4.1%	3.4%	6.2%	3.9%	4.9%
Never	Count	1	0	2	1	4
	% within Setting	1.0%	.0%	1.0%	1.3%	.9%
Total	Count	98	58	192	77	425
	% within Setting	100.0%	100.0%	100.0%	100.0%	100.0%

Appendix C Table 4.36 Scenario 2 M: Advise Victim to Obtain Temporary Restraining Order

			Setting			
		Urban	Urban Suburb	Large Suburban	Small Suburban	Total
Always	Count	86	55	169	74	384
	% within Setting	87.8%	94.8%	88.0%	96.1%	90.4%
Most of the time	Count	9	1	15	2	27
	% within Setting	9.2%	1.7%	7.8%	2.6%	6.4%
About half the time	Count	1	0	3	1	5
	% within Setting	1.0%	.0%	1.6%	1.3%	1.2%
Some of the time	Count	1	2	4	0	7
	% within Setting	1.0%	3.4%	2.1%	.0%	1.6%
Never	Count	1	0	1	0	2
	% within Setting	1.0%	.0%	.5%	.0%	.5%
Total	Count	98	58	192	77	425

Appendix C Table 4.37 Scenario 2 X: Victim to Sign "Victim Witness Notification Form"

			Setting			
		Urban	Urban Suburb	Large Suburban	Small Suburban	Total
Always	Count	86	55	172	72	385
	% within Setting	87.8%	94.8%	89.6%	93.5%	90.6%
Most of the time	Count	9	2	12	0	23
	% within Setting	9.2%	3.4%	6.2%	.0%	5.4%
About half the time	Count	1	0	6	0	7
	% within Setting	1.0%	.0%	3.1%	.0%	1.6%
Some of the time	Count	0	1	1	3	5
	% within Setting	.0%	1.7%	.5%	3.9%	1.2%
Never	Count	2	0	1	2	5
	% within Setting	2.0%	.0%	.5%	2.6%	1.2%
Total	Count	98	58	192	77	425

Appendix C Table 4.38 Scenario 2 A: Take No Police Action, Not an Offense or Crime

		Setting				
		Urban	Urban Suburb	Large Suburban	Small Suburban	Total
Always	Count	3	0	1	0	4
	% within Setting	3.1%	.0%	.5%	.0%	.9%
Most of the time	Count	2	1	0	1	4
	% within Setting	2.0%	1.7%	.0%	1.3%	.9%
About half the time	Count	2	0	5	0	7
	% within Setting	2.0%	.0%	2.6%	.0%	1.6%
Some of the time	Count	6	2	11	2	21
	% within Setting	6.1%	3.4%	5.7%	2.6%	4.9%
Never	Count	85	55	175	74	389
	% within Setting	86.7%	94.8%	91.1%	96.1%	91.5%
Total	Count	98	58	192	77	425

Appendix C Table 4.39 Scenario 2 N: Advise Victim to Sign Complaint Tomorrow

		Setting				
		Urban	Urban Suburb	Large Suburban	Small Suburban	Total
Always	Count	7	8	20	17	52
	% within Setting	7.1%	13.8%	10.4%	22.1%	12.2%
Most of the time	Count	13	5	13	4	35
	% within Setting	13.3%	8.6%	6.8%	5.2%	8.2%
About half the time	Count	4	5	23	9	41
	% within Setting	4.1%	8.6%	12.0%	11.7%	9.6%
Some of the time	Count	14	9	49	10	82
	% within Setting	14.3%	15.5%	25.5%	13.0%	19.3%
Never	Count	60	31	87	37	215
	% within Setting	61.2%	53.4%	45.3%	48.1%	50.6%
Total	Count	98	58	192	77	425

Appendix C Table 4.40 Scenario 2: Proper Classification to Document
Incident

		Setting				
		Urban	Urban Suburb	Large Suburban	Small Suburban	Total
Never document as "family problem"	Count	79	50	153	60	342
	% of subjects	81%	86%	80%	78%	81%
Never document as "Verbal Dispute"	Count	79	45	150	65	339
	% of subjects	70%	78%	78%	84%	80%
Never document as "Gone on Arrival"	Count	94	54	183	77	408
	% of subjects	96%	93%	95%	100%	96%
Never document as "Unfounded"	Count	96	56	186	75	413
	% of subjects	98%	97%	97%	97%	98%

Appendix C Table 4.41 Scenario 2: Arrest Offender not Under Domestic
Violence Laws

		Setting				
		Urban	Urban Suburb	Large Suburban	Small Suburban	Total
Always	Count	12	7	13	8	40
	% within Setting	12.2%	12.1%	6.8%	10.5%	9.5%
Most of the time	Count	3	5	13	8	29
	% within Setting	3.1%	8.6%	6.8%	10.5%	6.9%
About half the time	Count	9	8	14	7	38
	% within Setting	9.2%	13.8%	7.3%	9.2%	9.0%
Some of the time	Count	26	18	66	21	131
	% within Setting	26.5%	31.0%	34.6%	27.6%	31.0%
Never	Count	48	20	85	32	185
	% within Setting	49.0%	34.5%	44.5%	42.1%	43.7%
Total	Count	98	58	191	76	423

Appendix C Table 4.42 Scenario 3 H: Arrest Offender not Under Domestic Violence Laws

		Setting				Total
		Urban	Urban Suburb	Large Suburban	Small Suburban	
Always	Count	12	7	21	10	50
	% within Setting	12.4%	12.1%	11.1%	13.0%	11.8%
Most of the time	Count	4	2	9	7	22
	% within Setting	4.1%	3.4%	4.7%	9.1%	5.2%
About half the time	Count	5	7	15	6	33
	% within Setting	5.2%	12.1%	7.9%	7.8%	7.8%
Some of the time	Count	23	17	46	18	104
	% within Setting	23.7%	29.3%	24.2%	23.4%	24.6%
Never	Count	53	25	99	36	213
	% within Setting	54.6%	43.1%	52.1%	46.8%	50.5%
Total	Count	97	58	190	77	422

Appendix C Table 4.43 Scenario 3 A: No Police Action, Not an Offense or Crime

		Setting				Total
		Urban	Urban Suburb	Large Suburban	Small Suburban	
Always	Count	2	1	2	6	11
	% within Setting	2.0%	1.7%	1.0%	7.8%	2.6%
Most of the time	Count	3	0	6	2	11
	% within Setting	3.1%	.0%	3.1%	2.6%	2.6%
About half the time	Count	2	0	2	2	6
	% within Setting	2.0%	.0%	1.0%	2.6%	1.4%
Some of the time	Count	4	6	14	10	34
	% within Setting	4.1%	10.3%	7.3%	13.0%	8.0%
Never	Count	87	51	168	57	363
	% within Setting	88.8%	87.9%	87.5%	74.0%	85.4%
Total	Count	98	58	192	77	425

Appendix C Table 4.44 Scenario 3 M: Advise Victim to Obtain Temporary
Restraining Order

		Setting				
		Urban	Urban Suburb	Large Suburban	Small Suburban	Total
Always	Count	56	30	91	39	216
	% within Setting	59.6%	51.7%	48.9%	54.2%	52.7%
Most of the time	Count	5	1	16	6	28
	% within Setting	5.3%	1.7%	8.6%	8.3%	6.8%
About half the time	Count	0	3	4	4	11
	% within Setting	.0%	5.2%	2.2%	5.6%	2.7%
Some of the time	Count	6	4	10	4	24
	% within Setting	6.4%	6.9%	5.4%	5.6%	5.9%
Never	Count	27	20	65	19	131
	% within Setting	28.7%	34.5%	34.9%	26.4%	32.0%
Total	Count	94	58	186	72	410

Appendix C Table 4.45 Scenario 3 X: Victim to Sign "Victim Witness
Notification Form"

		Setting				
		Urban	Urban Suburb	Large Suburban	Small Suburban	Total
Always	Count	81	50	151	56	338
	% within Setting	83.5%	86.2%	79.5%	72.7%	80.1%
Most of the time	Count	7	1	15	1	24
	% within Setting	7.2%	1.7%	7.9%	1.3%	5.7%
About half the time	Count	2	0	6	2	10
	% within Setting	2.1%	.0%	3.2%	2.6%	2.4%
Some of the time	Count	6	4	8	7	25
	% within Setting	6.2%	6.9%	4.2%	9.1%	5.9%
Never	Count	1	3	10	11	25
	% within Setting	1.0%	5.2%	5.3%	14.3%	5.9%
Total	Count	97	58	190	77	422

Appendix C Table 4.46   Scenario 3 N: Advise Victim to Sign Complaint Tomorrow

		Setting				
		Urban	Urban Suburb	Large Suburban	Small Suburban	Total
Always	Count	8	10	23	20	61
	% within Setting	8.2%	17.2%	12.1%	26.7%	14.5%
Most of the time	Count	4	3	9	5	21
	% within Setting	4.1%	5.2%	4.7%	6.7%	5.0%
About half the time	Count	6	2	15	7	30
	% within Setting	6.2%	3.4%	7.9%	9.3%	7.1%
Some of the time	Count	17	4	29	6	56
	% within Setting	17.5%	6.9%	15.3%	8.0%	13.3%
Never	Count	62	39	114	37	252
	% within Setting	63.9%	67.2%	60.0%	49.3%	60.0%
Total	Count	97	58	190	75	420

Appendix C Table 4.47 Scenario 3: Proper Classification to Document Incident

		Setting				
		Urban	Urban Suburb	Large Suburban	Small Suburban	Total
Never document as "family problem"	Count	84	51	165	69	369
	% of subjects	87%	88%	86%	90%	87%
Never document as "Verbal Dispute"	Count	76	41	147	48	312
	% of subjects	78%	71%	77%	62%	74%
Never document as "Gone on Arrival"	Count	90	55	181	69	395
	% of subjects	93%	95%	95%	90%	93%
Never document as "Unfounded"	Count	91	54	179	72	396
	% of subjects	94%	95%	94%	94%	94%

Appendix C Table 4.48 Scenario 4 H: Arrest Offender not under Domestic Violence Laws

		Arrest offender not under DV laws					
		Always	Most of the time	About half the time	Some of the time	Never	Total
Male as offender	Count	26	17	28	95	131	297
	% within row	8.8%	5.7%	9.4%	32.0%	44.1%	100.0%
Female as offender	Count	2	2	1	4	8	17
	% within row	11.8%	11.8%	5.9%	23.5%	47.1%	100.0%
Both as offenders	Count	0	0	0	2	2	4
	% within row	.0%	.0%	.0%	50.0%	50.0%	100.0%
Neither as offender	Count	4	8	6	20	64	102
	% within row	3.9%	7.8%	5.9%	19.6%	62.7%	100.0%
Total	Count	32	27	35	121	205	420

Appendix C Table 4.49 Scenario 4 J: Officer to Sign Complaint

		Sign complaint against offender					
		Always	Most of the time	About half the time	Some of the time	Never	Total
Male as offender	Count	38	21	15	81	140	295
	% within row	12.9%	7.1%	5.1%	27.5%	47.5%	100.0%
Female as offender	Count	1	3	1	5	7	17
	% within row	5.9%	17.6%	5.9%	29.4%	41.2%	100.0%
Both as offenders	Count	0	0	0	2	2	4
	% within row	.0%	.0%	.0%	50.0%	50.0%	100.0%
Neither as offender	Count	7	6	2	12	75	102
	% within row	6.9%	5.9%	2.0%	11.8%	73.5%	100.0%
Total	Count	46	30	18	100	224	418

Appendix C Table 4.50 Scenario 4 L: Advise Victim to Seek Counseling

		Advise victim to seek counseling				
		Always	Most of the time	About half the time	Some of the time	Never	Total
Male as offender	Count	156	50	25	42	23	296
	% within row	52.7%	16.9%	8.4%	14.2%	7.8%	100.0%
Female as offender	Count	7	6	2	2	1	18
	% within row	38.9%	33.3%	11.1%	11.1%	5.6%	100.0%
Both as offenders	Count	2	2	0	0	0	4
	% within row	50.0%	50.0%	.0%	.0%	.0%	100.0%
Neither as offender	Count	45	17	15	6	17	100
	% within row	45.0%	17.0%	15.0%	6.0%	17.0%	100.0%
Total	Count	210	75	42	50	41	418

Appendix C Table 4.51 Scenario 4 M: Advise Victim to Obtain Temporary Restraining Order

		Advise victim to obtain TRO				
		Always	Most of the time	About half the time	Some of the time	Never	Total
Male as offender	Count	188	33	15	26	34	296
	% within row	63.5%	11.1%	5.1%	8.8%	11.5%	100.0%
Female as offender	Count	10	3	3	1	1	18
	% within row	55.6%	16.7%	16.7%	5.6%	5.6%	100.0%
Both as offenders	Count	3	0	1	0	0	4
	% within row	75.0%	.0%	25.0%	.0%	.0%	100.0%
Neither as offender	Count	54	12	9	8	20	103
	% within row	52.4%	11.7%	8.7%	7.8%	19.4%	100.0%
Total	Count	255	48	28	35	55	421

Appendix C Table 4.52 Scenario 4 O: Make No Written Report of Incident

| | | Setting | | | | |
		Urban	Urban Suburb	Large Suburban	Small Suburban	Total
Always	Count	6	2	5	3	16
	% within Setting	6.1%	3.4%	2.7%	3.9%	3.8%
Most of the time	Count	4	2	5	0	11
	% within Setting	4.1%	3.4%	2.7%	.0%	2.6%
About half the time	Count	9	2	7	3	21
	% within Setting	9.2%	3.4%	3.7%	3.9%	5.0%
Some of the time	Count	12	7	13	2	34
	% within Setting	12.2%	12.1%	6.9%	2.6%	8.1%
Never	Count	67	45	158	69	339
	% within Setting	68.4%	77.6%	84.0%	89.6%	80.5%
Total	Count	98	58	188	77	421

Appendix C Table 4.53 Scenario 4 V: Document with "Domestic Violence Offense Report"

| | | Document with "Domestic Violence Offense Report" | | | | | |
		Always	Most of the time	About half the time	Some of the time	Never	Total
Male as offender	Count	120	19	27	54	78	298
	% within row	40.3%	6.4%	9.1%	18.1%	26.2%	100.0%
Female as offender	Count	6	1	5	2	3	17
	% within row	35.3%	5.9%	29.4%	11.8%	17.6%	100.0%
Both as offenders	Count	2	0	1	0	1	4
	% within row	50.0%	.0%	25.0%	.0%	25.0%	100.0%
Neither as offender	Count	18	5	6	13	61	103
	% within row	17.5%	4.9%	5.8%	12.6%	59.2%	100.0%
Total	Count	146	25	39	69	143	422

Appendix C Table 4.54 Scenario 4 X: Victim to Sign "Victim Witness Notification Form"

		Victim to sign "Victim Witness Notification form"					
		Always	Most of the time	About half the time	Some of the time	Never	Total
Male as offender	Count	169	19	16	42	51	297
	% within row	56.9%	6.4%	5.4%	14.1%	17.2%	100.0%
Female as offender	Count	11	1	2	1	3	18
	% within row	61.1%	5.6%	11.1%	5.6%	16.7%	100.0%
Both as offender	Count	3	0	1	0	0	4
	% within row	75.0%	.0%	25.0%	.0%	.0%	100.0%
Neither as offender	Count	37	8	2	4	52	103
	% within row	35.9%	7.8%	1.9%	3.9%	50.5%	100.0%
Total	Count	220	28	21	47	106	422

Appendix C Table 4.55 Scenario 5 H: Arrest Offender not Under Domestic Violence Laws

		Setting				
		Urban	Urban Suburb	Large Suburban	Small Suburban	Total
Always	Count	21	17	31	25	94
	% within Setting	21.4%	29.8%	16.3%	32.5%	22.3%
Most of the time	Count	8	4	13	6	31
	% within Setting	8.2%	7.0%	6.8%	7.8%	7.3%
About half the time	Count	4	7	13	2	26
	% within Setting	4.1%	12.3%	6.8%	2.6%	6.2%
Some of the time	Count	20	6	45	15	86
	% within Setting	20.4%	10.5%	23.7%	19.5%	20.4%
Never	Count	45	23	88	29	185
	% within Setting	45.9%	40.4%	46.3%	37.7%	43.8%
Total	Count	98	57	190	77	422

Appendix C Table 4.56 Scenario 5 H: Identify and Arrest Offender not Under Domestic Violence Laws

		Arrest offender not Under DV laws					
		Always	Most of the time	About half the time	Some of the time	Never	Total
Male	Count	6	2	2	6	9	25
	% within row	24.0%	8.0%	8.0%	24.0%	36.0%	100.0%
Female	Count	61	20	20	72	145	318
	% within row	19.2%	6.3%	6.3%	22.6%	45.6%	100.0%
Both	Count	27	9	4	8	30	78
	% within row	34.6%	11.5%	5.1%	10.3%	38.5%	100.0%
Neither	Count	0	0	0	0	1	1
	% within row	22.3%	7.3%	6.2%	20.4%	43.8%	100.0%
Total	Count	94	31	26	86	185	422

Appendix C Table 4.57 Scenario 5 A: Take No Police Action

		Setting				
		Urban	Urban Suburb	Large Suburban	Small Suburban	Total
Always	Count	6	0	0	1	7
	% within Setting	6.1%	.0%	.0%	1.3%	1.6%
Most of the time	Count	1	0	0	0	1
	% within Setting	1.0%	.0%	.0%	.0%	.2%
About half the time	Count	1	0	3	0	4
	% within Setting	1.0%	.0%	1.6%	.0%	.9%
Some of the time	Count	3	1	3	0	7
	% within Setting	3.1%	1.7%	1.6%	.0%	1.6%
Never	Count	87	57	186	76	406
	% within Setting	88.8%	98.3%	96.9%	98.7%	95.5%
Total	Count	98	58	192	77	425

Appendix C Table 4.58 Scenario 5 M: Advise Victim to Obtain a Temporary Restraining Order

		Setting				
		Urban	Urban Suburb	Large Suburban	Small Suburban	Total
Always	Count	86	52	172	72	382
	% within Setting	89.6%	89.7%	90.5%	93.5%	90.7%
Most of the time	Count	4	1	6	4	15
	% within Setting	4.2%	1.7%	3.2%	5.2%	3.6%
About half the time	Count	3	1	4	1	9
	% within Setting	3.1%	1.7%	2.1%	1.3%	2.1%
Some of the time	Count	2	3	4	0	9
	% within Setting	2.1%	5.2%	2.1%	.0%	2.1%
Never	Count	1	1	4	0	6
	% within Setting	1.0%	1.7%	2.1%	.0%	1.4%
Total	Count	96	58	190	77	421

Appendix C Table 4.59 Scenario 5 X: Victim to Sign "Victim Witness Notification Form"

		Setting				
		Urban	Urban Suburb	Large Suburban	Small Suburban	Total
Always	Count	90	56	180	73	399
	% within Setting	91.8%	96.6%	93.8%	94.8%	93.9%
Most of the time	Count	3	1	5	2	11
	% within Setting	3.1%	1.7%	2.6%	2.6%	2.6%
About half the time	Count	2	1	3	0	6
	% within Setting	2.0%	1.7%	1.6%	.0%	1.4%
Some of the time	Count	3	0	3	2	8
	% within Setting	3.1%	.0%	1.6%	2.6%	1.9%
Never	Count	0	0	1	0	1
	% within Setting	.0%	.0%	.5%	.0%	.2%
Total	Count	98	58	192	77	425

Appendix C Table 4.60 Scenario 5 W: Seize Any Weapon that Poses a Threat to Victim

		Setting				
		Urban	Urban Suburb	Large Suburban	Small Suburban	Total
Always	Count	82	54	168	71	375
	% within Setting	83.7%	93.1%	88.0%	92.2%	88.4%
Most of the time	Count	7	0	8	1	16
	% within Setting	7.1%	.0%	4.2%	1.3%	3.8%
About half the time	Count	3	3	4	0	10
	% within Setting	3.1%	5.2%	2.1%	.0%	2.4%
Some of the time	Count	4	1	7	3	15
	% within Setting	4.1%	1.7%	3.7%	3.9%	3.5%
Never	Count	2	0	4	2	8
	% within Setting	2.0%	.0%	2.1%	2.6%	1.9%
Total	Count	98	58	191	77	424

Appendix C Table 4.61 Scenario 5 A: Take No Police Action

		Setting				
		Urban	Urban Suburb	Large Suburban	Small Suburban	Total
Always	Count	6	0	0	1	7
	% within Setting	6.1%	.0%	.0%	1.3%	1.6%
Most of the time	Count	1	0	0	0	1
	% within Setting	1.0%	.0%	.0%	.0%	.2%
About half the time	Count	1	0	3	0	4
	% within Setting	1.0%	.0%	1.6%	.0%	.9%
Some of the time	Count	3	1	3	0	7
	% within Setting	3.1%	1.7%	1.6%	.0%	1.6%
Never	Count	87	57	186	76	406
	% within Setting	88.8%	98.3%	96.9%	98.7%	95.5%
Total	Count	98	58	192	77	425

Appendix C Table 4.62 Scenario 5 N: Advise Victim to Sign Complaint Tomorrow

			Setting			
		Urban	Urban Suburb	Large Suburban	Small Suburban	Total
Always	Count	9	12	28	17	66
	% within Setting	9.2%	20.7%	14.7%	22.1%	15.6%
Most of the time	Count	7	6	5	5	23
	% within Setting	7.1%	10.3%	2.6%	6.5%	5.4%
About half the time	Count	3	5	9	4	21
	% within Setting	3.1%	8.6%	4.7%	5.2%	5.0%
Some of the time	Count	13	4	29	8	54
	% within Setting	13.3%	6.9%	15.3%	10.4%	12.8%
Never	Count	66	31	119	43	259
	% within Setting	67.3%	53.4%	62.6%	55.8%	61.2%
Total	Count	98	58	190	77	423

Appendix C Table 4.63 Scenario 5: Proper Classification to Document Incident

Never document as		Setting				
		Urban 98 Subjects	Urban Suburb 57 Subjects	Large Suburban 191 Subjects	Small Suburban 77 Subjects	Total 423 Subjects
"family problem"	Count	80	51	171	66	368
	% of subjects	82.5%	87.9%	89.5%	85.7%	87.0%
"Verbal Dispute"	Count	86	53	181	75	395
	% of subjects	87.8%	93.0%	94.8%	97.4%	93.4%
"Gone on Arrival"	Count	89	55	188	77	409
	% of subjects	90.8%	96.5%	98.4%	100.0%	96.7%
"Unfounded"	Count	92	55	186	77	410
	% of subjects	93.9%	96.5%	97.4%	100.0%	96.9%

Appendix C Table 4.64 Scenario 6 H: Arrest not Under the Domestic Violence Laws

		Setting				
		Urban	Urban Suburb	Large Suburban	Small Suburban	Total
Always	Count	15	11	29	27	82
	% within Setting	15.3%	19.0%	15.1%	35.1%	19.3%
Most of the time	Count	6	5	12	5	28
	% within Setting	6.1%	8.6%	6.2%	6.5%	6.6%
About half he time	Count	4	5	11	3	23
	% within Setting	4.1%	8.6%	5.7%	3.9%	5.4%
Some of the time	Count	19	11	43	10	83
	% within Setting	19.4%	19.0%	22.4%	13.0%	19.5%
Never	Count	54	26	97	32	209
	% within Setting	55.1%	44.8%	50.5%	41.6%	49.2%
Total	Count	98	58	192	77	425

Appendix C Table 4.65 Scenario 6 K: Dispatch Medical Assistance for Victim

		Setting				
		Urban	Urban Suburb	Large Suburban	Small Suburban	Total
Always	Count	79	54	147	65	345
	% within Setting	80.6%	93.1%	77.4%	84.4%	81.6%
Most of the time	Count	9	1	21	4	35
	% within Setting	9.2%	1.7%	11.1%	5.2%	8.3%
About half the time	Count	3	0	11	5	19
	% within Setting	3.1%	.0%	5.8%	6.5%	4.5%
Some of the time	Count	6	3	10	1	20
	% within Setting	6.1%	5.2%	5.3%	1.3%	4.7%
Never	Count	1	0	1	2	4
	% within Setting	1.0%	.0%	.5%	2.6%	.9%
Total	Count	98	58	190	77	423

Appendix C Table 4.66 Scenario 6: Advise Victim to Obtain Temporary
Restraining Order

		Setting				
		Urban	Urban Suburb	Large Suburban	Small Suburban	Total
Always	Count	93	56	184	75	408
	% within Setting	94.9%	96.6%	95.8%	97.4%	96.0%
Most of the time	Count	3	2	4	2	11
	% within Setting	3.1%	3.4%	2.1%	2.6%	2.6%
About half the time	Count	1	0	3	0	4
	% within Setting	1.0%	.0%	1.6%	.0%	.9%
Some of the time	Count	0	0	1	0	1
	% within Setting	.0%	.0%	.5%	.0%	.2%
Never	Count	1	0	0	0	1
	% within Setting	1.0%	.0%	.0%	.0%	.2%
Total	Count	98	58	192	77	425

Appendix C Table 4.67 Scenario 6 X: Victim to Sign "Victim Witness
Notification Form"

		Setting				
		Urban	Urban Suburb	Large Suburban	Small Suburban	Total
Always	Count	90	57	178	75	400
	% within Setting	92.8%	98.3%	92.7%	97.4%	94.3%
Most of the time	Count	5	1	9	0	15
	% within Setting	5.2%	1.7%	4.7%	.0%	3.5%
About half the time	Count	0	0	3	2	5
	% within Setting	.0%	.0%	1.6%	2.6%	1.2%
Some of the time	Count	2	0	2	0	4
	% within Setting	2.1%	.0%	1.0%	.0%	.9%
Total	Count	97	58	192	77	424

Appendix C Table 4.68 Scenario 6: Proper Classification to Document Incident

Never document as		Setting				Total 423 Subjects
		Urban 98 Subjects	Urban Suburb 55 Subjects	Large Suburban 192 Subjects	Small Suburban 77 Subjects	
Family problem	Count	81	53	168	65	367
	% of subjects	84.4%	91.4%	88.0%	84.4%	87.0%
Verbal dispute	Count	84	52	176	73	385
	% of subjects	86.6%	89.7%	92.1%	96.1%	91.2%
Gone on Arrival	Count	90	55	188	76	409
	% of subjects	91.8%	96.5%	98.4%	98.7%	96.7%
Unfounded	Count	93	55	186	75	409
	% of subjects	94.9%	96.5%	97.4%	97.4%	96.7%

APPENDIX D SUPPLEMENTAL TABLES

Appendix D Table 5.1: Multiple Comparisons of Arrest Mean Scores by Work Setting

(I) Setting	(J) Setting	Mean Difference (I-J)	Std. Error	Sig
Urban	Urban Suburb	-.181	.747	1.000
	Large Suburban	1.031	.563	.406
	Small Suburban	1.811	.692	.055
Urban Suburb	Urban	.181	.747	1.000
	Large Suburban	1.211	.676	.443
	Small Suburban	1.992	.787	.070
Large Suburban	Urban	-1.031	.563	.406
	Urban Suburb	-1.211	.676	.443
	Small Suburban	.780	.615	1.000
Small Suburban	Urban	-1.811	.692	.055
	Urban Suburb	-1.992	.787	.070
	Large Suburban	-.780	.615	1.000

Appendix D Table 5.2: Multiple Comparisons of Disorderly Persons Arrest Means by Shift Size

(I) PO shift	(J) PO shift	Mean Difference (I-J)	Std. Error	Sig.
1-3 Officers	4-6 Officers	2.641[*]	.872	.016
	7-9 Officers	3.347[*]	.928	.002
	More than 9 Officers	1.566	.961	.624

* The mean difference is significant at the 0.05 level.

Appendix D Table 5.3:Multiple Comparisons of Disorderly Persons Arrest
Means by Geographical Setting

(I) Setting	(J) Setting	Mean Difference (I-J)	Std. Error	Sig.
Urban Suburb	Urban	.231	.552	1.000
	Large Suburban	.790	.500	.687
	Small Suburban	1.557*	.583	.047

Appendix D Table 5.4: Multiple Comparisons by Arrest Mean Scores
Of Self-Report Compliance with AG Guidelines on Domestic Violence

(I) Enforcement of Domestic Violence	(J) Enforcement of Domestic Violence	Mean Difference (I-J)	Std. Error	Sig.
Sometimes	Often	-4.045*	1.387	.011
	Always	-6.470*	1.330	.000
Often	Sometimes	4.045*	1.387	.011
	Always	-2.425*	.522	.000
Always	Sometimes	6.470*	1.330	.000
	Often	2.425*	.522	.000

* The mean difference is significant at the 0.05 level.

Appendix D Table 5.5: Multiple Comparisons of Arrest Mean Scores by Officers Self-Report on the Practicality of Enforcement of Attorney General Guidelines Involving Domestic Violence

(I) Practicality of Domestic Violence Enforcement	(J) Practicality of Domestic Violence Enforcement	Mean Difference (I-J)	Std. Error	Sig.
Always	Never	4.586	2.594	.467
	Sometimes	2.829*	.585	.000
	Often	1.514*	.563	.045

* The mean difference is significant at the 0.05 level.

Appendix D Table 5.6: Arrest Mean Scores by Years of Police Service

Years of Police Service	N	Mean	Std. Deviation
6 years or less	99	23.20	4.477
More than 6 years , but 12 or less	120	25.28	4.629
More than 12 years, but 18 or less	74	24.42	4.338
More than 18 years, but 24 or less	86	25.23	4.487
More than 24 years, but 30 or less	31	25.23	4.485
More than 30 years	8	24.50	3.505
Total	418	24.61	4.538

References

Adams, K. (1999). What we know about police use of force. In *Use of force by police: Overview of national and local data.* (pp. 1-14). Washington, DC: National Institute of Justice and Bureau of Justice Statistics.

Adams, K., Alpert, G. P., Dunham R. G., Garner, J. H., Greenfield, L. A., Henriquez, M. A., Langan, P. A., Maxwell, C. D., & Smith, S. K. (1999). *Use of force by police: Overview of national and local data* (Publication No. NCJ 176330). Washington, DC: National Institute of Justice and Bureau of Justice Statistics.

Alpert, G., & Dunham, R. (1988). *Policing multi-ethnic neighborhoods.* New York: Greenwood.

Alpert, G., & Dunham, R. (1997). *Policing urban America.* Prospect Heights, IL: Waveland.

Alpert, G., & Smith, M. (1999). Police use-of-force data: Where we are and where we should be going. *Police Quarterly, 2,* 57-78.

Alpert, G. P., & MacDonald, J. (2001). Police use of force: An analysis of organizational characteristics. *Justice Quarterly, 18,* 393-409.

Alpert G. P., & Smith, W. C. (1994). Developing police policy: An evaluation of the control principle. *American Journal of Police, 13,* 1–20.

Avakame, E., & Fyfe, J. (2001). Differential police treatment of male-on-female spousal violence. *Violence Against Women, 7,* 22-45.

Avakame, E. F., Fyfe, J. J., & McCoy, C. (1999). "Did you call the police? What did they do?" An empirical assessment of Black's theory of mobilization of law. *Justice Quarterly, 16,* 765-792.

Bachman, R., & Coker, A. L. (1995). Police involvement in domestic violence: The interactive effects of victim injury, offender's history of violence, and race. *Violence and Victims, 10,* 91-106.

Balos, B., & Trozky, T. (1988). Enforcement of domestic abuse act in Minnesota: A preliminary study. *Law and Inequity, 6,* 83-125.

Bard, M. (1970). *Training police as specialist in family crisis intervention.* Washington, DC: U.S. Department of Justice.

Bard, M., & Connolly, H. (1978). The police and family violence: Practice and policy. In U.S. Civil Rights Commission, *Battered women: Issues of public policy.* (pp. 309-326). Washington, DC: U.S. Civil Rights Commission.

Barnett, O. W., Miller-Perrin, C. L., & Perrin, R. D. (1997). *Family violence across the lifespan.* Thousand Oaks, CA: Sage.

Bayley, D. H. (1991). Community policing: A report from the devil's advocate. In J. R. Greene & S. D. Mastrofski (Eds.), *Community policing: Rhetoric or reality?* (pp. 225-238). New York: Praeger.

Bayley, D. H. (1986). The tactical choices of police patrol officers. *Journal of Criminal Justice, 14,* 329-348.

Belknap, J. (1995). Law enforcement officers' attitudes about the appropriate responses to woman battering. *International Review of Victimology, 4,* 47-62.

Belknap, J. (1996). The invisible woman: Gender, crime, and justice. Belmont, CA: Wadsworth.

Belknap, J., & McCall, K. D. (1994). Woman battering and police referrals. *Journal of Criminal Justice, 22,* 223-236.

Bell, D. J. (1985). A multiyear study of Ohio urban, suburban, and rural police dispositions of domestic disputes. *Victimology, 10,* 301-310.

Bennett, W. W., & Hess, K. M. (2007). *Management and supervision in law enforcement* (5th ed.). Belmont, CA: Thomson Wadsworth.

Berk, R. A., & Newton, P. J. (1985). Does arrest really deter wife battery? An effort to replicate the findings of the Minneapolis spouse abuse experiment. *American Sociological Review, 50,* 253-262.

Berk, R. A., Campbell, A., Klap, R., & Western, B. (1992a). A Bayesian analysis of the Colorado Springs spouse abuse experiment. *Journal of Criminal Law & Criminology, 83,* 170-200.

Berk, R. A., Campbell, A., Klap, R., & Western, B. (1992b). The deterrent effects of arrest in incidents of domestic violence: A Bayesian analysis of four field experiments. *American Sociological Review, 57,* 698-708.

Berk, R., & Newton, P. J. (1985). Does arrest really deter wife battery? An effort to replicate the findings of the Minneapolis spouse abuse experiment. *American Sociological Review, 50,* 253-262.

Berk. S. F., & Loseke, D. R. (1981). Handling family violence: Situational determinants of police arrest in domestic disturbances. *Law & Society Review, 15,* 317-346.

Bittner, E. (1970). *The functions of police in a modern society.* Washington, DC: National Institute of Mental Health.

Black, D. (1971). The social organization of arrest. *Stanford Law Review, 23,* 1087-1111.

Black, D. (1976). *The behavior of law.* New York: Academic Press.

Black, D. (1980). *The manners and customs of the police.* New York: Academic Press.

Blackwell, B. S., & Vaughn, M. S. (2003). Police civil liability for inappropriate response to domestic assault victims. *Journal of Criminal Justice, 31,* 129-146.

Blau, P. M. (1968). The hierarchy of authority in organizations. *American Journal of Sociology, 73,* 453-467.

Blau, P. M. (1973). *On the nature of organizations.* New York: John Wiley.

Blount, W. R., Yegidis, B. L., & Maheux, R. M. (1992). Police attitudes toward preferred arrest: Influences of rank and productivity. *American Journal of Police, 11,* 35–52.

Bourg, S., & Stock, H. V. (1994). A review of domestic violence arrest statistics in a police department using pro-arrest policy: Are proarrest policies enough? *Journal of Family Violence, 9,* 177-189.

Bowker, L. H. (1982). Police services to battered women: Bad or not so bad. *Criminal Justice and Behavior, 9,* 476-494.

Bowman, C. G. (1992). The arrest experiments: A feminist critique. *Journal of Criminal Law and Criminology, 83,* 201-209.

Breci, M. (1989). The effect of training on police attitudes toward family violence: Where does mandatory arrest fit in? *Journal of Crime and Justice, 12,* 1, 35-49.

Brown, M. K. (1981). Working the street: Police discretion and the dilemmas of reform. New York: Russell Sage Foundation.

Browne, S. M. (1995). Due process and equal protection challenges to the inadequate response of the police in domestic violence situations. *Southern California Law Review, 68,* 1295–1334.

Brunetto, Y., & Farr-Wharton, R. (2005). The role of management post NPM in the implementation of new policies affecting police officers' practices. *Policing, 28,* 221-242.

Bruno V. Codd, 90 Misc. 2d 1047, 396 N.Y.S. 2d. 974, (1977) N.Y. Misc. Lexis 2217 (N.Y. Sup. Ct. 1977)

Buel, S. M. (1988). Recent developments: Mandatory arrest for domestic violence. *Harvard Women's Law Journal, 11,* 213–226.

Burris, C. A., & Jaffe, P. (1983). Wife abuse as a crime: The impact of police laying charges. *Canadian Journal of Criminology, 25,* 309-318.

Buzawa, E., & Buzawa, C. (Eds.). (1990). *Domestic violence: The criminal justice response.* Westwood, CT: Auburn House.

Buzawa, E. S., & Austin, T. (1993). Determining police response to domestic violence victims: The role of victim preference. *American Behavioral Scientist, 36,* 610-623.

Buzawa, E. S., Austin, T., & Buzawa, C. (1995). Responding to crimes of violence against women: Gender differences vs. organizational imperatives. *Crime & Delinquency, 41,* 443-466.

Buzawa, E. S., & Buzawa, C. G. (1993a). Opening the doors: the changing police response to domestic violence. In R. G. Dunham & G. P. Alpert (Eds.), *Critical issues in policing,* (pp. 551-67). Prospect Heights, IL: Waveland.

Buzawa, E. S., & Buzawa, C. G. (1993b). The scientific evidence is not conclusive: Arrest is no panacea. In R. J. Gelles & D. R. Loseke (Eds.), *Current controversies on family violence* (pp. 337–356). Newbury Park, CA: Sage.

Buzawa, E. S., Buzawa, C. G., & Stark, E, (2011). *Responding to Domestic Violence: The Integration of Criminal Justice and Human Services,* (4th ed.). Thousand Oaks, CA: Sage.

Buzawa, E. S., & Buzawa, C. G. (2003). *Domestic violence: The criminal justice response* (3rd ed.). Thousand Oaks, CA: Sage.

Buzawa, E. S., & Hotaling, G. T. (2006). The impact of relationship status, gender, and minor status in the police response to domestic assaults. *Victims & Offenders, 1,* 323-360.

Caldwell, R. G. (1947). *Red Hannah: Delaware's whipping post.* Philadelphia, University of Pennsylvania Press.

Campbell, J. C. (2005). Assessing dangerousness in domestic violence cases: History, challenges, and opportunities. *Criminology and Public Policy, 4,* 653-672.

Carter, D. L., Sapp, A. D., & Stephens, D. W. (1989). Higher education as a bona fide occupational qualification. *American Journal of Police, 7,* 1-28.

Chalk, R., & King, P. A. (1998). *Violence in the family: Assessing prevention and treatment programs.* Washington, DC: National Academy Press.

Chevigny, P. (1969). Police power: Police abuse in New York City. New York: Pantheon.

Christensen, W., & Crank J. P. (2001). Police work and culture in nonurban settings: An ethnographic analysis. *Police Quarterly, 1,* 69-98.

Cohen, B., & Chaiken, J. M. (1973). *Police background characteristics and performance.* Lexington, MA: Lexington Books.

Cohn, E. G., & Sherman, L. W. (1987). *Police policy on domestic violence, 1986: A national survey* (Report 5). Washington, DC: Crime Control Institute.

Connolly, C., Huzurbazar, S., & Routh-McGee, T. (2000). Multiple parties in domestic violence situations and arrest. *Journal of Criminal Justice, 28,* 181–188.

Cordner, G. W. (1998). Community policing: elements and effects. In G. P. Alpert & A. Piquero (Eds.), *Community policing: Contemporary readings* (pp. 45-62). Prospect Heights, IL: Waveland.

Cordner, G., & Williams, G. (1998). *Community policing and accreditation: Compatibility or conflict?* Washington, DC: National Institute of Justice, U.S. Department of Justice.

Coulter, M., Kuehnle, K., Byers, R., & Alfonso, M. (1999). Police-reporting behavior and victim-police interactions as described by women in a domestic violence shelter. *Journal of Interpersonal Violence, 14,* 1290-1298.

Crank, J. P. (1990). The influence of environmental and organizational factors on police style in urban and rural environments. *Journal of Research in Crime and Delinquency, 27,* 166-189.

Crank, J. P. (2004). *Understanding police culture.* Cincinnati, OH: Anderson/Lexis Nexis Publishing.

Crank, J. P., & Wells, L. E. (1991). The effects of size and urbanization on structure among Illinois police departments. *Justice Quarterly, 87,* 2, 169-185.

Davis, P. W. (1983). Restoring the semblance of order: Police strategies in the domestic disturbance. *Symbolic Interaction, 6*(2), 261-278.

Davis, R. C., & Taylor, B. G. (1997). A proactive response to family violence: The results of a randomized experiment. *Criminology, 35,*2, 307-333.

DeKeseredy, W. S., & Schwartz M. D. (2009). *Dangerous Exits: Escaping Abusive Relationships in Rural America.* New Brunswick, NJ: Rutgers University Press.

DeShaney v. Winnebago County Department of Social Services, 109 S. Ct. 998 (1989).

DiIulio, J. J. (1993). Measuring police when there is no bottom line. In *Performance measures for the criminal justice system* (pp. 143-156). Washington, DC: National Institute of Justice and Bureau of Justice Statistics.

Dobash, R. E., & Dobash, R. P. (1979). *Violence against wives: A case against the patriarch.* New York: The Free Press.

Dobash, R. E., & Dobash, R. P. (1992). *Women, violence and social change.* London: Routledge.

Dobash, R. P., Dobash, R. E., Wilson, M., & Daly, M. (1992). The myth of sexual symmetry in marital violence. *Social Problems, 39,* 71-91.

Dolon, R., Hendricks, J., & Meagher, M. S. (1986). Police practices and attitudes toward domestic violence. *Journal of Police Science & Administration, 14,* 3, 187-192.

Donnelly, D. A., Cook, K. J., & Wilson, L. A. (1999). Provision and exclusion: the dual face of services to battered women in three Deep South states. *Violence against Women, 5,* 710-741.

Dugan, L. (2003). Domestic violence legislation: Exploring its impact on the likelihood of domestic violence, police involvement, and arrest. *Criminology & Public Policy, 2,* 283- 312.

Dunford, F. W. (1992). The measurement of recidivism in cases of spouse assault. *Journal of Criminal Law and Criminology, 83,* 120-136.

Dunford, F. W., Huizinga, D., & Elliott, D. S. (1990). The role of arrest in domestic assault: The Omaha Police Experiment. *Criminology, 28,* 183-206.

Dutton, D., Hart, D. S., Kennedy, L. W., & Williams, K. R. (1996). Arrest and the reduction of repeat wife assault. In E. S. Buzawa & C. G. Buzawa (Eds.), *Domestic violence: The criminal justice response* (2nd ed., pp. 111–127). Thousand Oaks, CA: Sage.

Dutton, D. G. (1995). *The domestic assault of women* (2nd ed.). Boston: Allynn-Bacon.

Dutton, D. G., & McGregor, B. M. (1991). Symbiosis of arrest and treatment of wife assault: The case for combined intervention. In M. Steinman (Ed.), *Women battering: Policy responses* (NCJ-129473, pp. 131-154).

Eck, J. E., & Spelman, W. (1987). *Problem solving: Problem-Oriented policing in Newport News.* Washington, DC: National Institute of Justice.

Edleson, J. L. (1991). Coordinated community responses. In M. Steinman (Ed.), *Woman battering: Policy response* (pp. 203-219). Highland Heights, KY: Ashland.

Eigenberg, H. M., Scarborough, K. E., & Kappeler, V. E. (1996). Contributory factors affecting arrest in domestic and non-domestic assaults. *American Journal of Police, 15,* 27-54.

Eitle, D. (2005). The influence of mandatory arrest policies, police organizational characteristics, and situational variables on the probability of arrest in domestic violence cases. *Crime & Delinquency, 51,* 573-597.

Ellis, J. W. (1984). Prosecutorial discretion to charge in cases of spousal assault: A dialogue. *Journal of Criminal Law and Criminology, 75,* 56-102.

Engel, R., Sobol, J., & Worden, R. (2000). Further exploration of the demeanor hypothesis: The interaction of suspects' characteristics and demeanor and Police Behavior. *Justice Quarterly, 17,* 235-258.

Erez, E., & Belknap, J. (1998). In their own words: Battered women's assessment of the criminal processing system's responses. *Violence and Victims, 13,* 251-268.

Fagan, J. (1996). *The criminalization of domestic violence: Promises and limits.* Washington DC: National Institute of Justice.

Feder, L. (1996). Police handling of domestic calls: The importance of offender's presence in the arrest decision. *Journal of Criminal Justice, 24,*6, 481-490.

Feder, L. (1997). Domestic violence and police response in a pro-arrest jurisdiction. *Women and Criminal Justice, 8,*4, 79-98.

Feder, L. (1998). Police handling of domestic and nondomestic assault calls: Is there a case for discrimination? *Crime & Delinquency, 44,* 335-349.

Feder, L. (1999). Police handling of domestic violence calls: An overview and further investigation. *Women and Criminal Justice, 10,* 49–68.

Felson, R. B., & Ackerman, J. (2001). Arrest for domestic and other assaults. *Criminology, 39,* 655–676.

Felson, R. B., Ackerman, J. M., & Gallagher, C. A. (2005). Police intervention and the repeat of domestic assault. *Criminology, 43,* 563-588.

Ferraro, K. J. (2001). Women battering: More than a family problem. In C. Renzetti & L. Goodstein (Eds.), *Women, crime, and criminal justice: Original feminist readings,* (pp. 145–153). Los Angeles: Roxbury.

Ferraro, K. J. (1989). Policing woman battering. *Social Problems, 36,* 61-74.

Ferraro, K. J. (1995). Cops, courts, and woman battering in the United States. In J. Hanmer, J. Radford, & E. Stanko (Eds.), *Women, policing, and male violence* (pp. 155-184). London: Routledge Kegan Paul.

Ferraro, K. J., & Johnson, J. M. (1983). How women experience battering: The process of victimization, *Social Problems, 30,* 325-339.

Ferraro, K. J., & Pope, L. (1993). Irreconcilable differences: Police, battered women, and the law. In N. Z. Hilton (Ed.), *Legal response to wife assault: Current trends and evaluation* (pp. 96-126). Newbury Park, CA: Sage.

Finn, M. A., & Bettis, P. (2006). Punitive action or gentle persuasion: Exploring police officers' justifications for using dual arrest in domestic violence cases. *Violence Against Women, 12,* 268-287.

Finn, M. A., Blackwell, B. S., Stalans, L. J., Studdard, S., & Dugan, L. (2004). Dual arrest decision in domestic violence cases: The influence of departmental policies. *Crime and Delinquency, 50,* 565-589.

Fogelson, R. M. (1977). *Big-City police.* Cambridge, MA: Harvard University Press.

Foley, T., & Terrill, W. (2008). Police comfort and victims. *Victims and Offenders, 3,* 192-216.

Ford, D. A., Reichard, D., Goldsmith, S., & Regoli, M. J. (1996). Future directions for criminal justice policy on domestic violence. In E. S. Buzawa & C. G. Buzawa (Eds.), *Do arrests and restraining orders work?* (pp. 243-265). Thousand Oaks, CA: Sage.

Forst, B., Luicianovic, J., & Cox, S. J. (1977). *What happens after arrest? A court perspective of police operations in the District of Columbia.* Washington, DC: Institute for Law and Social Research.

Fosdick, R. (1920). *American police systems.* New York: Century.

Frattaroli, S., & Tertt, S. P. (2006). Understanding and informing policy implications: A case study of the domestic violence provisions of the Maryland Gun Violence Act. *Evaluation Review, 30,* 347-360.

Frantzen, D., Miguel. San Miguel, C. & Dae-Koon, K. (2011). Predicting case conviction and domestic violence recidivism: Measuring the deterrent effects of conviction and protection order violations. *Violence and Victims, 26*(4), 395-409.

Frisch, L. A. (1992). Research that succeeds, policies that fail. *Journal of Criminal Law & Criminology, 83,* 209-216.

Frye, V., Haviland, M., & Rajah, V. (2007). Dual arrest and other unintended consequences of mandatory arrest in New York City: A brief report. *Journal of Family Violence, 22,* 397-405.

Fyfe, J. (1998). In defense of police agency accreditation. *Policing, 21,* 192-201.

Fyfe, J. J., Greene, J. R., Walsh, W. F., Wilson, O.W., & McLaren, R. C. (1995). *Police administration* (5th ed.). New York: McGraw-Hill.

Fyfe, J. J., Klinger, D. A., & Flavin, J. M. (1997). Differential police treatment of male-on-female spousal violence. *Criminology, 35,* 455-473.

Gastil, R. D. (1971). Homicide and a regional subculture of violence. *American Sociological Review, 36,* 412-427.

Gelhaus, L. (1999). Civil suits against police change domestic violence response. *Trial, 35,* 103–105.

Geller, W., & Scott, M. (1992). Deadly force: What we Know-A practitioner's Desk reference on police-involved shootings. Washington, DC: Police Executive Research Forum.

Geller, W. A., & Swanger, G. (1995). *Managing innovation in policing: The untapped potential of the middle manager.* Washington, DC: Police Executive Research Forum.

Gelles, R. J. (1974). The violent home: A study of physical aggression between husbands and wives. Newbury Park, CA: Sage Publications.

Gelles, R. J. (1993). Constraints against family violence: How well do they work? *American Behavioral Scientist, 36,* 575-586.

Gelles, R. J., & Strauss, M. A. (1978). Determinants of violence in the family: Towards a theoretical integration. In W. R. Burr, R. Hill, F. I. Nye, I. L. Reiss (Eds.), *Contemporary theories about the family* (Vol. 1, Ch. 21). New York, Free Press.

Gellespie, C. K. (1989). *Justifiable homicide: Battered women, self defense, and the law.* Columbus, OH: Ohio State University Press.

Goldstein, H. (1964). Police discretion: The ideal versus the real. *Public Administration Review, 23,* 140-148.

Goldstein, H. (1987). Toward community-oriented policing: potential, basic requirements, and threshold questions. *Crime and Delinquency, 33,* 6-30.

Goldstein, H. (1990). *Problem-Oriented policing.* New York: McGraw-Hill.

Gondolf, E. W., & McFerron. J. R. (1989). Handling battering men: Police action in wife abuse cases. *Criminal Justice & Behavior, 16,* 429-439.

Goolkasian, G. A. (1986). *Confronting domestic violence: The role of criminal court judges.* Washington DC: National Institute of Justice

Gosselin, D. K. (2000). *Heavy hands: An introduction to the crimes of domestic violence.* Upper Saddle River, NJ: Prentice-Hall.

Gross, S. (1984). Women becoming cops: Developmental issues and solutions. *Police Chief, 51,*1, 32-35.

Hall, D. L. (2005). Domestic violence arrest decision making: The role of suspect availability in the arrest decision. *Criminal Justice & Behavior, 32*, 390-411.

Hall, R. H. (2002). *Organizations: Structures, processes, and outcomes* (8th ed.). Upper Saddle River, NJ: Prentice Hall.

Hammer, J., Radford, J., & Stanko, E. A. (1989). *Women, policing and male violence: International perspectives.* London: Routledge & Kegan Paul.

Hart, B. (1993). Battered women and the criminal justice system. *American Behavioral Scientist, 36,* 624-638.

Healey, K., Smith, C., & O'Sullivan, C. (1998). *Batterer intervention: Program approaches and criminal justice strategies.* Washington DC: National Institute of Justice.

Hendricks, J. E. (1992). Domestic violence legislation in the United States: A survey of the states. In E. C. Viano (Ed.), *Intimate violence: Interdisciplinary perspectives* (pp. 213-226). Washington, DC: Hemisphere.

Hepburn, J. R. (1978). Race and the decision to arrest: An analysis of warrants issued. *Journal of Research in Crime and Delinquency, 15,* 54-73.

Herbert, S. (1998). Police subculture reconsidered. *Criminology, 36*(2), 343-369.

Hirschel, J. D., & Hutchison, I. W. (1991). Police-preferred arrest policies. In M. Steinman (Ed.), *Woman battering: Police responses,* pp. 49-72. Cincinnati: Anderson.

Hirschel, J. D., & Hutchison, I. W. (1992). Female spouse abuse and the police response: The Charlotte, North Carolina experiment. *Journal of Criminal Law and Criminology, 83,* 73-119.

Hirschel, J. D., Hutchison, I. W., & Dean, C. W. (1992). The failure of arrest to deter spouse abuse. *Journal of Research in Crime and Delinquency, 29,* 7-33.

Ho, T. (2000). Domestic violence in a southern city: The effects of a mandatory arrest policy on male-versus-female aggravated assault incidents. *American Journal of Criminal Justice, 25,* 107-118.

Ho, T. (2003). The influence of suspect gender in domestic violence arrests. *American Journal of Criminal Justice, 27,* 183-195.

Hoff, L. A. (1990). *Battered women as survivors.* New York: Routledge.

Homant, J. R., & Kennedy, D. B. (1985). Police perceptions of spouse abuse: A comparison of male and female officers. *Journal of Criminal Justice, 13,* 29-47.

Horwitz, S. H., LaRussa-Trott, M., Santiago, L., Pearson, J., Skiff, D. M., & Cerulli, C. (2011). An inside view of police officers' experience with domestic violence. Journal of Family Violence, 26, 617-635.

Hotaling, G. T., & Buzawa, E. (June, 2001). *An analysis of assaults in rural communities: Final report.* Washington, DC: U.S. Department of Justice, Office of Community Oriented Policing Services.

Hoyle, C., & Sanders, A. (2000). Police response to domestic violence: From victim choice to victim empowerment? *British Journal of Criminology, 40,* 14-36.

Humphries, D. (2002). No easy answers: Public policy, criminal justice, and domestic violence. *Criminology and Public Policy, 2,* 91-96.

Illinois Department of State Police. (1986). *Crime in Illinois.* Springfield, IL: State of Illinois.

Independent Commission on the Los Angeles Police Department. (1991). *Report of the independent commission on the Los Angeles police department.* Los Angeles: Independent Commission on the Los Angeles Police Department.

International City Management Association. (1986). *The municipal yearbook.* Washington, DC: The International City Management Association.

Jaffe, P., Wolfe, D. A., Telford, A., & Austin, G. (1986). The impact of police charges in incidents of wife abuse. *Journal of Family Violence, 1,* 37-49.

Jiao, A. Y. (2001). Degrees of urbanism and police orientations: Testing preferences for different policing approaches across urban, suburban and rural areas. *Police Quarterly, 4, 361-387.*

Johnson, R. R. (2010). Making domestic violence arrests: A test of expectancy theory. P*olicing: An International Journal of Police Strategies & Management, 33*(3), 531-547.

Jolin, A, (1983). Domestic violence legislation: An impact assessment. *Journal of Police Science and Administration, 11,* 4, 451-456.

Jolin, A., & Moose, C. A. (1997). Evaluating a domestic violence program in a community policing environment: Research implementation issues, *Crime and Delinquency, 43,* 279-297.

Jones, D. A., & Belknap, J. (1999). Police responses to battering in a progressive pro-arrest jurisdiction. *Justice Quarterly, 15,* 249–273.

Kane, R. (1999). Patterns of arrest in domestic violence encounters: Identifying a police decision-making model. *Journal of Criminal Justice, 27,* 65-79.

Kane, R. J. (2000). Police responses to restraining orders in domestic violence incidents: Identifying the custody-threshold thesis. *Criminal Justice and Behavior, 27,* 561–580.

Kappeler, V. E. (2001). *Critical issues in police civil liability.* (3rd. ed.). Prospect Heights, IL: Waveland.

Kappeler, V. E., Sapp, A. D., & Carter, D. L. (1993). Police officer higher education, citizens complaints and departmental rules violations. *American Journal of Police, 7,* 37-54.

Kappeler, V. E., Sluder, R. D., & Alpert, G. P. (1998). *Forces of deviance: Understanding the dark side of policing* (2nd ed.). Prospect Heights, IL: Waveland.

Keilitz, S., Hannaford, P. L., & Efkeman, H. S. (1997). *Civil protection orders: The benefits and limitations for victims of domestic violence* (Publication R-201). Williamsburg, VA: National Center for State Courts Research.

Kelling, G., & Kliesmet, R. (1995). Police unions, police culture, the Friday crab club, and police abuse of force. In W. A. Geller, & H. Toch (Eds.), *And justice for all: A national agenda for understanding and controlling police abuse of force* (pp. 187-204). Washington, DC: Police Executive Research Forum.

Kelling, G. L., & Coles, C. M. (1997). Fixing broken windows: Restoring order and reducing crime in our communities. New York: Kessler.

Kelling, G. L., & Moore, M. H. (1988). The evolving strategy of policing. In V. E. Kappeler (Ed.), *The police and society* (pp. 3-27). Prospect Heights, IL: Waveland Press.

Kennedy, D. B., & Homant, R. J. (1983). Battered women's evaluation of the police response. *Victimology, 9,* 174-179.

King, W. R. (1999). Time, constancy, and change in American municipal police organizations. *Police Quarterly, 2,* 338-364.

Klein, A. R. (2007). Practical implications of current domestic violence research, part I: law enforcement. Washington DC: U. S. Department of Justice.

Klein, C. J. (1990–1991). Will the section 1983 equal protection claim solve the equal protection problem faced by victims of domestic violence? *Journal of Family Law, 29,* 635–658.

Klinger, D. A. (1994). Demeanor or crime? Why "hostile" citizens are more likely to be arrested. *Criminology, 32,* 475-493.

Klinger, D. A. (1995). Policing spousal assault. *Journal of Research in Crime and Delinquency, 32,* 308-324.

Klinger, D. A. (1996). More on demeanor and arrest in Dade County. *Criminology, 34,* 301-323.

Klofas, J. M. (2000). Metropolitan development and policing: The elephant in the living room. *Criminal Justice Review, 25,* 234-245.

Kowalewski, D., Hall, W., Dolan, J., & Anderson, J. (1984). Police environments and operational codes: A case study of rural setting. *Journal of Police Science and Administration, 12,* 363-372.

Langley, R., & Levy, R. C. (1977). *Wife beating: The silent crisis.* New York: Dutton.

Langworthy, R. H. (1985). Wilson's theory of police behavior: A replication of the constraint theory. *Justice Quarterly, 2,* 89-98.

Langworthy, R. H. (1986). *The structure of police organizations.* New York: Praeger.

Lanza-Kanduce, L., Greenleaf, R., & Donahue, M. (1995). Trickle-up report writing: The impact of a pro-arrest policy for domestic disturbances. *Justice Quarterly, 12,* 525-542.

Lawrenz, F., Lembo, R., & Schade, T. (1988). Time series analysis of the effect of a domestic violence directive on the number of arrests per day. *Journal of Criminal Justice, 16,* 493-498.

Lempert, R. (1984). From the editor. *Law and Society Review,18,* 4, 505-513.

Liederbach, J. (2005). Addressing the "elephant in the living room": An observational study of the work of suburban police. *Policing: An International Journal of Police Strategies and Management, 28,* 415-434.

Liebman, D. A., & Schwartz, J. (1973). Police programs in domestic crisis intervention: A review. In J. R, Snibbe & H.M. Snibbe (Eds.), *The urban policeman in transition,* (pp. 421-472). Springfield, Ill.: Charles C. Thomas.

Liska, A. E., Chamlin, M. B. (1984). Social structure and crime control among macro social units. *American Journal of Sociology, 90,* 383-395.

London, J. (1978). Images of violence against women. *Victimology, 2,* 510-524.

Logan, T., Shannon, L., & Walker, R. (2005). Protective orders in rural and urban areas: A multiple perspective analysis. *Violence Against Women, 11,* 896-911.

Logan, T., Shannon, L., & Walker, R. (2006). Police attitudes toward domestic violence offenders. *Journal of Interpersonal Violence, 21,* 1365-1374.

Logan, T., Walker, R., & Leukefeld, C. (2001a). Intimate and stranger violence history among drug-using incarcerated males. *International Journal of Offender Therapy and Comparative Criminology, 45,* 228-243.

Logan, T., Walker, R., & Leukefeld, C. (2001b). Rural, urban influenced and urban differences among domestic violence arrestees in Kentucky. *Journal of Interpersonal Violence, 16,* 266-283.

Logan, T., Walker, R., Jordan, C., & Leukefeld, C. (2006). *Women and victimization: Contributing factors, interventions, and implications.* Washington, DC: American Psychological Association Press.

Logan, T. K., & Walker, R. (2009). Civil protection orders outcomes: Justice and perceptions of effectiveness. *Journal of Interpersonal Violence, 24*(4), 675-692.

Logan, T. K., & Walker, R. (2010). Civil protection orders effectiveness: Justice or just a piece of paper? *Violence and Victims, 25*(3), 332-348.

Lundman, R. J. (1974). Routine police practices: A commonweal perspective. *Social Problems, 22,* 127-141.

Lundman, R. J. (1979). Organizational norms and police discretion. *Criminology, 17,* 159-171.

Lundman, R. J. (1996). Demeanor and arrest: Additional evidence from unpublished data. *Journal of Research in Crime and Delinquency, 33,* 306-323.

Lyon, A. D. (1999). Be careful what you wish for: An examination of arrest and prosecution patterns of domestic violence cases in two cities in Michigan. *Michigan Journal of Gender and Law, 5,* 253–276.

MacDonald, J. M. (2002). The effectiveness of community policing in reducing urban violence. *Crime & Delinquency, 48,* 592-618.

Maguire, E. R. (2003). Organizational structure in American police agencies: Context, complexity, and control. Albany, NY: State University of New York Press.

Mann, C. R. (1993). *Unequal justice: A question of color.* Indianapolis, IN: University Press.

Manning, P. K. (1984). Community policing. *American Journal of Police, 3,* 205-227.

Manning, P. K. (1997). *Police work: The social organization of policing* (2nd ed.). Prospect Heights, IL: Waveland.

Marjory D. Fields (2010). Diversion of DV cases endangers victims. *Domestic Violence Report, 15,* 33–34; 43–45.

Martin, D. (1981). *Battered wives (Rev. ed.).* San Francisco: Volcano Press.

Martin, M. E. (1997a). Policy promise: community policing and domestic violence victim satisfaction. *Policing: An International Journal of Police Strategies & Management, 20,* 519-531.

Martin, M. E. (1997b). Double your trouble: Dual arrest in family violence. *Journal of Family Violence, 12,* 139-157.

Marvell, T. B., & Moody, C. E. (1996). Specification problems, police levels, and crime rates. *Criminology, 34,* 609-646.

Mastrofski, S. (1986). Police agency accreditation: The prospects of reform. *American Journal of Police, 5,* 45-81.

Mastrofski, S. (1998). Police agency accreditation: A skeptical view. *Policing, 21,* 202-205.

Mastrofski, S., Parks, R., Reiss, A., Worden, R., DeJong, C., Snipes, J., & Terrill. W. (1998). *Systematic observation of public police: Applying field research methods to policy issues.* Washington, DC: National Institute of Justice.

Mastrofski, S. D. (1991). Community policing as reform: A cautionary tale. In J. R. Greene & S. D. Mastrofski (Eds.), *Community policing: Rhetoric or reality?* (pp. 47-68). New York: Praeger.

Mastrofski, S. D., Ritti, R. R., & Hoffsmaster, D. (1987). Organizational determinants of police discretion: The case of drinking and driving. *Journal of Criminal Justice, 15,* 387-402.

Mastrofski, S. D., Worden, R. E., & Snipes, J. B. (1995). Law enforcement in a time of community policing. *Criminology, 33* 4, 539-563.

Maxwell, C., Garner, J., & Fagan, J. (2001). The effects of arrest on intimate partner violence: New evidence from the spouse assault replication program. Washington, DC: National Institute of Justice.

McDermott, M. J., & Garofalo, J. (2004). When advocacy for domestic violence victims backfires: Types and sources of victim disempowerment. *Violence Against Women, 10,* 1245-1266.

McFarlane, L. (1991). The right to privacy one hundred years later : Domestic violence victims v. municipalities: Who pays when the police will not respond? *Case Western Reserve Law Review* 41 Case W. Res 929. Symposium conducted at Case Western Reserve University.

McFarlane, J., Wilson, P., Lemmy, D., & Malecha, A. (2000). Women filing assault charges on an intimate partner: Criminal justice outcomes and future violence experienced. *Violence Against Women, 6,* 396–408.

McEwen, T. (1996). *National data collection on police use of force.* Alexandria, VA: Institute for Law and Justice.

McKee v. City of Rockwall, 877 F.2d 409 (5th Cir. 1989).

McLeod, M. (1984). Women against men: An examination of domestic violence based on an analysis of official and national victimization data. *Justice Quarterly 1,* 171-192

Meagher, M. S. (1985). Police patrol styles: How pervasive is community variation? *Journal of Police Style and Administration, 13,* 36-45.

Meeker, J., & Binder, A. (1990). Reforms as experiments: The impact of the Minneapolis Experiment on police policy. *Journal of Police Science and Administration, 17,* 147-153.

Mederer, H., & Gelles, R. J. (1989). Compassion or control: Intervention in cases of wife abuse. *Journal of Interpersonal Violence, 4,* 25-43.

Miller, J. (2003). An arresting development: Domestic violence victim experiences and perceptions. *Journal of Interpersonal Violence, 18,* 695-716.

Miller, J., & Krull, A. (1997). Controlling domestic violence: Victim resources and police intervention. In G. Kantor & J. Jasinski (Eds.), *Out of the darkness: Contemporary perspectives on family violence* (pp. 235-254). Thousand Oaks, CA: Sage.

Miller, N. (2000). A legislative primer on state domestic violence-related legislation: A law enforcement and prosecution perspective. Alexandria VA: Institute for Law and Justice.

Miller, S. L. (1999). *Gender and community policing: Walking the talk.* Boston: Northeastern University Press.

Miller, S. L. (2000). Arrest policies for domestic violence and their implications for battered women. In R. Muraskin (Ed.), *It's a crime: Women and justice* (2nd ed. pp. 287–310). Upper Saddle River, NJ: Prentice-Hall.

Miller, S. L. (2001). The paradox of women arrested for domestic violence: Criminal justice professionals and service providers respond. *Violence Against Women, 7,* 12, 1339-1376.

Mignon, S. I., & Holmes, W. M. (1995). Police response to mandatory arrest laws. *Crime and Delinquency, 41,* 430-442.

Monk, R. C. (1993). Taking sides: Clashing views on controversial subjects in crime and criminology. Guilford, CT: Dushkin.

Muir, W. K. (1977). *Police: Street corner politicians.* Chicago: University of Chicago Press.

National Advisory Commission on Criminal Justice Standards and Goals. (1973). *Police.* Washington DC: U.S. Government Printing Office.

National Research Council of the National Academies (2004). *Fairness and effectiveness in policing: The evidence*. Washington DC: The National Academies Press.

New Jersey Criminal Code of Criminal Justice, Title 2C.

New Jersey Division of Criminal Justice, (2003). *Legal aspects of domestic violence: Instructor manual*. (July) Trenton, NJ.

Niederhoffer, A. (1967). Behind the shield: The police in urban society. New York: Anchor.

O'Dell, A. (2007). Why do police arrest victims of domestic violence? The need for comprehensive training and investigative protocols. *Journal of Aggression, Maltreatment and Trauma*, 75(3/4), 53-73.

Okun, L. (1986). *Woman abuse: Facts replacing myths*. Albany, NY: State University of New York Press.

Oppenlander, N. (1982). Coping or copping out: Police service delivery in domestic disputes. *Criminology, 20*, 449-465.

Ostrom, E., Parks, R. B., & Whitaker, G. P. (1978). Police agency size: Some evidence of its effects. *Policy Studies Journal, 1*, 34-36.

Pagelow, M. D. (1981). *Woman-Battering: Victims and their experiences*. Beverly Hills, CA: Sage.

Parsons, T. (1951). *The social system*. Glencoe IL: Free Press.

Paoline, E. A. (2003). Taking stock: Toward a richer understanding of police culture. *Journal of Criminal Justice, 31*, 199-214.

Paoline, E. A., Myers, S. M., & Worden, R. E. (2000). Police culture, individualism, and community policing: Evidence from two police departments. *Justice Quarterly, 17*, 575-605.

Pate, A. M., & Hamilton, E. E. (1992). Formal and informal deterrents to domestic violence: The Dade County Spouse Assault Experiment. *American Sociological Review, 57*, 691-697.

Pelfrey, W. J., Jr. (1998). Precipitating factors of paradigmatic shift in policing: The origin of the community policing era. In G. P. Alpert & A. Piquero (Eds.), *Community policing: Contemporary readings* (pp. 79-92). Prospect Heights, IL: Waveland.

Pleck, E. (1987). Domestic tyranny: The making of American social policy against family violence from the colonial times to the present. New York: Oxford University Press.

Pleck, E. (1989. Criminal approaches to family violence, 1640-1980. In L. Ohlin& M. Tonry (Eds.), *Family violence*. Vol. 11, *Crime and justice: A review of research*, pp 19-57. Chicago: University of Chicago Press.

President's Commission on Law Enforcement and the Administration of
Justice. (1968). *The challenge of crime in a free society.* Washington,
DC: U.S. Government Printing Office.

Quarto, D., & Schwartz, M. (1985). Domestic violence in criminal court: An
examination of new legislation in Ohio. In C. Schweber & C.
Feinman (Eds.), *Criminal justice politics and women: The aftermath
of legally mandated change* (pp. 29-46), New York: Haworth.

Quinney, R. (1970). *The social reality of crime.* Boston: Little, Brown.

Rajah, V., Frye, V., & Haviland, M. (2006). Aren't I a victim? Notes on
identity challenges relating to police action in a mandatory arrest
jurisdiction. *Violence Against Women, 12,* 897-916.

Reiss, A. (1992). Police organization in the twentieth century. In M. Tonry &
N. Morris (Eds.), *Modern policing* (pp. 51-97). Chicago: University
of Chicago Press.

Reisig, M. D., McCluskey, J. D., Mastrofski , S. D., & Terril, W. (2004).
Citizen disrespect toward the police. *Justice Quarterly, 21,* 241-268.

Rennison, C. M. (2003). *Intimate partner violence, 1993-2001* (Publication No.
NCJ 197838). Washington, DC: Bureau of Justice Statistics.

Rennison, C. M., & Welchans, S. (2000). *Intimate partner violence*
(Publication No. NCJ178247). Washington, DC: Bureau of Justice
Statistics.

Reuss-Ianni, E. (1983). *Two cultures of policing.* New Brunswick, NJ:
Transaction Books.

Rigakos, G. (1997). Situational determinants of police responses to civil and
criminal injunctions for battered women. *Violence Against Women, 3,*
204-216.

Riksheim, E., & Chermak, S. M. (1993). Causes of police behavior revisited.
Journal of Criminal Justice, 21, 353-382.

Robinson, A. L. (2000). The effect of a domestic violence policy change on
police officers' schemata. *Criminal Justice and Behavior, 27,* 600-
624.

Robinson, A. L., & Chandek, M. (2000). The domestic violence arrest decision:
Examining demographic, attitudinal and situational variables. *Crime
& Delinquency, 46,* 18-37.

Robinson, A. L., & Chandek, M. S. (2000). Differential police response to
black battered women. *Women and Criminal Justice, 12,* 29-61.

Rowe, M. (2007). Rendering visible the invisible: Police discretion,
professionalism and decision-making. *Policing and Society, 17,* 279-
294.

Rowe, K. (1985). The limits of the neighborhood justice center: Why domestic violence cases should not be mediated. *Emory Law Journal, 34,* 855-910.

Roy, M. (1977). A current survey of 150 cases. In M. Roy (Ed.), *Battered women* (pp. 25-44). New York: Van Nostrand Reinhold.

Sampson, R., & Cohen, J. (1988). Deterrent effects of the police on crime: A replication and theoretical extension. *Law and Society Review, 22,* 163-189.

Saunders, D. G. (1995). The tendency to arrest victims of domestic violence: A preliminary analysis of officer characteristics. *Journal of Interpersonal Violence, 10,* 147-158.

Schechter, S. (1982). Women and male violence: The visions and struggles of the battered women's movement. Boston: South End.

Schmidt, J. D., & Sherman, L. W. (1993). Does arrest deter domestic violence? *American Behavioral Scientist, 36,* 601-609.

Schroeder, D. J., Lombardo, F., & Strollo, J. (1995). *Management and supervision of law enforcement personnel.* Binghamton, NY: J.B.L. Publications.

Scott v. Hart, No. C-76-2395 (N.D. Cal., Oct 28, 1976).

Scott, W. R. (1992). *Organizations: Rational, natural, and open systems* (3rd ed.). Englewood Cliffs, NJ: Prentice Hall.

Sherman, L. W. (1992). The influence of criminology on criminal law: Evaluating arrests for misdemeanor domestic violence. *Journal of Criminal Law & Criminology, 83*(1), 1-45.

Sherman, L. W., & Berk, R. A. (1984). The specific deterrent effects of arrest for domestic assault. *American Sociological Review, 49,* 261-272.

Sherman, L. W., Schmidt J. D., & Rogan, D. P. (1992). *Policing domestic violence: Experiments and dilemmas.* New York: Free Press.

Sherman, L. W., Schmidt, J. D., Rogan, D. P., Smith, D. A., Gartin, P. R., Cohn, E. G., Collins, D. J., & Bacich. A. R. (1991). From initial deterrence to long-term escalation: Short-custody arrest for poverty ghetto domestic violence. *Criminology, 29,* 821-850.

Sherman, L. W., Schmidt, J. D., Rogan, D. P., Smith, D. A., Gartin, P. R., Cohn, E. G., Collins, D. J., & Bacich, A. R. (1991a). The variable effects of arrest on criminal careers: The Milwaukee Domestic Violence Experiment." *Journal of Criminal Law & Criminology, 83,* 137-169.

Sherman, L. W., Smith, D. A., Schmidt, J. D., & Rogan, D. P. (1991). *Ghetto poverty, crime and punishment: Legal and informal control of domestic violence.* Washington, DC: Crime Control Institute.

Sherman, L. W., Smith, D. A., Schmidt, J. D., & Rogan, D. P. (1992). Crime, punishment, and stake in conformity: Legal and informal control of domestic violence. *American Sociological Review, 57,* 680-690.

Sherman, L. W., & the National Advisory Commission on Higher Education for Police Officers. (1978). *The quality of police education.* San Francisco: Jossey-Bass.

Sheptycki, J. W. E. (1991). Using the state to change society: The example of domestic violence. *The Journal of Human Justice, 3,* 47-66.

Shernock, S. K. (1992). Effects of college education on professional attitudes among police. *Journal of Criminal Justice Education, 3,* 71-92.

Simpson, S. S., Bouffard, L., & Garner, J. (2006). The influence of legal reform on the probability of arrest in domestic violence cases. *Justice Quarterly, 23,* 297-316.

Sims, V. H. (1988). *Small town and rural police.* Springfield, IL: Charles C. Thomas.

Sinden, P., & Stephens, B. (1999). Police perceptions of domestic violence: The nexus of victim, perpetrator, event, self and law. *Policing: An International Journal of Police Strategies & Management, 22,* 313-326.

Skogan, W. G., & Hartnett, S. M. (1997). *Community Policing, Chicago Style.* New York: Oxford University Press.

Skolnick, J. (1985). A sketch of the policeman's working personality. In A. Niederhoffer, A. S. Blumberg, & E. Niederhoffer (Eds.), *The ambivalent force: Perspectives on the police* (3rd ed., pp. 80-90). New York: Holt, Rinehart and Winston.

Skolnick, J. H., & Bayley, D. H. (1986). *The new blue line: Police innovation in six American cities.* New York: Free Press.

Slovak, J. S. (1986). Styles of urban policing: Organization, environment, and police styles in selected American cities. New York: New York University Press.

Smith, A. (2000). It's my decision, isn't it? A research note on battered women's perception of mandatory intervention laws. *Violence Against Women, 6*(12), 1384-1402.

Smith, D. (1984). The organizational context of legal control. *Criminology, 22,* 19-38.

Smith, D. (1986). The neighborhood context of police behavior. In A. Reiss & M. Tonry (Eds.), *Communities and crime* (pp. 314-341). Chicago, IL: University of Chicago Press.

Smith, D. A. (1987). Police response to interpersonal violence: Defining the parameters of legal control. *Social Forces, 65,* 767-782.

Smith, D. A., & Klein, J. R. (1984). Police control of interpersonal disputes. *Social Problems, 31,* 468-481.

Smith, D. A., Visher, C. A., & Davidson, L. A. (1984). Equity and discretionary justice: The influence of race on arrest decisions. *Journal of Criminal Law and Criminology, 75,* 234-249.

Smith, N., & Flanagan, C. (2000). *Effective detective: Identifying the skills of an effective SIO.* London, England: Great Britain Home Office.

Stalans, L. J., & Finn, M. A. (1995). How novice and experienced officers interpret wife assaults: Normative and efficiency frames. *Law and Society Review, 29,* 287-321.

Stalans, L. J., & Finn, M. A. (2000). Gender differences in officer's perceptions and decisions about domestic violence cases. *Women & Criminal Justice, 11,* 1-24.

Stalans, L. J., & Finn, M. A. (2006). Public's and police officers' interpretation and handling of domestic violence cases: Divergent realities. *Journal of Interpersonal Violence, 21,* 1129-1155.

Stanko, E. A. (1989). Missing the mark? Policing battering. In J. Hanmer, J. Radford, & E. A. Stanko (Eds.), *Women, policing, and male violence* (pp. 46-69). London: Routledge.

Stark, E. (1993). Mandatory arrest of batterers: A reply to its critics. *American Behavioral Scientist, 36,* 651-680.

State of New Jersey. (2004). *Domestic violence procedures manual,* (July), Trenton, NJ.

State of New Jersey. (2007). *Uniform crime report 2006.* Department of Law and Public Safety, Division of the State Police, Uniform Crime Reporting Unit. Retrieved on April 20, 2008 from http://www.njsp.org/info/ucr2006/index.html.

State of New Jersey. (2009). *Uniform crime report 2008.* Department of Law and Public Safety, Division of the State Police, Uniform Crime Reporting Unit. Retrieved on October 30, 2009 from http://www.njsp.org/info/ucr2008/index.html.

Steinmetz, S. K. (1978). The battered husband syndrome. *Victimology: An International Journal, 2,* 499-509.

Stephens, B., & Sinden, P. (2000). Victims' voices domestic assault victims' perceptions of police demeanor. *Journal of Interpersonal Violence, 15,* 534-547.

Stewart, A. (2000). Policing domestic violence: An overview of emerging issues. *Police Practice & Research, 2,* 447-459.

Straus, M. A., & Gelles, R. J. (1986). Societal change and change in family violence from 1975 to 1985 as revealed in two national surveys. *Journal of Marriage and the Family, 48,* 465-479.

Straus, M. A., & Gelles, R. J. (1990). How violent are American families? Estimates from the National Family Violence Resurvey and other studies. In M. A. Straus & R. J. Gelles (Eds.), *Physical violence in American families: Risk factors and adaptations to violence in 8,145 families* (pp . 95-112). New Brunswick, N.J: Transaction Publishers.

Straus , M. A., & Lincoln, A. J. (1985). A conceptual framework for understanding crime and the family. In A. J. Lindon & M. Straus (Eds.), *Crime and the family.* Springfield, Il.: Charles C. Thomas Publishers.

Swanson, C. (1978). The influence of organization and environment on arrest policies in major U.S. cities. *Policy Studies Journal, 7,* 390-398.

Swanson, C. R., Territo, L., & Taylor R. W. (2005). *Police administration: Structures processes and behavior.* Upper Saddle River, NJ: Pearson Prentice Hall.

Talarico, S. M., & Swanson, C. R. Jr. (1978). Styles of policing: A preliminary mapping. *Policy Studies Journal, 7,* 398-406.

Thibault, E. A., Lynch, L. M., & McBride, R. B. (2004). *Proactive police management* (6th ed.). Upper Saddle River, NJ: Pearson Prentice Hall.

Thurman v. City of Torrington, 595 F. Supp. 1521 (D. Conn. 1984).

Tjaden, P., & Thoennes, N. (2000). Extent, nature, and consequences of intimate partner violence: Findings from the National Violence against Women Survey. Washington DC: U.S. Department of Justice

U.S. Attorney General's Task Force on Family Violence. (1984). *Final report.* Washington, DC: U.S. Government Printing Office.

U.S. Bureau of the Census. (1980a). *General population characteristics.* Washington, DC: U.S. Government Printing Office.

U.S. Bureau of the Census. (1980b). *General social and economic characteristics.* Washington, DC: U.S. Government Printing Office.

U.S. Bureau of the Census (1990). *1990 census: Detailed population characteristic.* Washington, DC: U.S. Government Printing Office.

U.S. Bureau of the Census (2010). *New Jersey quick facts.* Retrieved online December16,2010fromhttp://quickfacts.census.gov/qfd/states/34000.html.

U.S. Bureau of the Census (2010). *Guide to State and Local Census Geography- New Jersey.* Retrieved online December 16, 2010 from http://www.census.gov/www/Guidestloc/st34 nj.html.

U.S. Commission on Civil Rights. (1981). *Who Is guarding the guardians?* Washington, DC: U.S. Government Printing Office.

U.S. Department of Justice (1995). *Crime in the United States,* Washington, DC: U.S. Department of Justice, Federal Bureau of Investigation.

U.S. Department of Justice (1997). *Uniform crime reports.* 1996. Washington, DC: U.S. Department of Justice, Federal Bureau of Investigation.

U.S. Department of Justice (1999). The Clinton administration's law enforcement strategy: Combating crime with community policing and community prosecution. Washington, DC: U.S. Department of Justice.

Virginia Association of Chiefs of Police. (1994). *Use of force report.* Richmond, VA: Virginia Association of Chiefs of Police.

Vollmer, A. (1972). *The police and modern society.* (Montclair, NJ: Patterson Smith reprint of original 1936 manuscript).

Waaland, P., & Keeley. S. (1985). Police decision-making in wife abuse: The impact of legal and extra-legal factors. *Law & Human Behavior, 9,* 355-366.

Walker, J. (1981). Police in the middle: A study of small city police interventions in domestic disputes. *Journal of Police Science and Administration, 9,* 243-260.

Walker, L. E. (1979). *The battered woman.* New York, Harper & Row.

Walker, L. E. (1985). Psychological impact of the criminalization of domestic violence on Victims. *Victimology, 10,* 281-300.

Walker, L. E. (1991). Post traumatic stress disorder in women: Diagnosis and treatment of Battered Women Syndrome. *Psychotherapy, 28,* 1, 21-29.

Walker, S. (1999). *The police in America* (3rd ed.). Boston: McGraw-Hill.

Wallace, H. (1996). Family violence. Needham Heights, MA: Allyn Bacon.

Watson v. City of Kansas City, 857 F.2d 690; (10th Cir. 1988) Lexis 12640.

Websdale, N., & Johnson, B. (1997). The policing of domestic violence in rural and urban areas: The voices of battered women. *Policing and Society, 6,* 297-317.

Weis, J. G. (1989). Family violence research methodology and design. *Crime and Justice: An Annual Review of Research. 11,* 117-162.

Weisheit, R., Falcone, D., & Wells, L. (1999). *Crime and policing in rural and small-town America* (2nd ed.). Prospect Heights, IL: Waveland.

Wermuth, L. A. (1983). Wife beating: The crime without punishment. (Doctoral dissertation, University of Califorina, Berkley 1983).

White, M. D., Goldkamp, J. S., & Campbell, S. P. (2005). Beyond mandatory arrest: Developing a comprehensive response to domestic violence. *Police Practice & Research: An International Journal, 6,* 261-278.

Wilson, J. Q. (1968). Varieties of police behavior: The management of law and order in eight communities. Cambridge, MA: Harvard University Press.

Wilson, J. Q., & Kelling, G. L. (1982). Broken windows: The police and neighborhood safety. Atlantic Monthly, 249, 29-38.

Wilson, O. W., & McLaren. R. C. (1977). *Police Administration* (4th ed.). New York: McGraw-Hill.

Wilson, S., & Jasinski, J. L. (2004). Public satisfaction with the police in domestic violence cases: The importance of arrest, expectations, and involuntary contact. *American Journal of Criminal Justice, 28,* 235-254.

Wolfgang, M. (1958). *Patterns in criminal homicide.* Philadelphia: University of Pennsylvania Press.

Worden, A. P. (1993). The attitudes of women and men in policing: Testing conventional and contemporary wisdom. *Criminology, 31,* 203-237.

Worden, R. E. (1989). Situational and attitudinal explanations of police behavior: A theoretical reappraisal and empirical assessment. *Law and Society Review, 23,* 677-711.

Worden, R. E. (1990). A badge and a baccalaureate: Policies, hypotheses, and further evidence. *Justice Quarterly, 7,* 565-592.

Worden, R. E. (1995). Police officers' belief systems: A framework for analysis. *American Journal of Police, 14,* 49-81.

Worden, R. E., & Pollitz, A. A. (1984). Police arrests in domestic disturbances: A further look. *Law & Society Review, 18,* 105-119.

Wycoff, M. A., & Skogan, W. G. (1994). The effect of a community policing management style on officers' attitudes. *Crime and Delinquency, 40,* 371-383.

Wylie, P. B., Basinger, L. F., Heinecke, C. L., & Reuckert, J. A. (1976). *Approach to evaluating a police program of family crisis intervention in six demonstration cities: Final report.* Washington DC: National Criminal Justice Reference Service.

Yllo, K. A., & Straus, M. A. (1984). Patriarchy and violence against wives: The impact of structure and normative factors. *Journal of International and Comparative Social Welfare* 1:16-29.

Zalman, M. (1992). The courts' response to police intervention in domestic violence. In E. S. Buzawa & C. G. Buzawa (Eds.), *Domestic violence: The changing criminal justice response* (2nd ed., pp. 79–110). Westport, CT: Auburn House.

Zimring, F. E., Makherjee, S. K., & Van Winkle, B. (1983). *Deterrence: The legal threat in crime control.* Chicago: University of Chicago Press.

Zora, J. (1992). The criminal law of misdemeanor domestic violence, 1970-1990. *Journal of Criminal Law and Criminology, 83,* 46-72.

Zorza, J. (2010). Batterer manipulation and retaliation compounded by denial and complicity in the family courts. In Mo Therese Hannah & Barry Goldstein (Eds.), *Domestic Violence, Abuse, and Child Custody: Legal Strategies and Policy Issues.* Kingston, NJ: Civic Research Institute.

Zora, J. (2011). Restorative Justice: Does it work for DV victims? Part II. *Domestic Violence, 16*(4), 51-60

Index